BOOK
LUST

BOOK
LUST

NANCY PEARL

RECOMMENDED READING FOR EVERY
MOOD, MOMENT, AND REASON

SASQUATCH BOOKS
SEATTLE

Printed in the United States of America
Published by Sasquatch Books
Distributed by Publishers Group West
10 09 08 07 06 05   12 11 10 9 8 7 6

Art direction: Kate Basart
Cover and interior design: Rowan Moore/doublemranch.com
Cover photograph: Jason Koski
Copy editor: Phyllis Hatfield

Library of Congress Cataloging in Publication Data

Pearl, Nancy
Book Lust : recommended reading for every mood, moment, and reason /
by Nancy Pearl.
    p. cm.
Includes index.
ISBN 1-57061-381-8
1. Best books. 2. Books and reading—United States. 3. Pearl, Nancy—Books and reading. I. Title.

Z1035.9.P38 2003
011'73—dc21   2003045796

Sasquatch Books
119 South Main Street, Suite 400
Seattle, WA 98104
206/467-4300
www.sasquatchbooks.com
custserv@sasquatchbooks.com

Contents

Introduction

I love to read. And while I might not absolutely agree with the Anglo-American man of letters Logan Pearsall Smith, who said, "People say that life is the thing, but I prefer reading," I come awfully close to subscribing to his sentiment. In fact, back in the days when I did such things, I needlepointed the quotation onto a piece of canvas. I've never gotten around to framing it or turning it into a pillow. Too many books, and life, had my attention, I guess.

Reading has always brought me pure joy. I read to encounter new worlds and new ways of looking at our own world. I read to enlarge my horizons, to gain wisdom, to experience beauty, to understand myself better, and for the pure wonderment of it all. I read and marvel over how writers use language in ways I never thought of. I read for company, and for escape. Because I am incurably interested in the lives of other people, both friends and strangers, I read to meet myriad folks and enter their lives—for me, a way of vanquishing the "otherness" we all experience.

I grew up in a lower-middle-class neighborhood of Detroit in a family of readers, although my father only went to school through the sixth grade and didn't get his GED until he was seventy. My mother, a highly educated woman, was a disastrous combination of fury and depression. She read poetry (especially those depressed poets like A. E. Housman and Philip Larkin) and fiction. (She's the only person I know of who loved books of fantasy and science fiction with the same degree of intensity.) Mine was a family that today would be labeled dysfunctional. All I knew then was that I was deeply and fatally unhappy.

It was painful to live in our house, and consequently I spent most of my childhood and early adolescence at the public library. The librarians at the

Parkman Branch Library found me books that revealed worlds beyond what I saw and experienced every day. Although I remember very few specific events in my childhood, I have vivid memories of hundreds of books I read and loved during those years. Sometimes I can't quite come up with the plot, or the names of characters, but I do remember how I was transported when I read them.

I'm talking about books like **The Wonderful Flight to the Mushroom Planet** by Eleanor Cameron; Elizabeth Goudge's **The Little White Horse;** Robert Heinlein's **Space Cadet; Red Planet;** and **The Star Beast; Hitty: Her First Hundred Years** by Rachel Field; **Caddie Woodlawn** by Carol Ryrie Brink; **The Lion, the Witch, and the Wardrobe** by C. S. Lewis; **The Hobbit** and **The Lord of the Rings** by J. R. R. Tolkien; Elizabeth Enright's **The Saturdays;The Sea is Blue** by Marie Lawson; Eleanor Estes's **The Moffats** and **Ginger Pye;** the Betsy-Tacy books by Maud Hart Lovelace; the books about Beany Malone by Lenora Mattingly Weber; the Swallows and Amazons series by Arthur Ransome; Evelyn Sibley Lampman's **Crazy Creek; Wait for Marcy** by Rosamund du Jardin; **Green Eyes** by Jean Nielsen; **The Casket and the Sword** by Norman Dale; David Severn's **Dream Gold;** Betty Cavanna's young adult novels, especially **Going on Sixteen; Minnow on the Say** by Philippa Pearce; and John R. Tunis's **The Kid from Tomkinsville,** among many others. (Just listing them here makes me want to track down the ones I don't own and reread them.)

It's not too much of an exaggeration—if it's one at all—to say that reading saved my life.

By the time I was ten years old, I knew I wanted to become a children's librarian, just like Miss Long and Miss Whitehead, the two main influences on my reading life. And although for a few moments in college I was tempted to go to MIT to study transformational grammar with Noam

Chomsky, I've never since wavered in my belief that being a librarian is one of the best, and noblest, careers that anyone could have.

To paraphrase Robert Frost (from "Two Tramps in Mud Time"), my love and my work are one—and I feel extremely lucky to be able to say so. I've been fortunate to work in three great library systems—Detroit Public Library, Tulsa City-County Library, and Seattle Public Library—and a wonderful independent bookstore, Yorktown Alley, in Tulsa, Oklahoma, which have allowed me to grow as a reader and to share my knowledge and love with other readers. I'm also grateful that I have been given the opportunity to review books weekly on two public radio stations: KWGS in Tulsa, and KUOW in Seattle.

Whenever I begin reading a new book, I am embarking on a new, uncharted journey with an unmarked destination. I never know where a particular book will take me, toward what other books I will be led. How could I have predicted that reading Richard Bausch's **Hello to the Cannibals** would send me on a reading jag about Victorian lady travelers? Or that Salman Rushdie's **Midnight's Children** would lead me to **Freedom at Midnight** by Larry Collins and Dominique Lapierre and open up the world of India to me?

Each time I begin a new book (and any book I haven't read before is a "new" book), there's the very real chance that this is a book that I will fall in love with. Some books let me know from the very first sentence that I am in great hands, that this reading experience will offer me pure pleasure. When I began Pete Dexter's **The Paperboy**, Ward Just's **A Dangerous Friend**, Dave Eggers's **A Heartbreaking Work of Staggering Genius**, and Donna Tartt's **The Little Friend**, I had no doubt that I would fall in love with them. And I did.

One of my strongest-held beliefs is that no one should ever finish a book that they're not enjoying, no matter how popular or well reviewed the book is. Believe me, nobody is going to get any points in heaven by slogging their way through a book they aren't enjoying but think they ought to read. I live by what I call "the rule of fifty," which acknowledges that time is short and the world of books is immense. If you're fifty years old or younger, give every book about fifty pages before you decide to commit yourself to reading it, or give it up. If you're over fifty, which is when time gets even shorter, subtract your age from 100—the result is the number of pages you should read before deciding. Keep in mind that your mood has a lot to do with whether or not you will like a book. I always leave open the option of going back to a book that I haven't liked (especially if someone I respect has recommended it to me) sometime later. I've begun many books, put them down unfinished, then returned a month or two, or years, later and ended up loving them. This happened with Matthew Kneale's **English Passengers,** John Crowley's **Little, Big,** and Andrea Barrett's **The Voyage of the Narwhal.**

Book Lust grew out of my more than thirty years of work as a professional reader and book reviewer, and my ongoing experiences of talking to people all over the world about the books they most love. In many ways this was an easy book to write, because I've read and enjoyed so many books that I've wanted to tell other people about. The difficulty arose because the more lists of books I made, the more books I remembered that I wanted to include. Having to decide, once and for all, which books belonged here was agony. (Even as I write this introduction, other titles spring to mind—wonderful books that I hate to leave out.)

You will notice that many of the books I recommend are out of print. If you have a hankering to read them—and I hope you do—check at your local library, which, even if it doesn't own the book, will likely be able to borrow it from another library for you. Or take advantage of the power of the Internet in locating out-of-print books. (One result of working on **Book Lust** is that I've spent a lot of time—not to mention money—purchasing books that I realized I just had to own.)

So get yourself settled in a comfortable chair, grab a pen and paper, and enjoy yourself as you read through this book. Incidentally, I'm sure you'll be horrified about books I've left out or overlooked. I'd love to hear what books you think I should have included, or which books I could as easily have omitted, in your opinion. Sharing the books you've loved is one of the great pleasures in reading. You can reach me by email at nancy@nancypearl.com.

One of the most wonderful paragraphs about the joys of reading is in "How Should One Read a Book?," an essay in Virginia Woolf's collection **The Second Common Reader.** She writes:

> *I have sometimes dreamt . . . that when the Day of Judgment dawns and the great conquerors and lawyers and statesmen come to receive their rewards—their crowns, their laurels, their names carved indelibly upon imperishable marble—the Almighty will turn to Peter and will say, not without a certain envy when He sees us coming with our books under our arms, "Look, these need no reward. We have nothing to give them here. They have loved reading."*

It's an honor to share some of my favorite books with you. I hope some of them will become your favorites, too. Let me know.

Acknowledgments

This book could not have been written without the help of many people, including everyone I've greeted over the last umpteen years by asking whether they've read anything good lately.

I am grateful to my editors at **Library Journal** for allowing me to adapt some of The Reader's Shelf columns that I edit and/or write for them, and more specifically, to the following contributors who have given me permission to adapt their columns for use in this book: Andrea Kempf (Czech It Out; Balkan Specters; China Voices; Japanese Fiction; Polish Poems and Prose; Cuba Sí!); Jennifer Baker (King Arthur; Not Only for Kids: Fantasies for Grown-ups; African American Fiction); David Hellman (Grit Lit); Chris Higashi (Passage to India; Historical Fiction Around the World; Prose by Poets; as well as for her thorough vetting of this book in manuscript); and Jennifer Young (American Indian Literature).

A big thank-you, also, to David Wright, not only for advice about noir fiction, but because he always had just the right word for me; Susan Fort, for suggesting the "A ... My Name is Alice" and "Physicians Writing More Than Prescriptions" categories; Neal Wyatt for "Romans-Fleuves" and her part in "Romance Novels: Our Love Is Here to Stay"; Jennifer McCord for the other part of "Romance Novels: Our Love Is Here to Stay"; Jay Raman for introducing me to the South Sea Islands books; and Millie Loeb for the idea behind "Pawns of History."

Thank you to Libraries Unlimited for allowing me to use some particularly felicitous language from my books **Now Read This: A Guide to Mainstream Fiction, 1978–1998,** and **Now Read This II: A Guide to Mainstream Fiction, 1990–2001.**

Thanks to the wonderful people at Sasquatch Books: Gary Luke, Susan Quinn, Gina Johnston, and Sarah Smith, for loving the book, and to Phyllis Hatfield for her editing talent.

And I am grateful beyond words to my husband, Joe, who makes my reading life possible.

This book is dedicated to my granddaughter Sarah Lakshmi Raman, who I hope grows up loving to read, but not too much.

A . . . MY NAME IS ALICE

I once heard Anna Quindlen answer the question of what authors she most enjoyed reading by saying that, basically, she read "the Alices." I realized then that one could have a most enjoyable binge reading these Alices: Alice Adams, Alice Elliott Dark, Alice Hoffman, Alice Mattison, Alice McDermott, Alice Munro, Alice Walker, and first-time novelist Alice Sebold.

Alice Adams, an elegant writer of both short stories (which frequently appeared in *The New Yorker* magazine) and novels, wrote about the lives and emotional upheavals of women. Some of her best books include **Caroline's Daughters, After You've Gone: Stories, Superior Women,** and my favorite, her first novel, **Families and Survivors.** There's an excellent cross section of her short works in **The Stories of Alice Adams.**

Alice Elliott Dark writes highly polished and controlled (but frequently emotionally charged) fiction, including the award-winning **In the Gloaming: Stories** (the title story was selected by John Updike as one of the best stories of the century), **Naked to the Waist,** and a novel, **Think of England.**

Novelist Alice Hoffman is known for her magical realist fiction; she creates alternative universes rather than simply exploring everyday realities. Try an early novel, **The Drowning Season,** and then see how she's developed through **Illumination Night; Turtle Moon;** and **Blue Diary.**

Alice Mattison is a multitalented writer of short stories (**Men Giving Money, Women Yelling: Intersecting Stories,** which was a *New York Times* Notable Book), novels (**The Book Borrower** and **Hilda and Pearl**), and poetry (**Animals**). You'll find that her writing is marked by a fine delineation of characters and a wonderful use of language.

Among Alice McDermott's award-winning novels exploring Irish-American Catholic family relationships are **Child of My Heart; Charming**

Billy (which won the National Book Award); **At Weddings and Wakes; A Bigamist's Daughter;** and **That Night** (a finalist for the Pulitzer Prize, the National Book Award, and the *Los Angeles Times* Book Prize).

Canadian Alice Munro has been widely praised as one of the best contemporary short story writers; Cynthia Ozick described her as "our Chekhov." In her collections such as **Friend of My Youth: Stories, Open Secrets,** and **The Love of a Good Woman,** she writes about he **Lives of Girls and Women,** which is the title of another of her collections.

In her original and shocking first novel, the **Lovely Bones,** Alice Sebold tells the story of a murder (recounted by the teenage victim) and its aftermath, as her devastated family tries to cope with their grief.

Alice Walker writes fiction, nonfiction, and poetry. She is probably best known for her Pulitzer Prize– and American Book Award–winning novel, **The Color Purple,** but readers shouldn't miss her poetry (**Good Night, Willie Lee, I'll See You in the Morning: Poems**) and her other novels **Meridian** (an autobiographical novel about of the early years of the civil rights movement and an interracial marriage) and **Possessing the Secret of Joy.**

ACADEMIA: THE JOKE

Reading these academic satires, it's clear that the life of the mind is no match for all the jostling and jockeying for promotions and tenure and the intrigues of college politics. What with the incompetent administration and the egomaniacal faculty, there's tons of great material available.

Randall Jarrell took time away from his poetry and criticism to pen only one novel, but what a great novel it is. The witty and malicious **Pictures from an Institution** is the classic American academic satire, set at a progressive Eastern women's college and featuring the unpleasant novelist Gertrude Johnson, who bears a striking resemblance to writer Mary McCarthy, no favorite of Jarrell's.

In Mary McCarthy's own satire, **The Groves of Academe,** published in 1952, the plot might seem a bit dated (a professor professes to have been a communist so that his ultraliberal college won't fire him), but the academic infighting feels completely contemporary.

Jane Smiley's **Moo** is a raucous romp through the affectionately nicknamed Moo U., a state university located somewhere in the Midwest. A large cast of characters, including members of the administration, faculty, and students, are their normal eccentric selves, even as the college undertakes a secret research project involving a large hog named Earl Butz.

Ishmael Reed's **Japanese by Spring** relates the hilariously sad experiences of Benjamin "Chappie" Puttbutt, a very junior professor lusting after tenure, who becomes the head of the English department after his Japanese tutor buys the college.

When the mysterious feminist scholar and novelist Olga Kaminska arrives to teach at a university awfully much like Stanford, where John L'Heureux, the author of **The Handmaid of Desire**, teaches, she immediately begins manipulating the lives of all her fellow academicians in an attempt to give them what they think they most want. But is it?

And don't forget David Lodge's **Changing Places: A Tale of Two Campuses; Small World: An Academic Romance;** and **Nice Work,** which offer the British take on the academic follies; and Malcolm Bradbury's five witty novels about scholarly infighting and love and lust on Britain's redbrick campuses, which also include more than a few jabs at the pompous professorial types who populate these groves of academe (**Eating People Is Wrong; Stepping Westward; The History Man; Rates of Exchange;** and **To the Hermitage**); as well as Kingsley Amis's classic **Lucky Jim.**

ACADEMIC MYSTERIES

Mysteries set in academia are a vital part of the mystery canon. Fans of "cozy" mysteries (the murder-in-a-teacup sort) and the classic whodunit type will usually find academic mysteries to their liking. There is rarely any graphic sex or violence (no doubt a reflection of the real world of academia!).

In Dorothy Sayers's **Gaudy Night** (which is a rarity in that it is a mystery without a murder), Harriet Vane goes back to her Oxford college for a reunion (known as a "gaudy"), where she confronts a series of malicious and threatening anonymous notes and pranks and also her feelings for the dashing, wealthy, and brilliant Lord Peter Wimsey.

Kate Fansler, an English professor like her creator Carolyn Heilbrun (writing as Amanda Cross), was introduced in **In the Last Analysis.** A former student of Kate's is found stabbed to death on the couch in her psychiatrist's office, and Kate feels compelled to investigate whodunit. Other good books in this series are **The Theban Mysteries** and **The James Joyce Murder.**

Alfred Alcorn's **Murder in the Museum of Man** is the only academic mystery that I know of in which cannibalism is important to the plot.

Michael Innes's classic mystery, **Death at the President's Lodging,** features his regular sleuth, Inspector John Appleby, who investigates a murder at an Oxford college. The catch is that Appleby has only a few suspects from among whom to deduce the killer.

ACTION HEROINES

While the distaff side more than holds its own when it comes to mysteries (think of Kinsey Millhone or V. I. Warshawski or Carlotta Carlyle), there aren't too many action or suspense novels in which women have the lead role. In most adventure fiction women at best appear as sidekicks to the male hero and at worst merely provide the love or, more usually, the sex interest. There are, though, a few good adventure novels with women as protagonists. (Interestingly, they are usually written by men. Is this wish fulfillment [the women are unfailingly gorgeous, sexy, and brilliant], or what?) You go, girl!

Paul Eddy's **Flint** is a complicated thriller filled with dastardly villains who traffic in treachery. London police inspector Grace Flint is the victim of a sting operation that goes terribly awry—she is badly hurt (the descriptions of her attack are difficult to read) and determined to track down the man responsible, who happens to be involved in a high-level money-laundering operation. As Flint hunts down her man, risking life and limb, and not knowing whom to trust, British intelligence hunts for her, and the chase is on. Following with the almost equally good **Flint's Law.** Eddy is a writer to watch.

When Susan Van Meter's federal narcotics investigator husband is found murdered while in hot pursuit of a drug kingpin, she leaves her research position and takes on the task of tracking down and bringing to justice the murderer in **Saint Mike** by Jerry Oster.

Peter O'Donnell introduced Modesty Blaise, originally created as a comic strip, in the 1950s and has continued to showcase her talents in his over-the-top novels, which to my delight appear fairly frequently. Along with her longtime partner Willie Garvin, Modesty fights crime anywhere it shows its rotten head. A good introduction are the six stories that make up **Pieces of Modesty,** but you won't want to miss **Dragon's Claw.**

If you're willing to move away from the strictly realistic (as if the others in this list are realistic!) and into the realm of science fiction/fantasy, you can read about the exploits of Thursday Next, the intrepid literary detective heroine of Jasper Fforde's inventive and entertaining novels. Thursday must try to best the fiendish Acheron Hades, who has had the temerity to kid-nap Jane Eyre out of the pages of Brontë's novel, in **The Eyre Affair,** the first in the series.

ADVENTURE BY THE BOOK: FICTION

A h, the lure of the open road, or the open water, or simply the great unknown. Adventure fiction can be even more powerful than nonfiction (the best of which is plenty powerfully exciting) because novelists who tackle the genre have far more latitude than writers describing an actual event.

Although coming-of-age novels like Mark Twain's **Huckleberry Finn** or Robert Louis Stevenson's **Kidnapped** could rightly be considered adventure novels, as could many thrillers, I'm limiting this list to accounts of man (and/or woman) against nature.

Based on an actual event, Lisa Michaels's haunting **Grand Ambition** is the story of a honeymooning couple whose decision to raft down the Colorado River in 1928 ends in disaster.

The Birthday Boys by Beryl Bainbridge relates the exhilarating and poignant last days of the doomed 1912 Robert Falcon Scott–led Antarctic expedition that ended in the deaths of all five members of the group.

Ernest Shackleton's Antarctic expedition in 1914 is the subject of Melinda Mueller's **What the Ice Gets**—an epic poem told in the varied voices of members of Shackleton's crew and Shackleton himself.

An assignment to photograph bears in the Arctic wilderness turns into a struggle for survival for Beryl, the heroine of **The Cage**, by Audrey Schulman.

Two teenage adventure novels that make good reading for adults, too, are James Ramsey Ullman's long-out-of-print **Banner in the Sky**, in which a young Swiss boy is determined to climb the mountain on which his father died, and Gary Paulsen's **Hatchet**, a multi-award-winning story about a teenager surviving alone in the wilderness after an airplane crash.

ADVENTURE BY THE BOOK: NONFICTION

White knuckles and fear gnawing at the pit of your stomach: If you can't walk the walk (or climb the climb or sail the sea), at least you can read all about it.

Points Unknown: A Century of Great Exploration, edited by David Roberts, is a fabulous collection of classic adventure literature, from the famous (Robert Falcon Scott) to the perhaps less well known (Eric Newby, Francis Chichester, Joshua Slocum).

National Geographic Expeditions Atlas is less an atlas than a chronicle of adventures and a stunning compilation of the Society's trademark maps and photographs from expeditions that took place over the last 100-plus years. The diverse list of contributors includes Mary Leakey, Theodore Roosevelt, and John Glenn.

Although Jon Krakauer's devastating **Into Thin Air: A Personal Account of the Mount Everest Disaster** sets the standard for personal adventure books, other climbers also wrote movingly about the same 1996 tragic climb, as in Matt Dickinson's **The Other Side of Everest: Climbing the North Face Through the Killer Storm,** Anatoli Boukreev's **The Climb: Tragic Ambitions on Everest,** and **Left for Dead: My Journey Home from Everest** by Beck Weathers.

The Last River: The Tragic Race for Shangri-la by Todd Balf is the story of the disastrous 1998 trip by a highly skilled and gung-ho group of white-water kayakers on the Yarlung Tsangpo River in Tibet.

Fergus Fleming's chatty, entertaining, and historically accurate **Barrow's Boys: A Stirring Story of Daring, Fortitude, and Outright Lunacy** relates the experiences of the British explorers who searched in the first half of the nineteenth century for the Northwest Passage and, in Africa, sought the location of the fabled Timbuktu and searched for the mouth of the Niger River. Fleming's **Ninety Degrees North: The Quest for the North Pole** is another wonderful study of the brave and often misguided men who undertook dangerous journeys to satisfy their yearning for fame and adventure (or had a definite death wish!).

Derek Lundy's **Godforsaken Sea: Racing the World's Most Dangerous Waters** is the story of the 1996–97 Vendée Globe race, in which each of sixteen sailors attempted to sail single-handedly around the world (about 13,000 miles) through the world's most dangerous waters.

AFRICA: TODAY AND YESTERDAY

One of the best books to read in order to understand Africa is Thomas Pakenham's **The Scramble for Africa: White Man's Conquest of the Dark Continent from 1876 to 1912**, which describes how various colonial powers like France, England, and Belgium carved up a continent in a way that almost guaranteed the disasters and tragedies marking Africa's contemporary experiences.

The desert blooms in **Sahara: A Natural History** by Marq de Villiers and Sheila Hirtle, which brings to life the history, geography, legends, lore, and people of the great African desert, which was called The Endless Emptiness and The Great Nothing by early explorers.

A staff writer for *The New Yorker*, Philip Gourevitch visited Rwanda over a period of years to write what is perhaps the most personal and heart-wrenching account of genocide in the modern world, **We Wish to Inform You That Tomorrow We Will Be Killed with Our Families: Stories from Rwanda.**

King Leopold's Ghost: A Story of Greed, Terror, and Heroism in Colonial

Africa by Adam Hochschild is an account of the grim history of the Belgian Congo (the setting for Joseph Conrad's **Heart of Darkness**), under its plundering ruler-from-afar, the king of Belgium, who used "his" African colony to make himself wealthy beyond measure.

In **In the Footsteps of Mr. Kurtz: Living on the Brink of Disaster in Mobutu's Kenya,** Michela Wrong tries to make sense of the senseless: the economic failure of one of Africa's most blessed countries in terms of its natural resources. Wrong lays much blame at the feet of the Congo's ruler of thirty years, Mobutu Sese Seko, but blame can also be assigned to the United States and other countries that turned a blind eye—as is too often the case—to what was going on.

Ryszard Kapuscinski's **The Shadow of the Sun** is an intelligent and accessible collection of impressions gathered over forty years of covering postcolonial Africa for a variety of European publications.

AFRICAN AMERICAN FICTION: HE SAY

One of the earliest African American male novelists (he also wrote exceptional essays; check out **Nobody Knows My Name** and **The Fire Next Time**), James Baldwin, who always mixed elements of autobiography in his fiction, explored black life in America in novels like **Go Tell It on the Mountain** and **If Beale Street Could Talk**. He was also one of the best-known twentieth-century writers who dealt openly with issues of homosexuality in his fiction, most notably in **Giovanni's Room**. But in the nearly two decades since Baldwin's death, a whole new—and widely diverse—group of writers have written some terrific novels.

Two savagely funny novels explore the racial divide in decidedly unpolitically correct terms: Ishmael Reed's postmodern **Mumbo Jumbo** (with its indescribable plot, which involves the rise of black music and dancing even among the white middle class) and Percival Everett's **Erasure**, in which the determinedly upper-middle-class, unsuccessful African American writer Thelonius "Monk" Ellison, tiring of his literary fiction and nonfiction being ignored by the reading public, changes gears and pens a life-in-da-ghetto novel that, embarrassingly, catapults him to the top of his profession.

Ernest Gaines consistently writes brilliant, thought-provoking fiction. Two of his best are **A Lesson Before Dying**, which takes place in Louisiana in the 1940s and tells the story of a young man convicted and sentenced to die for a crime he didn't commit, and **The Autobiography of Miss Jane Pittman**, the fictional memoirs of a former slave.

In **High Cotton** by Darryl Pinckney, the protagonist (who bears a strong resemblance to the author) attempts to understand what it means to be a black man, both in the United States and as an expatriate in France in the 1960s.

Until **The Emperor of Ocean Park** was published in 2002, Stephen Carter was best known as a Yale law professor and author of several well-regarded nonfiction books, including **Reflections of an Affirmative Action Baby** and **The Culture of Disbelief: How American Law and Politics Trivialize Religious Devotion**. In his first novel Carter explores the world of upper-class African Americans, specifically a family coping with the mysteries resulting from the death of its patriarch, a conservative judge.

Other good examples of African American fiction by men include David Haynes's **Live at Five**; Colson Whitehead's **The Intuitionist** and **John Henry Days**; Bil Wright's **Sunday You Learn How to Box**; **Not a Day Goes By** by

E. Lynn Harris; Eric Jerome Dickey's **Liar's Game** and **Milk in My Coffee;** Omar Tyree's **For the Love of Money** and **A Do Right Man;** and John Edgar Wideman's **Two Cities** and **Sent For You Yesterday.**

AFRICAN AMERICAN FICTION: SHE SAY

Although fiction fans are probably familiar with the painful realities of Alice Walker's **The Color Purple,** and the magical realism of Toni Morrison's **Beloved** or the jazzy syncopation of **Jazz,** and know that Terry McMillan writes hip and sexy novels like **Waiting to Exhale; A Day Late and a Dollar Short;** and **How Stella Got Her Groove Back,** there's a whole new group of African American women writers who are writing about male/female relationships, women's friendships, and the plight of the upwardly mobile black woman.

In **What You Owe Me,** Bebe Moore Campbell sensitively explores the unlikely friendship between a refugee Jewish woman and a young black woman as it plays out over three generations and fifty years. Campbell's other novels include **Brothers and Sisters** and **Your Blues Ain't Like Mine.**

A convicted murderer and a woman infected with HIV fall reluctantly in love in Pearl Cleage's issue-filled and thoroughly enjoyable **What Looks Like Crazy on an Ordinary Day.**

Breezy and chatty, **He Say, She Say** by Yolanda Joe looks at relationships through the eyes of four narrators: two men and two women. Joe's other novels include **The Hatwearer's Lesson; Bebe's by Golly Wow;** and **This Just In** . . .

The heroine of Benilde Little's **The Itch** gradually realizes that, despite her

Ivy League education and wealthy husband, something important is missing from her life.

Verdi, the main character in **Blues Dancing** by Diane McKinney-Whetstone, is jolted from her sedate middle-class existence and thrust back into old passions by the sudden reappearance of a former lover from her college days. McKinney-Whetstone is also the author of **Tumbling**.

When her decade-old marriage ends, the main character in Valerie Wilson Wesley's **Ain't Nobody's Business If I Do** discovers that although change is difficult, it's not always bad.

And consider these for your reading list as well: Tina McElroy Ansa's **Baby of the Family** and **The Hand I Fan With**; Connie Briscoe's **A Long Way from Home**; **Big Girls Don't Cry**; and **Sisters & Lovers**; Anita Bunkley's **Wild Embers**; **Starlight Passage**; and **Black Gold**; Lorene Cary's **Pride**; Erika Ellis's **Good Fences**; Gayl Jones's **The Healing**; **Corregidora**; and **Mosquito**; Kristin Hunter Lattany's **Do Unto Others**; Helen Elaine Lee's **The Serpent's Gift** and **Water Marked**; Gloria Naylor's **Mama Day** and **Bailey's Cafe**; Connie Porter's **All-Bright Court**; Dori Sanders's **Her Own Place** and **Clover**; and A. J. Verdelle's **The Good Negress**.

AFRICAN COLONIALISM: FICTION

Europeans in Africa provide a terrific subject for fiction. Writers can explore not only the inevitable clashes of the cultures, but also the inscrutability of the land and its varied peoples. In many of the novels set in Africa, the characters go there to escape boredom or tragedy at home, and to search for new vistas and different lives.

In a sense, all novels about Africa are measured against one of the most powerful and affecting novels ever written by a non-African about Africa: Joseph Conrad's **Heart of Darkness.** It's the story of Marlow's journey into the heart of Africa in search of Kurtz, who originally came to Africa to "civilize" the natives.

A Scottish doctor's desire for adventure places him in 1970s Uganda, working for the Ministry of Health and then as personal physician to dictator Idi Amin, in **The Last King of Scotland** by Giles Foden.

Francesca Marciano's **Rules of the Wild** is a love story set among the world of expatriates in Nairobi, Kenya, in the 1990s—a group notorious for their life of indolence, addiction to pleasure, and lack of connection with and knowledge about black Africa and Africans.

When the other British colonial families leave newly independent Tanzania, Dr. Antonia Redmond, Africa-born and Harvard-trained, remains behind with one of her African patients, in Maria Thomas's **Antonia Saw the Oryx First.**

Two satirical novels about the culture clash in Africa are **White Man's Grave** by Richard Dooling (a young American goes to Sierra Leone in search of his missing best friend, a Peace Corps volunteer) and **Darkest England,** Christopher Hope's very funny novel about an African bushman who travels to London to confront Queen Elizabeth with the promises that Queen Victoria made to the Africans a century before.

Colonialism and cultural conflicts are the themes of M. G. Vassanji's **The Book of Secrets**, in which a diary written seventy years before is discovered in 1980s Dar es Salaam, and a retired schoolteacher tries to uncover the mystery it represents.

British ecologist Hope Clearwater goes to Africa both to escape a bad marriage and to study chimpanzees with a famous scientist in **Brazzaville Beach** by William Boyd.

In Ronan Bennett's political thriller **The Catastrophist**, Irish novelist James Gillespie arrives in the Congo in 1959 to woo back his former lover, now a follower of Patrice Lumumba, who became the first prime minister of the Democratic Republic of the Congo and was assassinated a short time later.

A nice companion read to **The Catastrophist** is **The Poisonwood Bible**, by Barbara Kingsolver, which is the story of an evangelical Baptist minister who, along with his wife and four daughters, comes to the Congo in 1959 in order to convert the heathen Africans.

AFRICAN LITERATURE IN ENGLISH

N ovels by Africans, like the fiction of Latin American writers, seem always to combine the personal and the political—ordinary lives coming up against the tragedy of colonial and postcolonial political reality. There is no escaping Africa's past in these novels, which gives a depth and resonance often lacking in American and British fiction.

Probably the best author with whom to begin reading African literature is Chinua Achebe, and the novel most emblematic of his overarching themes is his masterful **Things Fall Apart,** a book about British colonialism in Achebe's home country of Nigeria.

Ben Okri, one of the best of a new generation of African writers, won the Booker Prize for his novel **The Famished Road,** the story of the child Azaro, who endures the impoverishments and political upheavals in Nigeria while experiencing the wonders and terrors of a spirit world that only he can see.

In **Nervous Conditions,** set in Zimbabwe in the 1950s, Tsitsi Dangarembga describes the life of Tambu, who awakens to the realization of the possibilities beyond the limited (and limiting) expectations of her family and society.

In **The Rape of Shavi,** another Nigerian writer, Buchi Emecheta, tells the story of what happens when a group of Europeans, fleeing from what they believe is a nuclear holocaust, crash their plane near a desert tribe in Africa, and change the Shavi people's way of life forever.

A Senegalese woman reflects on her life, her marriage, and her place in society after her husband decides to take a second wife, in Mariama Bâ's **So Long a Letter.**

In J. Nozipo Maraire's **Zenzele: A Letter for My Daughter,** a mother in Zimbabwe tries to remind her daughter (in school in the United States) of their cultural heritage and their country's long political struggles.

Sembène Ousmane has written a deeply moving and tragic political novel of the struggle against French colonialism in Senegal, in **God's Bits of Woods.**

A Grain of Wheat by Ngugi wa Thiongó is a novel about the human price of revolution, as Kenyans struggle to shake off the yoke of British colonialism.

AGING

There are many nonfiction books that purport to explain and help the reader understand the process of getting old and all its attendant ills—a saggy body and less agile mind among them. But I find that good fiction on the subject of aging offers a more meaningful and moving experience. Here are the two best novels I've read on the topic:

Doris Lessing's **The Diaries of Jane Somers**
Elizabeth Taylor's **Mrs. Palfrey at the Claremont**
(no, this Taylor is not Michael Jackson's pal)

ALASKA

As Michelle Shocked says in her song "Anchorage," "You know you're in the largest state in the Union when you're anchored down in Anchorage." And the best books about Alaska (both fiction and nonfiction) acknowledge its sheer immensity and unforgiving nature.

Margaret E. Murie arrived in Alaska as a nine-year-old in 1911 (her stepfather was an assistant district attorney sent there from Seattle) and grew up in frontier Alaska before it became a state. As an adult, she and her husband Olaus devoted their lives to preserving the wilderness, an experience she shares in vivid detail in **Two in the Far North,** a wonderful introduction to the land and people of Alaska and to the heart of a remarkable woman who had enormous influence on the present-day conservation movement.

The poet, writer, and teacher Sheila Nickerson opens **Disappearance: A Map: A Meditation on Death and Loss in the High Latitudes** with this stunning sentence: "I live in a place where people disappear." She goes on to discuss what it means to live in a place where disappearances of people—of colleagues, friends of friends, hikers, pilots, tourists, thrill seekers—are common. She describes the ongoing erosion of the culture of the first peoples of Alaska, which is a constant troubling reminder of how "civilized" societies frequently treat groups of people whose oil they covet or whose wilderness they wish to tame.

One of the best memoirs I've ever read is Natalie Kusz's **Road Song,** which describes the life she and her family lived when they moved from Los Angeles to homestead in Fairbanks in 1969 and found that the challenges they faced (including crushing poverty and Natalie's being attacked by a neighbor's sled dog and losing an eye) only made them more determined to survive.

On a somewhat lighter note, there are several mystery writers who live, work, and set their novels in Alaska, including Dana Stabenow, Sue Henry, and John Straley. The central character in all the books by these writers is really Alaska itself—and despite the amount of crime that their protagonists have to cope with, it's hard to read them without wanting to call a travel agent immediately and book the next flight north.

Stabenow's best-known mystery series features former Anchorage district attorney, now turned private investigator, Aleut Kate Shugak, a fiercely independent and somewhat prickly young woman (similar in many respects to Sue Grafton's Kinsey Millhone). My favorite Shugak mystery is **A Cold-Blooded**

Business, set way off the beaten track in the oil fields of Prudhoe Bay, Alaska, north of the Arctic Circle and home to an oil company in trouble.

Sue Henry's first mystery, **Murder on the Iditarod Trail,** deservedly won two major mystery awards; in it she introduces her main series character, Jessie Arnold, who trains sled dogs and is Alaska's best-known female "musher." Henry's subsequent books only confirmed her talent for combining suspense-filled plots with vivid descriptive writing.

The main character in Straley's mystery series (which began with a doozy, **The Woman Who Married a Bear**), is Cecil Younger, a (somewhat troubled) private investigator in Sitka, a town he loves and that you will come to love, too.

Dorothy M. Jones was a professor of sociology at the University of Alaska for a number of years, and her heartfelt novel **Tatiana** is the moving story of the eponymous heroine attempting to remain true to herself and her heritage during the tumultuous twentieth century, a time that found great changes coming to Native Alaskan villages, particularly during World War II.

AMERICAN HISTORY: NONFICTION

Books about American history are probably a dime a dozen, from the high school textbooks we all groaned over to the quickie analyses of each presidential race that appear almost as soon as a winner is announced. But there are also some outstanding works, which appear far too infrequently, that help us understand the past and navigate the present. These books (all eminently, not to say compulsively, readable) encourage us to think about how we have been shaped by the past, personally as well as politically.

Whenever I ask a group of people about their favorite books, inevitably someone will rave about Howard Zinn's **A People's History of the United States**. Originally published in 1980, and frequently revised and updated, **A People's History** approaches its subject through an examination of the role of those who often did not appear in history books before: women, blacks, American Indians, and, especially, the working classes. Revolutionary when it first appeared, Zinn's work has been the model for many works of history ever since.

The Age of Gold: The California Gold Rush and the New American Dream by H. W. Brands is a wide-ranging and engaging history of the 1848 watershed event that drew people to California from all over the world and redefined how Americans thought about success. It's important when you're reading this book to be close to a library or bookstore, since you'll find yourself going down various fascinating byways and wanting to read more about them, too.

There Is a River: The Black Struggle for Freedom in America by Vincent Harding recounts the struggle against slavery and racism, beginning in West Africa with the first slave ships in the very early years of the seventeenth century, and continuing through the Civil War and Reconstruction.

Cadillac Desert: The American West and Its Disappearing Water by Marc Reisner is still considered the best book ever written about water issues in the arid western United States. Reisner is fascinated with geopolitics and discusses, among other topics: western history; the role of John Wesley Powell, the developers, and the environmentalists who continue to try to conserve the depleting water resources of our nation; and the largely horrifying position of many U.S. leaders toward the problems of aridity and shrinking aquifers.

The two classic, immensely readable books about the American Indian experience are Dee Brown's 1970 **Bury My Heart at Wounded Knee: An Indian History of the American West** and **The Long Death: The Last Days of the Plains Indian** by Ralph K. Andrist, which was originally published in 1964. Both books influenced later scholarship and the way Americans thought about the native population. Brown offers a well-documented (but quite controversial when first published) overview of the thirty dreadful years between 1860 and 1890, from the time of the Long Walk of the Navajos from their homelands to a reservation in New Mexico, and the massacre at Wounded Knee. Andrist lays out, in starkly evocative prose, the sorry plight of the Plains Indians as they were forced by the United States government to retreat in the face of western expansion.

AMERICAN HISTORY: FICTION

K evin Baker, a crackerjack researcher (he worked on Harold Evans's **The American Century**) and writer for *American Heritage,* makes great use of his talents in two novels. **Dreamland** vividly describes the lives of poor immigrant families on the Lower East Side of New York City, circa 1910, who find their lives made somewhat more bearable by the promise and excitement of Coney Island. **Paradise Alley** recounts the riots in New York City in 1863 that followed President Lincoln's decision to institute a draft to get soldiers to fight in the Civil War.

In the Fall by Jeffrey Lent charts the lives of the Pelham family after the Civil War, when young Norman comes home to Vermont having married Leah, a runaway slave. Lent's novel shows how no one can ever escape the effects of slavery—not the slave owners, nor the slaves themselves, nor the descendants of either.

With liberal doses of romance and mystery woven into the plot, it's easy to overlook the historical basis for Lauren Belfer's **City of Light.** Set during the Buffalo, New York, Pan-American Exposition in 1901, Belfer's novel looks at the early years of the skirmish between conservationists and the developers of natural resources in the Northeast. You'll never look at Niagara Falls the same way again after reading this novel.

In **Underworld** Don DeLillo explores, through multiple voices and psyches, the last half of the twentieth century, beginning with Bobby Thomson's 1951 home run that propelled the New York Baseball Giants into the World Series in the same year as the Soviet Union detonated an atomic bomb.

Frederick Busch's **The Night Inspector,** set in the years after the Civil War, follows the experiences of a horribly scarred (in both body and mind) Union veteran as he makes his way through the dark and menacing streets of New York.

E. L. Doctorow has a fictional family in **Ragtime** interacting with many of the most famous and infamous people of the first years of the twentieth century, including Henry Ford, Harry Houdini, Sigmund Freud, and Booker T. Washington.

AMERICAN INDIAN LITERATURE

A merican Indian literature began coming into its own in the 1960s, and the succeeding decades saw the publication of a number of new writers as well as renewed interest in older ones. Check out these anthologies for a good introduction to new writers as well as to reacquaint yourself with those who have made it into the literary mainstream:

Reinventing the Enemy's Language: Contemporary Native Women's Writings of North America, edited by Joy Harjo; Smoke Rising: The Native North American Literary Companion, edited by Joseph Bruchac et al.; Here First: Autobiographical Essays by Native American Writers; and Voices Under One Sky: Contemporary Native Literature, edited by Trish Fox Roman. Take a look, too, at Red on Red: Native American Literary Separatism by Craig S. Womack, a thoughtful assessment of the state of Native American literature today.

My favorites among American Indian writers include Leslie Marmon Silko (Ceremony and others); D'Arcy McNickle (Wind from an Enemy Sky); Louise Erdrich (Love Medicine and others); N. Scott Momaday (House Made of Dawn and others); Michael Dorris (A Yellow Raft in Blue Water); as well as Susan Power's The Grass Dancer; Thomas King's Green Grass, Running Water and Truth & Bright Water; Diane Glancy's Flutie; Sherman Alexie's The Lone Ranger and Tonto Fistfight in Heaven (don't miss Alexie's poetry, which is sharp, bitter, and often very funny); James Welch's The Heartsong of Charging Elk; Louis Owens's The Sharpest Sight; and Debra Magpie Earling's magnificent first novel Perma Red.

ARMCHAIR TRAVEL

There are lots of good reasons to travel—uncharted horizons to explore and new friends to make among them—but there are also lots of good reasons to stay home—a comfortable chair, a good reading light, and a mug of hot tea among them. So why not combine the two alternatives and stay at home to read books about other people's travels? Here are some great reads that will take you to Asia, Africa, India, and the far edges of North America.

Three classics of travel literature with which to begin your journey are Eric Newby's **A Short Walk in the Hindu Kush** (in fact, everything by Newby is worth reading); Wilfred Thesiger's **Arabian Sands;** and **News from Tartary: A Journey from Peking to Kashmir** by Peter Fleming.

The Great Railway Bazaar: By Train Through Asia by Paul Theroux is in some ways the granddaddy of contemporary armchair travel books. Although Theroux's later travelogues display a kind of nasty, cynical view of the people and places he encounters, here his descriptions of his trip via such famed trains as the Orient Express, the Khyber Mail, and the Trans-Siberian Express come across as merely eccentric.

Looking for Lovedu: A Woman's Journey Across Africa relates the sometimes hilarious adventures of Ann Jones as she traverses the continent in an ancient Land Rover, from Tangier to the southernmost tip of South Africa, in search of the last Queen of Lovedu, and in the company—for the first half of the trip—of the incomparable Muggleton, a young British photographer. (Incidentally, the hard word in the title is pronounced *low-bay-due.*)

In Colin Thubron's **In Siberia** we accompany the author on his journey across this enormous and enormously mysterious land, from Mongolia to the Arctic Circle, as he travels by car, boat, train, bus, and on foot.

Passage to Juneau by Jonathan Raban details a trip that is both exterior and interior: his voyage up the Inside Passage from Seattle to Juneau, on his 35-foot sailboat *Penelope,* and his ruminations on a wonderful diversity of topics.

In 1983, Chinese dissident Ma Jian took a three-year walk throughout his native country, as related in **Red Dust: A Path Through China.**

Another journey on foot—under much more fraught conditions—is Salvomir Rawicz's **The Long Walk,** in which he describes his 1941 escape from the Soviet gulag and his arduous hike to India.

In **Rowing to Latitude: Journeys Along the Arctic's Edge,** Jill Fredston describes how she and her husband spend their summers making their way around the edges of the Arctic by rowboat and kayak. No four-star hotels and gourmet dining experiences, no splendor on the Orient Express for this couple. They are at sea for weeks at a time, encountering polar bears, mosquitoes, killer storms, and big winds.

ART APPRECIATION

Probably the best way (some would argue the only way) to appreciate a work of art is to immerse yourself in viewing it, not reading about it. But I've found that three of the books I've most enjoyed are books about the world of art and how we experience art.

John Berger's **Ways of Seeing,** originally written as part of a BBC television series on art and art criticism aired in the early 1970s, offered the public a Marxist interpretation of the making and popularization of visual artworks. Berger expanded his thinking on these topics in later books like **About Looking** and **The Sense of Sight,** but his first book gives the clearest exposition of his theories. After reading Berger I found that I looked at works of art in a whole new way.

Robert Hughes, *Time* magazine's art critic, is a historian (he wrote a wonderful history of Australia, **The Fatal Shore**), cultural commentator (take a look at his spirited **Culture of Complaint**), and voracious reader with diverse interests. He brings all of his interests together in **The Shock of the New: The Hundred-Year History of Modern Art—Its Rise, Its Dazzling Achievement, Its Fall** (which, like Berger's book, was the basis for a television series in the 1970s and which, unlike Berger's, has a shocking misprint—"it's" for "its"—on the front cover of the 1991 revised edition). Hughes's book is filled with wonderful reproductions and insightful, thought-provoking commentary.

Novelist, poet, and essayist John Updike turns his considerable talents to writing winningly and winsomely about art, in **Just Looking: Essays on Art**, covering such topics as the Museum of Modern Art, children's book illustrators, Renoir, cartoonist Ralph Barton, and Andrew Wyeth, among others.

ASIAN AMERICAN EXPERIENCES

When Putnam published Amy Tan's first novel, **The Joy Luck Club**, in 1989, the book immediately hit the best-seller lists and brought the Asian American experience to a wide audience. Prior to Tan's novel there had been memoirs about growing up as a "hyphenated" American (most notably Jade Snow Wong's **Fifth Chinese Daughter** and Maxine Hong Kingston's **The Woman Warrior**), but nothing before had caught the imagination of American readers as Tan's novel did, and her success opened the door to other Asian writers exploring what it's like to grow up between two cultures.

Here are some of the best examples of Asian American coming-of-age writings: **Growing Up Asian American,** edited by Maria Hong, a collection of more than thirty short stories and essays by Frank Chin, Garrett Hongo, Mary Paik Lee, Susan Ito, and others; **Bone** by Fae Myenne Ng; Wayson Choy's autobiographical **The Jade Peony,** set in Vancouver's Chinatown in the 1940s; Lois-Ann Yamanaka's **Blu's Hanging** and **Wild Meat and the Bully Burgers;** Andrea Louie's **Moon Cakes; Donald Duk** by Frank Chin; Shawn Wong's **Homebase** and **American Knees;** Gish Jen's **Typical American** and **Mona in the Promised Land;** Lydia Minatoya's **The Strangeness of Beauty;** Gus Lee's **China Boy;** Chang-rae Lee's **Native Speaker.**

ASTRONOMICAL IDEAS

Authoritative" and (mostly) "comprehensible" (to the motivated but not scientific reader) are two adjectives that describe the prolific science writer Timothy Ferris. His books range from a look at amateur stargazers (**Seeing in the Dark: How Backyard Stargazers Are Probing Deep Space and Guarding Earth from Interplanetary Peril**) to a discussion of the way the mind works and the search for extraterrestrial intelligence (**The Mind's Sky: Human Intelligence in a Cosmic Context**) to an investigation of the concept of an expanding universe (**The Red Limit: The Search for the Edge of the Universe**) to **Coming of Age in the Milky Way,** a fascinating overview of the history of astronomy, from ancient times to the present.

Of course, Carl Sagan's **Cosmos** should be high on everyone's must-read list for this subject, even though the book is now more than two decades old. More than anyone before or since, Sagan turned "astronomy" into a household word. From its mind-catching opening sentence ("The Cosmos is all that is or ever was or ever will be") to its last line, this makes for interesting, informative, and enlightening reading.

In **Stardust: Supernovae and Life: The Cosmic Connection,** John Gribbin discusses the relationship between the creation of the universe (what scientists call "the big bang") and the atoms and molecules that make up humankind.

Two books trace the myriad myths and legends from all over the world that have evolved around the sun, planets, and solar system: E. C. Krupp's **Beyond the Blue Horizon: Myths and Legends of the Sun, Moon, Stars, and Planets** and Catherine Tennant's interactive **The Box of Stars: A Practical Guide to the Night Sky and Its Myths and Legends.**

The Soul of the Night: An Astronomical Pilgrimage by Chet Raymo (who also wrote **The Dork of Cork,** one of my favorite novels) is a bit off the scientific track, but these essays, which explore the links between science and religion, nevertheless offer much food for contemplation.

Two wonderful coffee-table books about space are Ken Croswell's **Magnificent Universe,** with many photos taken by the Hubble telescope, and **Full Moon** by Michael Light.

AUSTRALIAN FICTION

The text or subtext of much Australian fiction is both the vastness of the continent and its settlement by British convicts. Australian novels convey the idea that place somehow defines who and what you are. (Canadian fiction shares this sense of place to some degree.) Many Australian novelists write about journeys, road trips, people running away from their pasts or their presents (or their presence in their own life), challenged by the terrain, the weather, the impossibility of leaving (and the equal impossibility of staying), their own history, and the inner demons that plague them.

Martin Boyd's **The Cardboard Crown; A Difficult Young Man; When Blackbirds Sing;** and **Outbreak of Love** comprise a wonderful (and little-known) series written in the 1950s about an Australian family who move to England when things go wrong in Australia, and move back to Australia when things go wrong in England. The first two books are especially good.

Other notable Australian novels include Jessica Anderson's **Tirra Lirra by the River** and **The Only Daughter;** James Bradley's **Wrack;** Peter Carey's **True History of the Kelly Gang** and **Oscar and Lucinda;** Miles Franklin's **My Brilliant Career** (first published in 1901 and still a delight to read); Nikki Gemmell's **Alice Springs;** Janette Turner Hospital's **Oyster;** Thomas Keneally's **Woman of the Inner Sea;** David Malouf's **Remembering Babylon;** and Tim Winton's **Cloudstreet; That Eye, The Sky;** and **Dirt Music.**

Novels set in Tasmania form their own subgenre within the broader category of "Australia." Some of my favorites are Richard Flanagan's **The Sound of One Hand Clapping; Death of a River Guide;** and **Gould's Book of Fish;** and Matthew Kneale's **English Passengers.**

Two of the best novels set in Australia are by Nevil Shute: **A Town Like**

Alice and **The Breaking Wave** (**Requiem for a Wren** is its title in the United Kingdom). Shute, who was born in England, moved to Australia when he was nearly fifty and dearly loved his adopted country.

BABIES: A READER'S GUIDE

These four books won't tell you what to do when your child has a high fever, or how to identify a mysterious rash, or even how to get your baby to sleep through the night, but they all offer fascinating insights—and food for thought—on the emotional and psychological needs of children. Understanding those needs will almost inevitably lead to better parenting and better relationships between parents and their children. None of these books is new, but their wisdom is timeless.

Although it's generally accepted that in his personal life Bruno Bettelheim was not the nicest of men, his book **A Good Enough Parent: A Book on Child-Rearing** is a must-read for any new parent. What comes through in this book is Bettelheim's profound understanding of children and his deep compassion and respect for them. Be forewarned: Bettelheim's perspective is very psychoanalytic.

Selma H. Fraiberg's **Every Child's Birthright: In Defense of Mothering** rests upon her belief that "our survival as a human community may depend as much upon our nurture of love in infancy and childhood as upon the protection of our society from external threats."

Between Parent and Child by Haim Ginott offers concrete suggestions for dealing with daily situations and psychological problems faced by all parents. His focus is on parent-child communications, and he advocates giving a child choices rather than orders.

Summerhill by A. S. Neill has become a classic in the literature of permissive (which was a good adjective in the 1960s, when this book was written) education and child rearing. It's fun to read (lots of case studies of kids), even if you disagree with Neill's extremely Freudian-influenced ideas.

BALKAN SPECTERS

There's always trouble in the Balkans in the spring, as Rudyard Kipling (almost) said in The Light That Failed. This is an area of Central Europe where hatreds run deep, where memories are long, and where peace has nearly always seemed an impossible dream. These books, all of which are gut-wrenching and extremely painful to read, lay out the horrors and sorrows and complexities that have marked Bosnia's history.

A good background work on the region is Rebecca West's Black Lamb and Grey Falcon: A Journey Through Yugoslavia, which provides context and history, that makes the book still relevant years after it was first published in 1941.

Both Peter Maass in Love Thy Neighbor: A Story of War and Robert Kaplan in Balkan Ghosts: A Journey Through History expose the horror of life during wartime in the former Yugoslavia. Although there is inevitably some overlap between the two, it is surprisingly minimal, and both bear reading and rereading. Maass, a former war correspondent, is the more visceral writer (which is not meant to imply undisciplined emotion about his subject).

British war correspondent Anthony Loyd's troubled, honest, and unabashedly one-sided My War Gone By, I Miss It So compares the highs and the lows of war to his experiences with heroin, which might sound a bit off-putting but the metphor actually works amazingly well.

David Rohde won a Pulitzer Prize for his reporting from Bosnia, and you can see why in **Endgame: The Betrayal and Fall of Srebrenica, Europe's Worst Massacre Since World War II,** his tragic account of a battle in which more than seven thousand Muslims were murdered.

Bosnian novelists have frequently used issues of ethnic hatred as a subject for their plots. Nobel Prize winner Ivo Andrić's **The Bridge on the Drina** describes the relationships between the various ethnic groupings in a small Bosnian town from the sixteenth to the twentieth centuries.

In **S.: A Novel About the Balkans,** her book about a Bosnian who left the war zone and lives in Sweden, Slavenka Drakulić sounds a chilling note (in the most dispassionate tone) about the brutality of war, particularly as it is visited on women.

HAMILTON BASSO: TOO GOOD TO MISS

Sadly all but forgotten now, New Orleans native Hamilton Basso was a relatively important Southern writer in the 1940s and '50s. Although he spent most of his adult life in New York, where he was an associate editor at *The New Yorker* for more than twenty years, Basso's major subject was the South. He wrote with great affection, but not uncritically, about the South, in particular about its attitudes toward race and what he saw as Southern ancestry worship.

He wrote two novels still well worth reading: **The View from Pompey's Head** and **The Light Infantry Ball.** They were intended to be part of a trilogy, unfortunately never finished, about a fictional town, Pompey's Head, South Carolina.

The View from Pompey's Head was a best-seller in 1954. It's the story of a New York attorney who goes home to Pompey's Head to investigate a mystery surrounding a famous writer—in essence an exploration of Thomas Wolfe's dictum that "you can't go home again," and what can happen when you do.

The Light Infantry Ball, a finalist for the 1960 National Book Award for fiction, is a prequel to **The View from Pompey's Head.** It takes place during the Civil War and introduces many of the families whose descendants play important roles in that novel.

Basso's last novel was also one of my favorites. **A Touch of the Dragon** is both a love story and a character study of a particularly self-possessed and wealthy young woman, someone who is, to quote the poet A. E. Housman, "too unhappy to be kind," and who wanders in and out of the life of the narrator.

Other novels by Basso (not nearly as good as these three) include **The Greenroom; Sun in Capricorn; Days Before Lent; Court House Square;** and **Cinnamon Seed.**

BBB: BEST BUSINESS BOOKS

Although these books don't address specific issues such as how to run a company or what to look for when you're buying mutual funds, they offer fascinating insights into American business and financial practices, circa the late twentieth and early twenty-first centuries, and as such are perfect for literary readers who want to expand their knowledge of the arcane.

Malcolm Gladwell's **The Tipping Point: How Little Things Can Make a Big Difference** (much of which appeared in *The New Yorker* magazine) explores the virus-like spread of ideas and products through society—for example, how best-selling books are made, not born; why certain television shows succeed and others fail, despite their similarities; and how rumors travel at the speed of light.

You'll look at your behavior in shopping situations much differently after you read **Why We Buy: The Science of Shopping** by urban anthropologist Paco Underhill, an often troubling, always interesting analysis of what makes retail stores successful. (I found his message equally useful and valid for non-retail entities such as libraries, too.)

Liar's Poker: Rising Through the Wreckage on Wall Street by Michael Lewis is an up-close and personal (and very cautionary) view of the author's experiences working for a big Wall Street investment firm.

Two frightening books on the culture of avarice and greed in corporate America in the 1980s, as seen through the rise and fall of the king of the junk bond, Wall Street trader Michael Milken, are Connie Bruck's **The Predators' Ball: The Inside Story of Drexel Burnham and the Rise of the Junk Bond Raiders** and **Den of Thieves** by *Wall Street Journal* reporter (now editor) James B. Stewart. (Incidentally, a very good novel about working on Wall Street around this same period is the semiautobiographical **Moral Hazard** by Kate Jennings.)

BICYCLING

In How I Learned to Ride the Bicycle, Frances Willard (probably best known for her spirited work with the Woman's Christian Temperance Union) describes learning to ride a bicycle when she was nearly fifty-four years old. She quotes an English naval officer who, having just mastered a two-wheeler himself, said to her: "You women have no idea of the new realm of happiness which the bicycle has opened to us men." It's this realm of happiness that comes across so wonderfully in these entertaining accounts of great bicycle adventures.

No list of good bicycling books is at all complete without a mention of the unquenchable Dervla Murphy, who describes her bike trip across two continents in the frigid winter of 1961 in Full Tilt: Ireland to India With a Bicycle. Murphy's many other bicycle adventures are recounted in books like The Ukimwi Road: From Kenya to Zimbabwe and Wheels Within Wheels.

French Revolutions: Cycling the Tour de France by thirty-six-year-old Tim Moore is a very funny account of his experiences while trying to ride all 2,256 miles of the Tour de France several weeks before the real race began.

Many people were first inspired to travel by bicycle by Miles from Nowhere: A Round-the-World Bicycle Adventure, Barbara Savage's now classic story of a two-year trip that took her and her husband from their home in Santa Barbara, California, to the far corners of the world.

American Erika Warmbrunn spent eight months cycling from Siberia to Saigon in Where the Pavement Ends: One Woman's Bicycle Trip Through Mongolia, China & Vietnam. Her memoir is striking not only because of her description of the difficulties inherent in such a journey, but because of her appreciation for the people and places she encounters.

Back when bicycling was still in its infancy, Evelyn McDaniel Gibb's father and his best friend—both teenagers—set off on an amazing two-wheeled trip: riding north from Santa Rosa, California, up to Seattle for the Alaska-Yukon-Pacific Exposition. In **Two Wheels North: Bicycling the West Coast in 1909,** Gibb retells her father's grand adventure.

Goran Kropp describes his bicycle trip from Sweden to Nepal in **Ultimate High: My Everest Odyssey.** (Following this event-studded bike trip, Kropp went on to climb Everest alone, without supplemental oxygen or help from a Sherpa to carry his equipment, and bicycled on home!)

Two Wheels in the Dust: From Kathmandu to Kandy, by English senior citizen Anne Mustoe, details her spiritual pilgrimage from Nepal to Sri Lanka as she follows in the footsteps of the main characters in the Ramayana, the Sanskrit epic.

If you're up for rough bicycling in an unfamiliar terrain, share Andrew X. Pham's experiences in **Catfish and Mandala: A Two Wheeled-Voyage Through the Landscape and Memory of Vietnam.**

BIOGRAPHICAL NOVELS

Most biographical novels mix imagined characters in with the real ones. This allows the author to follow Emily Dickinson's dictum: "Tell all the truth but tell it slant." And that's the reason I love good biographical novels: The subjects seem to me to be even more "real" than they do in a straight biography. I also frequently find myself, upon finishing a biographical novel, reading a biography of the person, then comparing the two. Here are some of the best biographical novels I've read:

Amanda Burden looks back at her thirteenth year—when her stepmother was bludgeoned to death, and everyone's favorite suspect was the family's next-door neighbor, Lizzie Borden, who had been acquitted of the axe-murder of her own parents three decades before—in **Miss Lizzie** by Walter Satterthwait.

The Other Boleyn Girl, by Philippa Gregory, vividly retells the story of the tempestuous marriage of Anne Boleyn and Henry VIII from the point of view of Mary, Anne's older sister and Henry's mistress long before her sister caught the eye of the king.

Janet Stevenson's **Weep No More** illuminates the sad yet ultimately noble life of Elizabeth Van Lew, who disguised her activities as a Union spy in Richmond, Virginia, by appearing to be simply insane.

The protagonist of **The Untouchable,** a wonderful character study by John Banville, is based on Sir Anthony Blunt, art historian, Keeper of the Queen's Pictures, and one of the infamous group of Cambridge spies that included Kim Philby and Guy Burgess.

Max Byrd's **Grant** isn't set during the Civil War, when Ulysses S. Grant distinguished himself on the battlefield (and accepted Lee's surrender at

Appomattox) or during his two presidential terms (marked by general ineptitude and scandals), but instead begins five years before Grant's death, in 1885, from cancer of the throat. Byrd has also written outstanding biographical novels about Presidents Jefferson and Jackson.

Two writers have tried to contain the great abolitionist and rabble-rouser John Brown within the confines of a novel with some degree of success, if only because the books are so well written. Read them together, because no single interpretation or point of view can do John Brown justice, if justice he deserves: Russell Banks's **Cloudsplitter,** told from the point of view of Owen Brown, John's son, humanizes the leader of the attack on the federal arsenal at Harpers Ferry, and describes Brown as a difficult and demanding father. Bruce Olds's **Raising Holy Hell** is a postmodern interpretation of Brown's life and death, told from various points of view and written in the form of journal entries, letters, and interior monologues.

The Last Canyon by John Vernon is a beautiful retelling of John Wesley Powell's 1869 exploration of the Grand Canyon and his and his men's inevitable and tragic clash with a tribe of Paiute Indians who lived on the canyon's northern edge.

Reading **The Death of Ché Guevara** by Jay Cantor makes it easy to see how charismatic Castro's closest pal during the Cuban Revolution was. The book is fast moving and sympathetic to both Ché Guevara and the cause. Cantor was clearly as captivated by the energy and humanity of the man as were Ché's many followers.

BIRD BRAINS

After reading Lyanda Lynn Haupt's elegant meditation, Rare Encounters with Ordinary Birds: Notes from a Northwest Year, I found myself much more aware of the sights and sounds of the birds I saw and heard as I went through my ordinary activities and everyday life.

Warm, humorous, and filled with (unobtrusively presented) information, Red-tails in Love: A Wildlife Drama in Central Park, by *Wall Street Journal* columnist Marie Winn, relates the excitement in the New York birding community (and throughout the world) when two rare red-tail hawks are sighted in Central Park.

Traveling to Iceland, the Galapagos, Texas, Alberta, and beyond, naturalist and nature photographer Tim Gallagher has observed and written about birds of prey (falcons, eagles, condors, and other raptors) and other birds for more than twenty years. The beautifully written essays that make up Parts Unknown: A Naturalist's Journey in Search of Birds and Wild Places display Gallagher's love and appreciation for these magnificent birds and the wild and untamed world in which they live.

Birders: Tales of a Tribe by Mark Cocker distinguishes bird-watching (a rather passive activity) and birders (an active, aggressive, quirky lot of folks, which includes Cocker) and is a most entertaining look at what makes birders so passionate about their hobby that they'll endure extremes of climate, put up with total discomfort, and even take risks to accomplish their sighting goals.

Christopher Cokinos explores the last days of several different species of once-plentiful, now extinct birds, such as the passenger pigeon, the ivory-billed woodpecker, the great auk, the Labrador duck, and the Carolina parakeet in

Hope Is the Thing with Feathers: A Personal Chronicle of Vanished Birds. (The title is based on a line by Emily Dickinson.)

David Allen Sibley's **The Sibley Guide to Birds** is a beautifully illustrated guide for birders and armchair bird enthusiasts by an author squarely in the tradition of such long-famous three-named bird fanciers as John James Audubon and Roger Tory Peterson, while **The Sibley Guide to Bird Life & Behavior** is an indispensable collection of essays by well-known avian experts, for those who want even more information on all aspects of the subject.

In **The Birds of Heaven: Travel with Cranes**, Peter Matthiessen seeks out the world's fifteen species of cranes—eleven of which fall into the endangered category. The book is beautifully illustrated by Robert Bateman.

Providence of a Sparrow: Lessons from a Life Gone to the Birds by Chris Chester is his charming account of how an English sparrow changed his life.

In **The Beak of the Finch: A Story of Evolution in Our Time**, Jonathan Weiner writes about the scientists who are investigating successive generations of finches on Daphne Major, an island in the Galapagos.

BLACK HUMOR

I am not usually a fan of black humor, which seems to me to turn on the cruelty and nastiness of its characters. But for some reason, these three books—one very, very dark and the other two more a very pale shade of gray—are favorites of mine.

In **Lost** by Hans-Ulrich Treichel, the eight-year-old German narrator records his conflicted feelings when he discovers that the older brother he always believed had died during World War II might actually be alive. His parents have identified an orphan as their likely son Arnold, and now they have to prove that the orphan actually is their son. This lands the family in a Kafkaesque world of institutes, mad doctors, and scientific testing to determine the true parentage of the perhaps-Arnold.

The Lecturer's Tale by James Hynes might best be described as comic horror. On the day that he is fired, Nelson Humboldt, a lecturer in the English department of a prestigious university (where his brand of academic investigation has fallen out of favor, replaced by the deconstructionists, the multiculturalists, the feminists, and countless other "ists"), severs his finger in a freak collision with a bicycle. After the finger is reattached, Nelson discovers that by merely touching people with it, he can bend them to his will. So what will he do with this newfound power? Just about anything to get back at his enemies.

Terence Blacker's **Kill Your Darlings** is blacker than black, complete with a slimy antihero. Gregory Keays's failure to live up to his predicted career as a notable novelist stings particularly when he compares himself to the fabulously successful Martin Amis, who did live up to his promise. In addition, both his marriage (to the deliciously named Marigold, a fabulously successful feng shui practitioner) and his relationship with his teenage son have fallen apart. Sick of his life and his part-time gig teaching creative writing in a fifth-rate community college, Gregory decides to appropriate a novel written by one of his students, a young man who committed suicide after finishing the book, and use the manuscript to gain all the fame and fortune he feels he so richly deserves. This is a novel to love, with a main character to despise—an unreliable narrator to top all other unreliable narrators.

BOMB MAKERS

The making of the atom bomb and its subsequent use are the subject of some awfully interesting books.

Richard Rhodes's exceptionally readable **The Making of the Atomic Bomb** is the place to start. This sweeping chronicle of the difficult and sobering history of the endeavor called the Manhattan Project is marked by Rhodes's insightful studies of the complicated people who were most involved in the creation of the bomb, from Niels Bohr to Robert Oppenheimer. Rhodes followed this book with **Dark Sun: The Making of the Hydrogen Bomb.**

In **Heisenberg's War: The Secret History of the German Bomb,** Thomas Powers examines the life and work of the controversial German scientist who chose to remain in Germany after many of his physicist contemporaries had moved to the United States, and who led his country's nuclear research efforts. Powers tries to answer the question of why Germany never developed a nuclear bomb.

General Leslie Groves, who was put in charge of the Manhattan Project at its inception late in 1943, describes what went on from the time he set up the project through the bombing of Japan and the postwar years, in **Now It Can Be Told: The Story of the Manhattan Project.**

Gregg Herken, in **Brotherhood of the Bomb: The Tangled Lives and Loyalties of Robert Oppenheimer, Ernest Lawrence, and Edward Teller,** tells the history of the nuclear age through the intertwined biographies of three of the colleagues who were most involved in creating it. They began as friends yet ended up in strong disagreement about how the bomb should be used, both during the war and after.

Sometimes fiction can be valuable for broadening and deepening one's understanding of a difficult topic. In his Tony Award–winning play *Copenhagen,* Michael Frayn uses a (real) meeting between Werner Heisenberg and Niels Bohr in Denmark in 1941 to explore the way we interpret history.

E. V. Cunningham's **Phyllis** is one of the most moving novels set during the height of the Cold War, when the fear of nuclear spies was pervasive. In this story some missing uranium is traced to a physicist at a New York university. (E. V. Cunningham is the pseudonym for the blacklisted leftie Howard Fast.)

BOOKS ABOUT BOOKS

Bibliophiles love nothing better than making the acquaintance of other book lovers—especially between the pages of a book. Here are some people whose books about books I've especially enjoyed.

Wendy Lesser writes about the joys of loving books in **Nothing Remains the Same: Rereading and Remembering.**

Those of us who grew up enchanted by the world of literature will particularly celebrate Francis Spufford's **The Child That Books Built: A Life in Reading.**

Nicholas Basbanes explores the world of the book lover in **A Gentle Madness: Bibliophiles, Bibliomanes, and the Eternal Passion for Books** and **Patience & Fortitude: A Roving Chronicle of Book People, Book Places, and Book Culture.**

No real reader could resist a book with a title like **A Passion for Books: A Book Lover's Treasury of Stories, Essays, Humor, Lore, and Lists on Collecting, Reading, Borrowing, Lending, Caring for, and Appreciating Books,** edited by

Harold Rabinowitz and Rob Kaplan, with a foreword by Ray Bradbury.

It's always interesting to read about the books loved by writers whom you love, and you can feast to your heart's content in **For the Love of Books: 115 Celebrated Writers on the Books They Love Most** by Ronald B. Shwartz.

Novelist and essayist Anna Quindlen describes her relationship with books in **How Reading Changed My Life.**

Anne Fadiman's **Ex Libris: Confessions of a Common Reader** is a particularly lovely collection of essays, including a priceless one on combining the libraries of two heavy-duty readers who are joined in marriage.

Despite the title of her book, Fadiman is no common reader. Her father was the well-known writer, critic, book editor of *The New Yorker,* senior judge at the Book-of-the-Month Club, and all-around bookworm Clifton Fadiman, whose own book **The Lifetime Reading Plan** had enormous influence for more than forty years and is still worth looking at today.

In **Ruined by Reading: A Life in Books,** novelist Lynne Sharon Schwartz grapples with a question that I have long pondered: Is an addiction to reading—in which one prefers reading to real life—good or bad?

Editor Steven Gilbar collected selections from writers like Stanley Elkins, Michel de Montaigne, John Fowles, and Vladimir Nabokov on the pleasures and perils of an addiction to books, in **Reading in Bed: Personal Essays on the Glories of Reading.**

Fifty-seven writers (among them Sherman Alexie, Howard Norman, Larry Watson, Mona Simpson, and Nicholson Baker) share their recollections of the events and people that turned them into readers, in **The Most Wonderful Books: Writers on Discovering the Pleasures of Reading,** edited by Michael Dorris and Emilie Buchwald.

BOYS COMING OF AGE

Boys becoming men is an enduring theme in fiction. It's difficult to find anyone who didn't read at least one of the two best-known (and best) examples of the genre—John Knowles's **A Separate Peace** and J. D. Salinger's **The Catcher in the Rye**—in high school or college (and sometimes in both). Coming-of-age novels describe a search for understanding, not only of oneself, but also of the often mysterious, contradictory, and sometimes frightening adult world. They help readers reflect on their own experiences and offer a (sometimes minimal) consolation that one's feelings are not unique. Although many coming-of-age novels are, perforce, autobiographical in nature and earnest in tone (often overly so), many are filled with vivid characters and fresh insights.

Cormac McCarthy's novels are usually far too violent for me, but I found **All the Pretty Horses** difficult to put down. This gorgeously written contemporary classic, set in the late 1940s, is the story of John Grady Cole who, along with a friend, leaves his Texas home in search of adventure in Mexico, where he encounters experiences that turn him, unwillingly, into a man.

In **Testing the Current** by William McPherson, Tommy McAllister grows up awfully quickly during his ninth year, when he becomes aware of the inconsistencies and outright lies in the lives of his parents and their friends.

As an adult, Anton Steenwijk tries to come to terms with the 1945 murder near his childhood home of a Nazi collaborator, and the subsequent brutal retaliation suffered by his family, in Harry Mulisch's **The Assault**.

Alan Brown lays out a complicated childhood and difficult coming-of-age for his protagonist, Toshi, in **Audrey Hepburn's Neck**. Toshi's belated discovery of his mother's awful past in war-torn Japan leads him finally to understand and, perhaps, forgive her for deserting him and his father.

In **Isaac and His Devils** by Fernanda Eberstadt, young genius Isaac Hooker moves slowly toward adulthood, trying to balance the competing visions for his future of his overbearing mother and his passive father.

In Nick Hornby's lighthearted **About a Boy**, thirty-something, rich, self-ish, and very hip Will Freeman finally grows up only after becoming involved in the lives of Fiona and Marcus, Fiona's twelve-year-old son, who is solidly square and very unhappy.

Set in 1970s Birmingham, England, Jonathan Coe's **The Rotters' Club** explores the pangs and pains of adolescence through the experiences of Ben Trotter and his friends, which include unrequited love, faltering attempts to start a rock band, and subversion of the school newspaper.

BROTHERS AND SISTERS

In novels, if not in life, the relationship between siblings is composed of a dose or two of resentment, a sense of competition, a bit of admira-tion, some green-eyed jealousy, and sometimes hatred, with (occasion-ally) love and affection making up the rest.

The complex bonds between brothers and sisters are explored in David James Duncan's **The Brothers K,** the engrossing story of the Chance family, who are united by their love of baseball but torn apart by the mother's obsessive devotion to her Seventh-day Adventist beliefs.

Sometimes the death of a parent can bring children together, for better or for worse, as in J. Robert Lennon's **The Funnies.** When well-known car-toonist Carl Mix dies, his four estranged children, whose only real connec-tion is that they each suffered through the experience of having their lives transformed into humorous subject matter for their father's immensely popular "Family Funnies" comic strip (think "The Family Circus"), find themselves becoming a family for the first time.

In Annie Waters's first novel, **Glimmer,** Sage, who is the daughter of a divorced black father and a white mother and the youngest sibling in a family of five, reaches a crisis point during her first year of college. It's only with the (unexpected) support and love of her brothers and sisters that she is able to recover from a suicide attempt, cope with her sorrow over her mother's death, and come to accept her biracial identity.

After they're orphaned by a terrorist explosion, the McWilliams kids each deal with the tragedy in their own particular way, while together they star in a wildly successful comedy television series written by the eldest sibling, Sam, in Susan Richards Shreve's **Plum & Jaggers.**

Judith Rossner's very early novel **Nine Months in the Life of an Old Maid** shows how the entrance of an outsider can force a reassessment of the long-standing and sometimes unfair roles played by different members of a family.

In Sara Maitland's **Ancestral Truths,** a mountain-climbing accident—in which her lover disappeared and she had to have her right hand amputated—forces Claire Kerslake to go home to Scotland, where she is alternately nurtured and frustrated by her siblings, each with their own problems.

Living to Tell, by Antonya Nelson, is the story of an eventful year in the life of the Mabie family of Wichita, Kansas—a year in which thirty-three-year-old Winston returns home after spending five years in prison for killing his grandmother while driving drunk; his oldest sister, single-mother Emily, moves back in with her parents; and his seriously depressed sister Mona (whose affair with Emily's husband contributed to the breakup of their marriage) desperately searches for someone (not married) to love.

FREDERICK BUSCH:
TOO GOOD TO MISS

Frederick Busch is a prolific writer whose books are wildly diverse: from a novel about Charles Dickens (**The Mutual Friend**) to a legal thriller with sexual over- (and under-) tones (**Closing Arguments**) to a story about a marriage gone horribly awry after the death of the couple's daughter (**Girls**) to a masterful collection of short stories (**Don't Tell Anyone**) to a story of a maimed veteran of the Union Army wandering the dark streets of New York (**The Night Inspector**), which is also an homage to Herman Melville, to the story of an on-again, off-again relationship between two people no longer young (**Harry and Catherine**), to the tale of a psychologist forced to rethink his family's history (**A Memory of War**). Busch is also the author of a fascinating book about the art and craft of creating literature: **A Dangerous Profession: A Book about the Writing Life**.

All of Busch's work is marked by a meticulous attention to detail—both of place (it's hard to think of anyone who can bring a setting alive the way Busch can) and of character. His ability to present characters in crisis—a lawyer and Vietnam veteran obsessed with the woman he's defending, a husband who suspects his wife of a terrible deed, a woman forced to acknowledge that perhaps the man she loves is not the man she thinks he is, a Civil War sniper who has never recovered from his experiences in combat—is simply stunning. No one who's read **Closing Arguments** can forget it. Indeed, reading it once was so exhausting and disturbing for me that I could never even open the book again, nor will I soon forget the painful relationship between Jack and Fanny in **Girls**.

Other fiction by Busch includes **The Children in the Woods; Long Way** from Home; War Babies; Sometimes I Live in the Country; Absent Friends; Too Late American Boyhood Blues; Invisible Mending; Take This Man; Rounds; Hardwater Country: Domestic Particulars; Manual Labor; Breathing Trouble; and I Wanted a Year Without Fall.

His nonfiction includes Letters to a Fiction Writer; When People Publish; and Hawkes.

CALIFORNIA, HERE WE COME

With the exception of New York, probably no state is the setting for more novels than California. There's a lot of irony in the fiction set in California; the authors often seem to have a love-hate relationship with their subject.

The Los Angeles and Southern California contingent is led by Alison Lurie's The Nowhere City, which is probably my favorite California novel, followed closely by Dan McCall's Bluebird Canyon and Carolyn See's apocalyptic Golden Days.

Two breezy and warmhearted novels describing happily dysfunctional family relationships are Leslie Brenner's Greetings from the Golden State and The Diamond Lane by Karen Karbo.

Another take on the Southern California lifestyle is offered by the comedian and writer Sandra Tsing Loh's If You Lived Here, You'd Be Home By Now, the very funny story of a yuppie couple who are tired of their dreary apartment in a far Los Angeles suburb.

San Francisco is the setting for a wonderful assortment of novels, including Vikram Seth's novel-in-verse The Golden Gate, Armistead Maupin's delectable Tales of the City, the first volume in a series that includes More

Tales of the City, Further Tales of the City, Babycakes, Significant Others, and Sure of You; Tim Mahoney's We're Not Here; and Fae Myenne Ng's Bone.

Coming of age in California is a popular subject for novelists, as can be seen in China Boy by Gus Lee (San Francisco); Donald Duk by Frank Chin (San Francisco); Joy Nicholson's The Tribes of Palos Verdes (Palos Verdes); Eric Miles Williamson's East Bay Grease (Oakland); and The Last Bongo Sunset by Les Plesko (Venice).

Other novels with a strong California setting include Ernest Finney's The Lady with the Alligator Purse; Leslie Schwartz's Jumping the Green; and Bebe Moore Campbell's Brothers and Sisters.

CANADIAN FICTION

The most prestigious literary prize in Canada is the Governor-General's Literary Award, established in 1937. Anyone interested in sampling outstanding Canadian fiction or in seeing where Canadian fiction has been and where it's headed would do well to use these winning novels as a guide to good reading:

Whatever the setting—the prairies of Saskatchewan (Elizabeth Hay's A Student of Weather), the Toronto of Margaret Atwood (The Robber Bride), the Montreal of Mordecai Richler (The Apprenticeship of Duddy Kravitz), or the small towns of Ontario as seen in the stories of Alice Munro (Hateship, Friendship, Courtship, Loveship, Marriage: Stories or The Moons of Jupiter), or the Vancouver Chinatown of Sky Lee's Disappearing Moon Café and Wayson Choy's The Jade Peony—all have a distinctly evoked sense of place that I think distinguishes Canadian fiction.

Here are my favorite Canadian writers, and the books I've most enjoyed by them: Marianne Ackerman's **Jump**; David Bergen's **A Year of Lesser**; Bonnie Burnard's **A Good House**; Robertson Davies's **Fifth Business** and **What's Bred in the Bone** (and others); Sara Jeanette Duncan's **The Pool in the Desert**; Timothy Findley's **Headhunter**; Barbara Gowdy's **Mister Sandman** and **The Romantic**; Wayne Johnston's **The Colony of Unrequited Dreams**; Farley Mowat's **The Dog Who Wouldn't Be**; Michael Ondaatje's **Anil's Ghost**; Eden Robinson's **Monkey Beach**; Diane Schoemperlen's **In the Language of Love**; Jane Urquhart's **The Underpainter**; Guy Vanderhaeghe's **The Englishman's Boy**; and Carol Shields, who brings the city of Winnipeg to life in novels like **Larry's Party** and **The Republic of Love**.

There is one writer who, while not Canadian in fact, seems to be so in the spirit of his books: Howard Norman, author of three novels that take place in Newfoundland, the best being **The Bird Artist**.

CAT CRAZY

Sneaky Pie Brown, coauthor with Rita Mae Brown of a series of mysteries (including **Catch as Cat Can** and **Claws and Effect**), once opined, "Dogs have masters, cats have staff." Nowhere is this more evident than in the wide array of books—both fiction and nonfiction—about this four-legged, somewhat domesticated animal.

Caroline Alexander's **Mrs. Chippy's Last Expedition: The Remarkable Journal of Shackleton's Polar-Bound Cat** offers a singularly unique perspective on Ernest Shackleton's epic Antarctic adventure.

The stories in Nina de Gramont's **Of Cats and Men: Stories** include a cast of alluring felines who manage to inform their human companions of the ways of the world.

One of the best cat stories ever is "Queen of the Jungle," the first story in **Publish and Perish: Three Tales of Tenure and Terror** by James Hynes, in which a cat expresses his displeasure at his owner's caddish behavior in wickedly funny ways.

The eponymous Metzger, a cat who knows when (and when not) to use his power, plays an important role in Thomas Perry's **Metzger's Dog,** a thriller about shutting down the Los Angeles freeways.

(Reading Hynes and Perry is a good antidote to the sometimes-cloying sweetness of cat literature.)

Besides the Sneaky Pie Brown books, other mystery series featuring cats include those by Lilian Jackson Braun (**The Cat Who Saw Red; The Cat Who Could Read Backwards;** and my favorite, **The Cat Who Ate Danish Modern;** as happens with many mystery series, the early novels are much better than the later ones), Lydia Adamson's Alice Nestleton cat-sitter series (which began with **A Cat in the Manger**), and Carole Douglas's Midnight Louie series, all set in Las Vegas (the first is **Catnap**). Marion Babson's **Nine Lives to Murder** is pure delight—a Shakespearean actor falls from a ladder onto a cat and in the ensuing tangle they exchange bodies, so while the actor lies comatose, the cat searches for the would-be murderer. Although they are not the main characters in the mysteries by Frances and Richard Lockridge, Sherry, Gin, and Martini, the Siamese cats owned by (or who own) Pam and Jerry North, are wonderfully portrayed in such books as **The Norths Meet Murder** and **A Key to Death.**

While I know that many people enjoyed Cleveland Amory's **The Cat Who Came for Christmas** and May Sarton's **The Fur Person,** my all-time-favorite cat nonfiction consists of Doreen Tovey's very funny accounts of her love affair with Siamese cats, including **Cats in the Belfry** and **Cats in May.**

CHICK LIT

There was certainly always a category of fiction that explored the lives of primarily young, mostly single women—think of Mary McCarthy's **The Group** or Rona Jaffe's **The Best of Everything,** Jacqueline Susann's **Valley of the Dolls** or even Jane Austen's **Pride and Prejudice**—but with the publication of Helen Fielding's **Bridget Jones's Diary,** novels about the experiences of single women (or "singletons" in Bridget-speak) took on a whole new life.

Candace Bushnell's *New York Observer* columns were the basis for the hit television show *Sex and the City,* and her first novel, **Four Blondes,** could be read as more of the same, as it describes four New Yorkers in search of satisfying relationships and good sex (and not necessarily in that order).

The linked short stories of Melissa Bank's **The Girls' Guide to Hunting and Fishing** spoof those ever-so-popular self-help tomes that pontificate on how to get and keep your man.

Lucinda Rosenfeld's **What She Saw In** . . . is the story of Phoebe Fine's relationship with fifteen different men, including the first boy she kissed (Stinky Mancuso), her married lover Bruce Bledstone, and artist Pablo Miles (born Peter Mandelbaum).

Although Kate Reddy is married with children and is a successful bond trader, as the heroine of Allison Pearson's **I Don't Know How She Does It** she can be seen as Bridget Jones's older, no less harried and worried sister.

Christina Bartolomeo's delightful **Cupid and Diana** is "a novel about finding the right man, the right career, and the right outfit."

Other chick-lit novels are Isabel Wolff's **The Trials of Tiffany Trott** and **Making Minty Malone;** Lisa Jewell's **Thirty Nothing;** Sophie Kinsella's

Confessions of a Shopaholic; *Dog Handling* by Clare Naylor; **Girls' Poker Night** by Jill A. Davis; Anna Maxted's **Getting Over It**; Jennifer Weiner's **Good in Bed**; and Marian Keyes's **Lucy Sullivan Is Getting Married** (and her other novels).

CHINA VOICES

When many people think about Chinese literature, Pearl Buck is the first name that comes to mind. While **The Good Earth,** a moving novel of a Chinese peasant and his family, is still quite engaging, you'd be doing your reading life an injustice if you didn't go on and explore the works of native Chinese writers.

Undoubtedly, the place to start with Chinese fiction is with Cao Xueqin's eighteenth-century classic, **A Dream of Red Mansions,** a sweeping epic about family life and Confucian practices in feudal China, including numerous subplots, a gazillion characters, and a touching love story.

The works of Gao Xingjian, unknown to all but a few Americans before the author won the Nobel Prize for literature in 2000, demand much from the reader. His best-known translated work is **Soul Mountain,** a semiautobiographical account of his actual and metaphysical journey in search of health and enlightenment.

The so-called "scar literature" first appeared in China in the late 1970s, when the men and women who survived the turmoil of Mao's Cultural Revolution began writing about their experiences in both fiction and nonfiction. Two of the best novels are **Balzac and the Little Chinese Seamstress** by Dai Sijie, the story of two young boys—children of the hated intelligentsia—who are sent to a remote mountain village to be reeducated, and Dai Houying's **Stones of the Wall,** one of the earliest (and still one of the best) novels about the effects of the Cultural Revolution, which is set in the late 1970s around a group of college professors who are trying to rebuild lives thrown into despair and uncertainty by the cataclysm. (This is a novel I've remembered vividly since I first read it in 1985.)

Ha Jin won the National Book Award for Fiction in 1999 for his novel **Waiting**, set during and after the Cultural Revolution, but I think he's an even better short story writer. Try "A Tiger-Fighter Is Hard to Find" and "After Cowboy Chicken Came to Town," two of the best stories in his collection **The Bridegroom**.

Anchee Min has written both fiction (**Wild Ginger**) and nonfiction (**Red Azalea**) about people's lives during the Cultural Revolution. Other nonfiction examples of "scar literature" include books by Rae Yang (**Spider Eaters**), Liang Heng and Judith Shapiro (**Son of the Revolution**), Jung Chang (**Wild Swans**), Jan Wong (**Red China Blues: My Long March from Mao to Now**), and Nien Cheng (**Life and Death in Shanghai**).

CHRISTMAS BOOKS
FOR THE WHOLE FAMILY TO READ

I've always loved the tradition of reading **The Night Before Christmas** and Dr. Seuss's **How the Grinch Stole Christmas** aloud during the holiday season, but why stop with these? Here are some other wonderful books that will delight the whole family:

In **The Polar Express**, written and illustrated by Chris Van Allsburg, a little boy takes a railroad trip to the North Pole and receives a special gift from Santa Claus.

Santa Calls, written and illustrated by William Joyce, is set at the turn of the twentieth century in Abilene, Texas, where three children are unexpectedly summoned to the North Pole by none other than Santa Claus himself.

Joseph Slate (the writer) and Felicia Bond (the illustrator) combined to create **Little Porcupine's Christmas** (sometimes called **How Little Porcupine Played Christmas**), the story of how Little Porcupine gets a part in his school's Christmas play. If this picture book, originally published in 1982 and perfect for beginning readers, doesn't define "heartwarming," I don't know what does.

In **Red Ranger Came Calling,** cartoonist Berkeley Breathed (of *Bloom County* comics fame) tells the story of the time his father met Santa Claus, way back in 1939, on Vashon Island, off the coast of Seattle.

In **Hilary Knight's The Twelve Days of Christmas,** Knight takes a classic Christmas song and turns it into a beguiling picture book featuring Benjamin and Bedelia, two bears in love.

J. R. R. Tolkien is best known for **The Hobbit** and **The Lord of the Rings** trilogy, but don't miss **The Father Christmas Letters.** Tolkien wrote these letters for his children, beginning in 1920 and ending in 1939. Whimsical pictures complement the descriptions of Father Christmas's life at the North Pole.

CIVIL WAR FICTION

I t's interesting that in every generation since the War Between the States, fiction writers' explorations of that war have reflected their own generation's dreams, desires, fears, and beliefs.

This is as true of Stephen Crane's 1895 classic, **The Red Badge of Courage,** as it is of Margaret Mitchell's **Gone with the Wind,** which pictured a society far removed from the grim realities of 1936 and post-Depression America. In MacKinlay Kantor's Pulitzer Prize–winning **Andersonville,** published in 1955, the horrors of the notorious Confederate prison camp are described in terms that will inevitably remind readers of the concentration camps of World War II.

So, given the events of the years between 1955 and the present, including the women's and the civil rights movements and the Vietnam War, it should come as no surprise that many contemporary Civil War novels tend to be strongly antiromantic, antiwar, and concerned with issues of racism, male-female relationships, and the search for identity.

Among the best—in a crowded field of recent Civil War fiction—are these three: **The Killer Angels,** Michael Shaara's Pulitzer Prize–winning novel centered around the bloody Battle of Gettysburg, believed by many to be the finest Civil War novel ever written; Frederick Busch's **The Night Inspector,** in which the main character is a sharpshooter for the Union army; and **A Soldier's Book** by Joanna Higgins, which explores the life of Ira Stevens, a Union soldier forced to endure the horrors of a prisoner-of-war camp.

And hot on their heels are Howard Bahr's **The Year of Jubilo** and **The Black Flower;** Charles Frazier's **Cold Mountain;** Paulette Jiles's **Enemy**

Women; Jeffrey Lent's **In the Fall**; Janet Stevenson's **Weep No More**; Daniel Woodrell's **Woe to Live On**; and William Trotter's **The Sands of Pride.**

CIVIL WAR NONFICTION

The list of excellent books about the Civil War is awesomely large and extremely varied. There are general histories, such as James M. McPherson's Pulitzer Prize winner, **Battle Cry of Freedom: The Civil War Era** (in fact, anything by McPherson is worth reading), and Shelby Foote's three-volume set, **The Civil War: A Narrative: Fort Sumter to Perryville; Fredericksburg to Meridian; Red River to Appomattox;** also his accounts of individual battles, such as **Stars in Their Courses: The Gettysburg Campaign, June–July 1863.** (As with McPherson, whatever Foote writes—fiction or nonfiction—is well-researched, well-written, and worth a read.) Another good general history is **Landscape Turned Red** by Stephen W. Sears. Among biographies, I like **With Malice Toward None: A Life of Abraham Lincoln** by Stephen B. Oates; Lee and **Lee's Lieutenants: A Study in Command** by Douglas Southall Freeman; and a spate of personal writings from officers, soldiers, and civilians, including **Personal Memoirs: Ulysses S. Grant; All for the Union: The Civil War Diary and Letters of Elisha Hunt Rhodes;** and **Co. Aytch: A Confederate's Memoir of the Civil War.**

If you want to delve deeper into the subject, try these: John C. Waugh's **Class of 1846: From West Point to Appomattox: Stonewall Jackson, George McClellan, and Their Brothers;** Mary Chesnut's **A Diary from Dixie** or **Mary Chesnut's Civil War;** Jay Winik's **April 1865: The Month That Saved America;** Thomas Keneally's **American Scoundrel: The Life of the Notorious Civil War General Dan Sickles;** William C. Davis's **Battle at Bull Run: A History of the**

First Major Campaign of the Civil War; James M. McPherson's **The Atlas of the Civil War; The Blue and the Gray: The Story of the Civil War as Told by Participants,** edited by Henry Steele Commager; and Fletcher Pratt's **A Short History of the Civil War: Ordeal by Fire.**

THE CLASSICAL WORLD

F ans of historical fiction will be eager to extend the reach of their reading into ancient Greece and Rome.

One of my top ten favorite novels in any category is Stephanie Plowman's **The Road to Sardis,** a heartbreaking retelling of the events of the Peloponnesian War, which broke out in 431 B.C. between longtime rivals Athens and Sparta, and lasted for twenty-seven years.

Both Steven Pressfield's **Gates of Fire: An Epic Novel of the Battle of Thermopylae** and **Tides of War: A Novel of Alcibiades and the Peloponnesian War** are well-told accounts of crucial events in Greek history.

The story of the Greek commander Xenophon's escape from Persia with his army is thrillingly recounted in **The Ten Thousand: A Novel of Ancient Greece** by Michael Curtis Ford.

Alcibiades, one of the most interesting and complicated historical figures at the time of the Peloponnesian War, is also the subject of Rosemary Sutcliff's **The Flowers of Adonis.**

Mary Renault wrote several well-regarded and very readable historical novels about ancient Greece, including **Fire from Heaven** and **The Persian Boy,** both about the life of Alexander the Great.

Many mysteries are set in ancient Greece, including **Aristotle Detective** by the classicist Margaret Anne Doody. Here the great philosopher is called on to use his analytical powers to defend an alleged murderer. Others set in Greece are **The Eye of Cybele** by Daniel Chavarria, which is marked by a kind of dense, erotic goofiness; P. C. Doherty's **The Godless Man,** the fourth in his series featuring Alexander the Great (the first two were written under the pseudonym Ana Apostalou); and **The Athenian Murders** by José Carlos Somoza, which takes place partly in the fourth century and partly in the twentieth.

The classic novel on ancient Rome is Robert Graves's **I, Claudius: From the Autobiography of Tiberius Claudius, Born 10 B.C., Murdered and Deified A.D. 54,** a fictional autobiography set during the heyday of decadent Rome and filled with political intrigue and an exploration of the trappings of power. Graves followed this up with **Claudius the God and His Wife Messalina.**

Both Steven Saylor (**The Venus Throw; Roman Blood; Last Seen in Massilia; A Twist at the End;** and others) and Lindsey Davis (**Silver Pigs; Shadows in Bronze; Venus in Copper;** and more) write superior historical mysteries, in which you get not only a great mystery but also an accurate rendition of a particular time period—and no anachronisms.

One of the finest chroniclers of ancient Rome is Australian author Colleen McCullough, whose six-volume Masters of Rome series brings to life such historical personages as Caesar, Pompey, Cato, Brutus, and just about any other noble (and ignoble) Roman you've ever heard of. The series is composed of **The First Man in Rome; The Grass Crown; Fortune's Favorites; Caesar's Women; Caesar;** and **The October Horse.**

COLD WAR SPY FICTION

The only reason to lament the end of the Cold War is that its demise also meant the end of spy fiction as we knew it. An Us-versus-Them mentality and a clearly defined enemy animate these terrific novels, which take place during the height of the conflict between East and West:

John le Carré's **Tinker, Tailor, Soldier, Spy** in many ways defines the spy genre; it introduces the grand theme of ferreting out the Russian agent high up in British intelligence.

Betrayal, treachery, and unmasking a Russian spy are also the subjects of Len Deighton's best trilogy, **Berlin Game; Mexico Set;** and **London Match,** all featuring Bernard Sampson, who works for the British Secret Service.

Alec Hillsden, the hero of **The Endless Game** by Bryan Forbes, sets out to investigate why the KGB has tortured and murdered a female British agent, who just happens to be his former lover.

In William Hood's **Spy Wednesday,** Alan Trosper, retired CIA agent, is called back into action when a potential defector offers information that may or may not be true.

One of the most intricate Cold War spy novels I've ever read is David Quammen's **The Soul of Viktor Tronko,** based on the real-life case of a Cold War–era Russian defector who tells his debriefers that a Russian agent has infiltrated the upper echelons of the CIA.

Charles McCarry's **The Last Supper** also concerns the search for a Russian spy in the CIA. An earlier novel of McCarry's, **The Tears of Autumn,** offers a most plausible (could it possibly be true?) explanation for who killed President John F. Kennedy.

Set in the diplomatic community in a small Middle Eastern country at the height of the Cold War, Henry Bromell's **Little America** is the story of a son's search for the truth about his father, a CIA intelligence officer.

COMPANION READS

One reason I so love reading is that books often take me on journeys. Have you noticed the way some books grab you by the hand and pull you from one to another? Some books simply beg to be read sequentially, linked as they are by theme or subject matter (or both). I find that the experience of reading them together is far greater than the sum of each individual book; linking them broadens and deepens my experience of each separate book.

These are wonderful for book discussion groups, too. Incidentally, I'd suggest reading each grouping in the order in which I've listed them.

Three moving memoirs about growing up Hispanic in America:

Down These Mean Streets *by Piri Thomas*

When I Was Puerto Rican
and **Almost a Woman** *by Esmeralda Santiago*

Two views of Southern life, one fiction, one memoir:

Charms for the Easy Life *by Kaye Gibbons*

Addie: A Memoir *by Mary Lee Settle*

Two novels about single women, written almost one hundred years apart, one by a man and one by a woman:

The Odd Women *by George Gissing*

The Odd Woman *by Gail Godwin*

Three books set in Iran—first a novel about two lovers caught up in the

Iranian Revolution, then two books about Iran since the Revolution:

The Persian Bride *by James Buchan*

The Last Great Revolution:
Turmoil and Transformation in Iran
by Robin B. Wright

Persian Mirrors: The Elusive Face of Iran
by Elaine Sciolino

Into the heart of the Dark Continent in three novels and one riveting work of history:

Heart of Darkness *by Joseph Conrad*

Things Fall Apart *by Chinua Achebe*

The Poisonwood Bible *by Barbara Kingsolver*

King Leopold's Ghost: A Story of Greed, Terror, and Heroism in Colonial Africa
by Adam Hochschild

One novel and one work of nonfiction consider whether Bigfoot exists:

Wild Life *by Molly Gloss*

Where Bigfoot Walks: Crossing the Dark Divide *by Robert Michael Pyle*

America in Vietnam is the common theme of these two powerful and moving novels, set decades apart in that war-torn country:

The Quiet American *by Graham Greene*

A Dangerous Friend *by Ward Just*

Travel down the Mississippi with the man who said that he learned all he needed to know about human nature by traversing the Mississippi, and with an Englishman who yearns to discover America.

Life on the Mississippi *by Mark Twain*

Old Glory, an American Voyage *by Jonathan Raban*

Several writers have taken a classic work of fiction and written a novel about a minor character in it—but few have done it as well as Jean Rhys. And Jasper Fforde's delightful fantasy is a pure joy for any Jane Eyre fan.

Jane Eyre *by Charlotte Brontë*

Wide Sargasso Sea *by Jean Rhys*

The Eyre Affair *by Jasper Fforde*

Dick and Nicole Diver, the main characters in Fitzgerald's novel, were based on the lives of Sara and Gerald Murphy, big players during the era of the Lost Generation (the 1920s and '30s). Tomkins and Vaill explore the lives of this tragic couple in their biographies.

Tender Is the Night *by F. Scott Fitzgerald*

Living Well Is the Best Revenge *by Calvin Tomkins*

Everybody Was So Young: Gerald and Sara Murphy, a Lost Generation Love Story *by Amanda Vaill*

Fiction and nonfiction about the West offer contrasts and similarities:

Close Range: Wyoming Stories *by E. Annie Proulx*

Lasso the Wind: Away to the New West *by Timothy Egan*

Women's lives in the Far East are explored in two different novels:

The Moon Pearl *by Ruthanne Lum McCunn*

Women of the Silk *by Gail Tsukiyama*

Wallace Stegner actually based the life of the main character in **Angle of Repose** on the life of Mary Hallock Foote, and you can appreciate his appropriation (including the title of his novel, which comes from Foote's diaries) and his literary artistry in reading these two books together:

A Victorian Gentlewoman in the Old West
by Mary Hallock Foote

Angle of Repose *by Wallace Stegner*

Four novels about watching life without fully participating in it:

The Spectator Bird *by Wallace Stegner*

The Moviegoer *by Walker Percy*

The Remains of the Day *by Kazuo Ishiguro*

A Gesture Life *by Chang-rae Lee*

The great Victorian explorer Mary Kingsley is a wonderful subject, as can be seen in this collection—a novel, a biography, her own memoir, and a book that recreates her travels:

Hello to the Cannibals *by Richard Bausch*

A Voyager Out *by Katherine Frank*

Travels in West Africa *by Mary Kingsley*

One Dry Season: In the Footsteps of Mary Kingsley *by Caroline Alexander*

LES CRIMES NOIR

Generally, we're talking here about nonmysteries, typically tragic tales of greed, obsession, compulsion. You get the picture: doomed heroes, grifters, desperate men, femmes fatales.

The best place to begin is with the Library of America's two-volume collection, **Crime Novels: American Noir of the 1930s & 40s** and **Crime Novels: American Noir of the 1950s**. Together they include all the major writers as well as bring some lesser-known authors to a wider audience. In general chronological order, here are some depths to which you can lower yourself:

Paul Cain is an early, influential figure in this genre, who is now quite hard to find even in used bookstores and libraries. His 1932 **Fast One** was a noir landmark; it defined the honed-down, direct, choppy prose that slams the reader through the book.

Even nonfans of noir know the name James M. Cain. He wrote classic Depression-era noir, filled with desperate, scheming men and women, all looking for the main chance. His **The Postman Always Rings Twice** and **Double Indemnity** typify crime noir. Cain was fascinated with sordid tales about crime; the tabloid murder was his specialty. (You can see his influence on a contemporary writer like James Ellroy.)

Horace McCoy is another great Depression-era noir writer. His best-known work is **They Shoot Horses, Don't They?**, that wonderfully grungy dance-marathon nightmare novel (and film).

Gerald Kersh is a British practitioner of noir. The "hero" of **Night and the City** is a pimp and petty thug, a wrestling promoter who would sell his sister for a shot at the big time.

Cornell Woolrich did a big series of books with "black" in the title—**The Bride Wore Black; The Black Curtain; Black Alibi; The Black Angel; Black Path of Fear; Rendezvous in Black**—all filled with melodramatic plot twists, doom, and dread. With Woolrich, noir starts to slip into paranoia and psychosis. Where James M. Cain's people are simply horny and greedy, Woolrich's are anxious and afraid, stuck in a world that is full of shocking and dangerous surprises.

Kenneth Fearing wrote poetry as well as noir fiction, all deploring the mind-numbing existence we have been forced into by great impersonal forces. Read **The Big Clock** to get a feel for him as social critic, spinning out an edgy corporation-as-hell thriller: "The eye saw nothing but innocence, to

the instincts she was undiluted sex, the brain said here was a perfect hell."
(Fearing's novel was the basis for the great Kevin Costner film *No Way Out*.)

Jim Thompson, writing in the 1950s (a decade that fulfilled all of Kenneth
Fearing's fears), took noir to a new level of degradation. His crass sprees
break every convention; his heavies are twisted, unredeemable, savage out-
casts, outrageous and sometimes hilarious. **The Killer Inside Me** is a chilling
first-person story of an evil lawman, while **Pop. 1280** is a strangely funny
version of the same plot. Of all the noir writers, Thompson is the most popular today, in part because several of his novels, including **The Grifters,** were
successfully adapted for film.

Other great noir writers include David Goodis, the troubadour of the lost
and lonely, whose lyric, bleak, obsessive books like **Shoot the Piano Player**
are filled with lost people, lost hope, lost worlds; Chester Himes, whose
impressive work ranges from social realism (about a chaotic, superviolent
Harlem) to mysteries to noirs, of which **Run Man Run** and **The End of a
Primitive** are good examples; the very little-read today Dorothy B. Hughes,
whose **In a Lonely Place** is a great novel about a listless serial killer hanging
around Los Angeles; Charles Willeford, that granddaddy of Southern grit-
lit, who wrote **Cockfighter,** about a guy pursuing the Cockfighter of the
Year award, as well as a great Western noir (is there another one?), **The
Difference;** Frederic Brown (**The Fabulous Clipjoint**); and Jonathan Latimer
(**Murder in the Madhouse**).

CUBA SÍ!

There's a lot of good fiction and nonfiction written by Cubans about their homeland, the small island ninety miles south of Florida, and the vast majority of the books explore, either overtly or covertly, the themes of politics and exile.

The three grand old men of Cuban literature are Alejo Carpentier (his masterpiece is **The Lost Steps**); José Lezama Lima (whose autobiographical novel **Paradiso** infuriated Castro); and Guillermo Cabrera Infante (the setting of his novel **Three Trapped Tigers**—pre-Castro Havana—reminded me of Oscar Hijuelos's **A Simple Habana Melody From When the World Was Good**).

Hijuelos also wrote about the world of the Cuban émigré in his Pulitzer Prize–winning novels, **The Mambo Kings Play Songs of Love** and **Empress of the Splendid Season**.

For a biting view of Castro's Cuba, try **The Color of Summer, or, The New Garden of Earthly Delights** by Reinaldo Arenas (best known, probably, for **Before Night Falls,** his memoir of life as a gay man in Cuba).

A large group of Cuban émigrés are turning out wonderful novels, all exploring the lives of men and women in exile from their native land: Cristina García (**Dreaming in Cuban** and **The Agüero Sisters**), Beatriz Rivera (**Midnight Sandwiches at the Mariposa Express**), Zoé Valdés (**Yocandra in the Paradise of Nada**), Ernesto Mestre (**The Lazarus Rumba**), Ana Veciana-Suarez (**The Chin Kiss King**), and Ana Menéndez (whose collection, **In Cuba I Was a German Shepherd,** merits reading not only for the wonderful title story).

Two collections of Cuban-American fiction, both edited by Delia Poey, are excellent introductions to many writers who are likely to be unfamiliar to mainstream American readers: **Little Havana Blues: A Cuban-American**

Literature Anthology and **Iguana Dreams: New Latino Fiction.**

For a non-Cuban view of contemporary Cuba, Isadora Tattlin's **Cuba Diaries: An American Housewife in Havana** is a sympathetic yet clear-eyed account of the four years the author spent there with her European business-man husband and two young children. I don't think anyone can read this and not want to jump on the next flight to Havana. (I'm certainly planning to go.)

CYBERSPACE.COM

O f all the genres, science fiction is the one that has most embraced and endorsed postmodernism, with its dark visions of nuclear and environmental threats.

If you read no other work of what's known as "cyberpunk" (which looks at the ever-thinner line between humans and machines), at least read the novel that began it all: William Gibson's **Neuromancer,** which won every major science fiction award (the Nebula, the Hugo, and the Philip K. Dick award) in 1984, the year it was published. Gibson introduced words (including "cyberpunk" itself), themes, and a dystopic vision of the future that have been liberally reworked in the writings of many other authors.

Among other great examples of the melding of science fiction with post-modernism are Neal Stephenson's **Snow Crash** and **Cryptonomicon;** Eric S. Nylund's **Signal to Noise;** Pat Cadigan's **Tea from an Empty Cup** and **Dervish is Digital; Software** and **Wetware** by Rudy Rucker; John Brunner's **The Shockwave Rider,** written in the 1970s, before the official advent of cyber-punk; Bruce Sterling's **Zeitgeist; Heavy Weather;** and **Holy Fire** (or any of his other novels); William Gibson's **Pattern Recognition;** and **Hackers,** a collec-tion of short stories edited by Jack Dann and Gardner Dozois.

(You could do far worse than read almost anything else by William Gibson, Bruce Sterling, or Neal Stephenson.)

In the excellent collection **Storming the Reality Studio: A Casebook of Cyberpunk and Postmodern Science Fiction,** Larry McCaffery offers examples of cyberpunk's reach by including both fiction and nonfiction as well as artworks.

CZECH IT OUT

Although the Czech Republic has a population of only slightly more than ten million people, it's made a significant contribution to world literature in the twentieth century—a contribution that shows no signs of diminishing. Few countries can boast of a literary president (former playwright Vaclav Havel) or a similar range of wildly original authors who wrote between the two world wars and gave us many of the classics we continue to enjoy today.

In his fiction, Franz Kafka, whose frightening view of reality still rings eerily true, conjured the capital Prague into a weirdly compelling city where ordinary men became giant beetles (**The Metamorphosis**); where law-abiding citizens found themselves accused of crimes they did not commit (**The Trial**); and the populace looked in vain for recognition from the ruling entity, symbolized by a mysterious castle that eerily resembled the real castle dominating the Prague skyline (**The Castle**).

Kafka's hard-drinking contemporary Jaroslav Hasek wrote about the meaninglessness of World War I in **The Good Soldier Svejk and His Fortunes in the World War,** a black comedy of an unwilling soldier caught up in an insane military bureaucracy—which will sound familiar to any fan of Joseph Heller's **Catch-22.**

During the difficult years of the Soviet occupation of Czechoslovakia, when many writers were in prison or doing hard labor, Bohumil Hrabal wrote a series of vigorous and funny novels that are filled with acute observations of the effects of war, occupation, and politics on the lives of ordinary Czechs. These include **Closely Watched Trains,** the story of a young train dispatcher during the Nazi occupation who is more interested in sex than in seeing that the trains run on time, and **I Served the King of England,** a comic saga of a waiter-turned-millionaire, who loses everything when the Communists take over the country.

My favorite novel by the prolific Ivan Klima, who survived the Holocaust in the Terezin concentration camp, is **Judge on Trial,** the story of Adam Kindl, who discovers that the trial he is overseeing is actually a test of his loyalty to the Communist Party.

In **Sins for Father Knox** and his other noir-ish mysteries, Josef Skvorecky introduces police Lieutenant Boruvka, who is forced to work within the political realities of life under a dictatorship. In **The Miracle Game,** which features the author's alter ego Danny Smiricky, he paints a picture of the tragedy following the Prague Spring and the transient hope for a free Czechoslovakia. However, my favorite Skvorecky novel is **The Engineer of Human Souls.**

While Milan Kundera's **The Unbearable Lightness of Being** is his best-known novel, **The Joke,** the story of an innocent joke gone awry and written in the form of a musical quartet in which each of four narrators relates the same events from a different perspective, beautifully demonstrates Kundera's talent for well-drawn, believable characters.

Other writers to Czech out include Daniela Fischerova (**Fingers Pointing Somewhere Else: Stories**); Jáchym Topol (**City, Sister, Silver**); and Martin Šimečka (**The Year of the Frog**).

A DICKENS OF A TALE

It's too bad that most readers had Dickens (which was either **A Tale of Two Cities** or **Great Expectations**, I suspect) foisted on them in high school, so that his novels will forever be remembered as something you have to gag down, like a dose of castor oil. To many (too many) Dickens will always be relegated to the hopeless category of assigned readings (and by a dead white male, to boot), but to his contemporaries and a few generations thereafter, Dickens was a popular, even trashy author who wrote his novels in the form of breathless serial installments. There's a story I love about the time when chapters of **The Old Curiosity Shop** were being serialized in England before they arrived in America, and frantic readers would greet each boat from England and ask debarking passengers, "Is Little Nell dead?"

There are many contemporary Dickensian writers, grand storytellers all, whose plots are brilliantly byzantine and circuitous, peopled with a huge assortment of characters from all walks of Victorian life.

Michel Faber addresses the reader directly (the book is written in the second person), inviting him or her into 1870s London in **The Crimson Petal and the White,** an 800-plus-page journey in the company of a prostitute named Sugar who is brought into the world of William Rackham, a reluctant and self-absorbed heir to a perfume company who is besotted with her, Rackham's sickly wife, and his mysterious daughter. Along the way we meet a cross section of gentlemen, ladies, servants, guttersnipes, and whores.

Although **The Quincunx** by Charles Palliser is ostensibly the story of a young man's search for his true identity, the main character is early 1800s London itself—its smells, its sights, and above all its people.

Peter Carey has set a couple of books in the Victorian era, including **Oscar** and **Lucinda** and his postmodern reinterpretation of Dickens's **Great Expectations, Jack Maggs,** the story of a man illegally returning to England from prison in Australia in order to track down his son.

Fans of Dickens will find a familiar pathos and passion for justice in the pages of Émile Zola, whose sagas teem with characters in a dizzying atmosphere of suffering, sin, and grace, enveloping the reader in a million vivid details. Not much of Zola's vast oeuvre is available in English, but **The Belly of Paris** (**Le Ventre de Paris**) is worth seeking out.

Those who appreciate Dickens for his rhetorical fecundity may enjoy Alexander Theroux's verbal tour de force, **Darconville's Cat.** While presumably the story of a teacher's affair with one of his students, the novel's real energy comes from its author's almost perverse infatuation with language. Have a dictionary handy.

DINOSAUR HUNTING

Mark Jaffe's **The Gilded Dinosaur: The Fossil War Between E. D. Cope and O. C. Marsh and the Rise of American Science** is a chatty and often fascinating look at two notable characters in the history of what came to be known as the science of paleontology.

In **The Bonehunters' Revenge: Dinosaurs, Greed, and the Greatest Scientific Feud of the Gilded Age,** David Rains Wallace argues that this simple "bone war" had far-reaching implications for the settlement of the western United States.

Michael J. Novacek was a dinosaur-obsessed kid who never grew out of his fascination with the creatures from the past. He writes of his life's work excavating and studying dinosaurs all over the world in **Time Traveler: In Search of Dinosaurs and Ancient Mammals from Montana to Mongolia.**

To whet the appetite of youngsters for good books about dinosaurs, **The Dinosaurs of Waterhouse Hawkins** by Barbara Kerley and illustrated by Brian Selznick is a delight; it's also a children's book that adults will enjoy. This is the true story of a nineteenth-century British artist whose interest in dinosaurs led him to America, and a career creating reproductions of them for the public to enjoy, until he ran afoul of the notorious Boss Tweed.

Deborah Cadbury's **Terrible Lizard: The First Dinosaur Hunters and the Birth of a New Science** explores the earliest years of the study of paleontology, and the men (and a few women) who devoted their lives to the new science.

Christopher McGowan, a Canadian paleobiologist, introduces some of the major characters at the dawn of the science of paleontology in **The Dragon Seekers: How an Extraordinary Circle of Fossilists Discovered the Dinosaurs and Paved the Way for Darwin.**

If what you want is great illustrations and lots of useful information, it's almost impossible to go wrong with a National Geographic book. Dinosaur lovers won't want to miss **National Geographic Dinosaurs** by Paul M. Barrett, which includes hundreds of color photographs and various charts and timelines in its description of more than fifty different dinosaurs.

DO CLOTHES MAKE THE MAN
(OR WOMAN)?

Does what we wear define who we are? How have the different styles in clothing shaped our society? Would the Victorians have been less repressed had they not been so tightly corseted? What's the fashion industry really like? All these issues and more are considered—in one way or another, in tones ranging from humorous to semischolarly—in these books:

In **Love, Loss, and What I Wore**, Ilene Beckerman tells the delightful story (complete with drawings) of the ups and downs of her life, remembered through the clothes she wore, including her Brownie uniform, prom and wedding dress attire, and maternity togs. (Although not strictly related to clothes—it's often found in the weddings section of libraries and bookstores—Beckerman's **Mother of the Bride: The Dream, the Reality, the Search for the Perfect Dress** is the perfect book for any woman about to marry off a daughter.)

As befits a writer for *The New Yorker,* Kennedy Fraser (fashion critic for the magazine in the 1970s) writes entertainingly but oh-so-knowledgeably about her love affair with the world of fashion, in **The Fashionable Mind: Reflections on Fashion, 1970–1981** and **Scenes from the Fashionable World.**

In her books about fashion, **Sex and Suits** and **Seeing Through Clothes,** art historian Anne Hollander ponders the sociology, anthropology, and psychology of men's and women's clothing—and how beliefs in what's appropriate for each group have changed over the centuries.

DREAMING OF AFRICA

From Elspeth Huxley to Isak Dinesen to Carolyn Slaughter to Alexandra Fuller, memoirs of living in colonial and postcolonial Africa deliver a strong sense of place along with the personal stories of the authors.

Two memoirs that have shaped the vision that many of us have of colonial Africa are Elspeth Huxley's **The Flame Trees of Thika: Memories of an African Childhood** and Isak Dinesen's **Out of Africa.** Although Huxley's is told from the point of view of a child and Dinesen's of an adult, both present impressionistic tales of life on Kenyan coffee plantations in the first part of the twentieth century. What's especially interesting about both of them is the picture they give us of British East Africa at the height of the colonial period.

Other memoirs about life in colonial Africa include a good portion of Beryl Markham's **West with the Night,** about growing up in East Africa to become a bush pilot and then the first woman to fly solo across the Atlantic from east to west.

Doris Lessing's novel **Martha Quest,** the first in her Children of Violence series, is an accurate representation of her teenage years in Southern Rhodesia (now Zimbabwe). Lessing also covered much the same ground in **Under My Skin: Volume One Of My Autobiography to 1949.**

In recent years, other writers have written about their lives and experiences in Africa following World War II. They include **Before the Knife: Memories of an African Childhood** by Carolyn Slaughter; Kuki Gallmann's **I Dreamed of Africa;** and **Don't Let's Go to the Dogs Tonight: An African Childhood** by Alexandra Fuller.

Although it's not a memoir, I can't recommend books about life in colonial Africa without mentioning **White Mischief: The Murder of Lord Erroll** by James Fox, which portrays the deliciously dissolute lives of white colonialists in Africa.

ECOFICTION

I'm using the term ecofiction here to describe novels whose theme is the interconnectedness between humans and the natural world and the attendant dangers we face should that connection be severed through the continued degradation or destruction of the environment and our natural resources.

The defining fictional work in this field is Edward Abbey's 1975 comic novel **The Monkey Wrench Gang,** the story of a group of ecosaboteurs who are intent on preventing any further exploitation of the wilderness. Abbey followed this up with **Hayduke Lives!**

Pleasure of Believing by Anastasia Hobbet is about a woman whose devotion to rehabilitating injured birds and her unbridled anger at the common use of pesticides to control livestock predators set her at odds with both her husband and her Wyoming-rancher neighbors.

Chris Bohjalian's **Water Witches** pits environmentalists against developers in a small New England town. The effects of the struggle are reflected in the dynamics of one particular family.

In **Skywater,** by Melinda Worth Popham, a band of coyotes, faced with a diminishing water supply, set out across the Southwestern desert in search of the mythical and mystical source of all water. Believe me, you'll never view coyotes in the same way again.

Dick Pierce, the fisherman hero of John Casey's **Spartina,** finds himself at sea among the buffeting waves of his life—financial, environmental, and personal.

Barbara Kingsolver's **Animal Dreams** is the story of Cosi Noline, who comes home to Grace, Arizona, and finds not only personal upheaval—an ill father and complications in love—but also a town that's facing an environmental threat.

By showing how rampant industrial development compares to a cancer (caused by pollutants from a particular manufacturing company) growing inside a young woman, Richard Powers, in **Gain,** shines a spotlight on the human cost of industrial pollution.

Woven into Carl Hiaasen's comic romps through South Florida's criminal classes (in novels like **Sick Puppy** and **Lucky You**) is a darker note, as he exposes the venality and poor thinking of Florida's developers and politicians as they continue to bulldoze nature and rebuild it into condominiums and parking lots.

ELVIS ON MY MIND

Both novelists and biographers have been fascinated by the rise and fall of Elvis Presley and the role he played in shaping American popular culture. Books about Elvis seem never to stop coming, covering everything from his favorite recipes, to the houses he lived in, to his wife's view of their marriage, to a day in the King's life.

Hands down, the best biography of Presley is by Peter Guralnick. The two volumes are **Last Train to Memphis: The Rise of Elvis Presley** and **Careless Love: The Unmaking of Elvis Presley.**

Novelists use the facts of Elvis's life to explore themes of love, family relationships, and even religious and socioeconomic issues. Laura Kalpakian's **Graced Land** is the story of Joyce (born Rejoice) Jackson, a young welfare mother who has a shrine to Elvis on her front porch in a small California town and believes that he is her personal savior.

Other novels in which Presley either plays a role or exerts a strong influence are:

Maureen McCoy's	**Walking After Midnight**
Mark Childress's	**Tender**
Samuel Charters's	**Elvis Presley Calls His Mother After the Ed Sullivan Show**
P. F. Kluge's	**Biggest Elvis**
Jack Womack's	**Elvissey**
Kathryn Stern's	**Another Song About the King**

EPISTOLARY NOVELS: TAKE A LETTER

Despite the fact that they are difficult to do well, epistolary novels—novels in which the story unfolds in a series of letters from one character to another—have a long and respected history. Some of the earliest novels were written in the form of letters, including two of Samuel Richardson's published in the 1740s, **Pamela** and **Clarissa,** as well as Henry Fielding's **Shamela,** which is a portion of his novel **Joseph Andrews.** Another eighteenth-century novel, **The Sorrows of Young Werther** by Johann Goethe (originally published anonymously), was also written mostly in the form of letters.

There are lots of contemporary epistolary novels, including my two favorites: **Ella Minnow Pea: A Progressively Lipogrammatic Epistolary Fable** by Mark Dunn, and Steve Kluger's **Last Days of Summer,** which includes newspaper clippings, report cards, and other correspondence, in addition to the letters between the two main characters, a rookie baseball player and the twelve-year-old boy who worships him.

If this literary technique appeals to you, here are some other good ones: Carol Shields's **A Celibate Season; Zenzele: A Letter to My Daughter** by J. Nozipo Maraire, in which a Zimbabwean mother writes to her daughter at school in the United States about the cultural heritage and political struggle that shaped their family and country; **H** by Elizabeth Shepard, which is filled with letters from ten different characters, including some from a toy that belongs to a twelve-year-old autistic boy; Nick Bantock's inventive **Griffin and Sabine,** where you can actually see some of the individual postcards and letters sent between the title characters; Elizabeth Forsythe Hailey's **A Woman of Independent Means,** everyone's favorite novel when it first came out in 1978; Lee Smith's **Fair and Tender Ladies,** the life and times of Ivy Rowe, as she relates the details of her long life in the hills of Virginia through letters to friends and family; and **The City and the House** by Natalia Ginzburg.

ESSAYING ESSAYS

The best personal essays are those that open up a window on a particular subject that the author feels passionate about. The subject may be one that the reader isn't interested in, but the author's knowledge and enthusiasm, and the high quality of the writing, should draw the reader in immediately.

A good way of keeping up with contemporary essay writing is to check out the annual **The Best American Essays.** For an immersion into twentieth-century essay writing, you can't do better than **The Best American Essays of the Century,** with an introduction by Joyce Carol Oates. Among the fifty-five essayists are such notables as John Muir ("Stickeen"), Mark Twain ("Cornpone Opinions"), Henry Adams ("A Law of Acceleration") and Jane Addams ("The Devil Baby at Hull-House"), F. Scott Fitzgerald ("The Crack-up"), Richard Wright ("The Ethics of Living Jim Crow: An Autobiographical Sketch"), James Thurber ("Sex Ex Machina"), Martin Luther King, Jr. ("Letter from Birmingham Jail"), and Loren Eiseley ("The Brown Wasps").

Of my two favorite contemporary essayists—Joseph Epstein and Cynthia Ozick—only Ozick ("A Drugstore in Winter") is included in **The Best American Essays of the Century,** and one essay doesn't do nearly enough to display her brilliant mind and incisive writing. These are showcased to perfection in three essay collections, of which the first is the best: **Art and Ardor; Metaphor and Memory;** and **Fame and Folly.**

Joseph Epstein's **Plausible Prejudices: Essays on American Writing** is a terrific collection of opinionated, well-informed, beautifully written essays, including a section on the literary scene of the 1980s; another on contemporary writers such as Bernard Malamud, Ann Beattie ("Ann Beattie and the Hippoisie"), John Updike, Gabriel García Márquez, and Cynthia Ozick; and yet another section on older writers such as John dos Passos and Willa Cather.

Other essayists not to miss are James Baldwin writing about race in **Notes of a Native Son; Nobody Knows My Name;** and **The Fire Next Time;** Nobel Prize–winning Joseph Brodsky in his wide-ranging **On Grief and Reason,** which includes essays about his life and analyses of some of his favorite poems; **Reflections on Exile and Other Essays** by Edward W. Said, a collection of personal and political essays (perhaps, for Said, the two cannot be separated); and John Updike, whose many collections include **Hugging the Shore: Essays and Criticism; More Matter: Essays and Criticism;** and **Odd Jobs: Essays and Criticism.**

FAMILIES IN TROUBLE

A
lthough unhappy families have been the subject of fiction almost since fiction began—look at **Anna Karenina**, the 1875 novel that Leo Tolstoy opened with the sentence, "Happy families are all alike; every unhappy family is unhappy in its own way"—novels about the "dysfunctional family" seem to have come of age in recent years. Of course, there are different degrees of family unhappiness, from the normally neurotic to the seriously disturbed, but it's not too much of an overstatement to say that much popular fiction of late has as its text or subtext a family in trouble—from Philip Roth's **American Pastoral**, to Alice Hoffman's **White Horses** and **The Drowning Season**, to Jonathan Franzen's **The Corrections**, and everything in between.

Sometimes the novels describe life with a raging maniac for a father (**The Prince of Tides** by Pat Conroy) or a difficult mother (**Dinner at the Homesick Restaurant** by Anne Tyler, David James Duncan's **The Brothers K**) or the general dis-ease of coping with all that the late twentieth century threw at us (**Living to Tell** by Antonya Nelson; Donna Tartt's **The Little Friend**). Dysfunctional families, for better or worse, provide the plots for a great many well-written, interesting works of fiction.

In general, these novels are characterized and redeemed by the fact that most end happily, or at least with some sense of hope. And in the case of the novels listed below, the writer's skill is such that the endings don't seem false or merely tacked on, but rather an organic outgrowth of the characters and plot.

I always thought that Pat Conroy's **The Prince of Tides** (a book I love) defined the dysfunctional novel. The story of the Wingo family siblings— Tom (the narrator), Savannah, his suicidal twin sister, his brother, Luke—and their troubled and abusive parents has stayed with many readers long after the last page has been turned over.

But then I discovered **Life in the Air Ocean** by Sylvia Foley, a collection of linked stories that is surely one of the most depressing books I have ever read in a lifetime of reading grim and depressing books. We read, drawn inexorably on by the fine writing, the accounts of a family whose members seem to pass on the absolute worst of themselves to their children. For those who love books about miserably unhappy people seemingly unrelieved by any humor whatsoever (and I know there are many readers who do), this is the perfect book.

The family in Susanna Moore's **My Old Sweetheart** is certainly screwed up—a mentally ill mother and a distant and emotionally cold father make growing up difficult for Lily and her siblings, even in that most beautiful of settings, Hawaii.

And if these aren't enough, read António Lobo Antunes's **Act of the Damned**; Russell Banks's **Rule of the Bone**; Greg Bills's **Consider This Home**; Tim Binding's **In the Kingdom of Air**; Sheila Bosworth's **Almost Innocent**; Larry Brown's **Joe**; Joan Chase's **During the Reign of the Queen of Persia**; J. M. Coetzee's **Disgrace**; Angela Davis-Gardner's **Forms of Shelter**; James Bennett Gordon's **My Father's Geisha**; Philip Graham's **How to Read an Unwritten Language**; J. Robert Lennon's **The Funnies**; Diane Leslie's **Fleur de Leigh's Life of Crime**; Lynne McFall's **Dancer with Bruised Knees**; and Rebecca Wells's **Divine Secrets of the Ya-Ya Sisterhood**.

FATHERS AND DAUGHTERS

Many contemporary novelists explore the frequently fraught relationship between fathers and their daughters. Here are some of my favorites:

Teenage Saskia learns some difficult things about her long-absent father when he unexpectedly invites her and her best friend to spend a summer traveling in Scandinavia in Brian Hall's coming-of-age tale **The Saskiad**. The well-drawn and complicated characters add poignancy and depth to this novel, which can be appreciated by older teens but is aimed at the adult reader.

When his daughter Merry sets off a bomb in a suburban post office as a protest against the Vietnam War, Swede finds his own life in turmoil as well, in Philip Roth's **American Pastoral**.

Imaginary Crimes by Sheila Ballantyne limns the unhappy childhood of Sonya Weiler, who lives with a father interested only in his get-rich-quick schemes. Like **The Saskiad**, Ballantyne's intense novel is fine for older teens as well as the adult readers for whom it was written.

James Field, the protagonist of **Mr. Field's Daughter** by Richard Bausch, is mightily disappointed when his only daughter elopes with a ne'er-do-well, but he is less than happy when she returns home five years later, a child in tow and a broken marriage behind her.

The shadows left on a family by a daughter's troubled adolescence are explored with great sympathy for all concerned in **Solomon's Daughter** by C. E. Poverman.

Wise Children by Angela Carter tells the story of Dora Chance, a vaudeville veteran now in her seventies, who looks back over a lifetime spent in show business with her twin sister Nora, and their consistently futile attempts to get the man they believe is their father—a famous Shakespearean actor—to acknowledge them as his daughters.

When his daughter Mary Grace is diagnosed with a fatal kidney disease, Frank Thompson, a North Carolina highway patrolman, tries to find the strength to comfort his daughter, coexist with his estranged wife, and work through his own grief, in Doris Betts's moving novel, **Souls Raised from the Dead.**

The Sound of One Hand Clapping by Richard Flanagan describes the events following Sonja Buloh's return home, pregnant and unmarried, to face her abusive father and learn the truth about her mother.

FATHERS AND SONS

From the biblical story of Abraham's planned slaying of his son Isaac, to the classical Greek tale of Oedipus murdering (albeit unknowingly) his father, to the present, the dicey relationship between fathers and sons is a frequent theme in contemporary fiction. While these six books will probably not have the staying power of Abraham's or Oedipus's stories, each does a particularly good job of exploring the relationship between fathers and sons:

When Charlie, the son of a sailor and con man, falls in love, he decides that he wants no more scams and con games in his life, which comes as a shock and betrayal to his father, in G. W. Hawkes's **Gambler's Rose.**

Foreign service officer William North finds his life thrown into disarray and danger when he discovers that his son is a member of a terrorist organization, in **The American Ambassador** by Ward Just.

Obsessive love and a father's betrayal of his son are Josephine Hart's themes in **Damage,** a disturbing and riveting first novel.

So what would you do if your father escaped from his hospital bed and ran off in a large yellow convertible with a beautiful young woman? Raleigh Whittier Hayes tries to chase down his father in **Handling Sin** by Michael Malone, in which the humor is broad, but the sticky relationship between a father and son is deadly serious.

In **The Mosquito Coast** by Paul Theroux, Charlie Fox is forced to come to terms with an increasingly deranged and megalomaniac father, who has quixotically uprooted the family from the United States and moved them to Honduras.

FIRST LINES TO REMEMBER

I love good first lines. In some ways, a book's first line is probably the most important sentence in the book for me. The best first lines beckon and lure us into the author's imagination. They challenge us, implicitly saying, "I bet you can't stop here," and they usually win the bet. What avid reader doesn't remember Charles Dickens's first line in **A Tale of Two Cities** (even if they never read the novel itself all the way through): "It was the best of times, it was the worst of times. . . ."

Of course, it's always terrifically disappointing when these great first lines promise much and deliver little, but I promise you that these eight books not only have enticing first lines, but are perfectly wonderful all the way to the last line.

Pete Dexter's **The Paperboy** begins with a line that captures you with its world of possibilities: "My brother Ward was once a famous man."

Rhian Ellis opens **After Life,** her first novel, with a definite hint of mystery, not to say menace: "First I had to get his body into the boat."

It's hard to read the beginning of Dodie Smith's **I Capture the Castle** without a smile: "I write this sitting in the kitchen sink."

A Primate's Memoir: A Neuroscientist's Unconventional Life Among the Baboons, by Robert Sapolsky, starts this way: "I joined the baboon troop during my twenty-first year. I had never planned to become a savanna baboon when I grew up; instead, I had always assumed I would become a mountain gorilla."

The long first line of Scott Spencer's **Endless Love** effectively sets the stage for this amazing novel of adolescent passion: "When I was seventeen and in full obedience to my heart's most urgent commands, I stepped far from the pathway of normal life and in a moment's time ruined everything I loved— I loved so deeply, and when the love was interrupted, when the incorporeal body of love shrank back in terror and my own body was locked away, it was hard for others to believe that a life so new could suffer so irrevocably."

Jon Cohen's **The Man in the Window** begins thus: "Atlas Malone saw the angel again, this time down by the horse chestnut tree."

"'You'll want to scratch,' said the nurse. 'Don't,' said the orderly." is how **No One Thinks of Greenland** begins, by John Griesemer.

The almost forgotten but delightful **The Towers of Trebizond** by Rose Macaulay begins, "'Take my camel, dear,' said my Aunt Dot, as she climbed down from this animal on her return from High Mass."

FIRST NOVELS

I have an inordinate fondness for first novels. There's something so exciting about discovering new work and a new writer. What sometimes happens, of course, is that their first novels were the best they ever wrote, or sometimes (as is the case for Harper Lee's **To Kill a Mockingbird**), the *only* novel they wrote. So without reference to any other books by these authors, I present here some first novels (in alphabetical order by author) that I am delighted to have read:

Kate Atkinson's	Behind the Scenes at the Museum
Charlotte Bacon's	Lost Geography
Bonnie Burnard's	A Good House
John Derbyshire's	Seeing Calvin Coolidge in a Dream
Helen DeWitt's	The Last Samurai
Harriet Doerr's	Stones for Ibarra
Tom Drury's	The End of Vandalism
Mark Dunn's	Ella Minnow Pea: A Progressively Lipogrammatic Epistolary Fable
Gloria Emerson's	Loving Graham Greene
Jeffrey Eugenides's	The Virgin Suicides
Jasper Fforde's	The Eyre Affair
Jonathan Safran Foer's	Everything Is Illuminated
Jonathan Franzen's	The Twenty-Seventh City
Elizabeth Gilbert's	Stern Men
John Griesemer's	No One Thinks of Greenland
Elizabeth Hay's	A Student of Weather
Elizabeth Inness-Brown's	Burning Marguerite
Heidi Julavits's	The Mineral Palace

FLYING ABOVE THE CLOUDS

The best way to understand the thrill of flying without actually getting into a plane and making a solo takeoff or landing is to read the memoirs of the men and women who were among the early pioneers of flight. There's something about flying above the clouds that seems to make even the most prosaic of men into poets. Here are the best:

Antoine de Saint-Exupéry's **Wind, Sand and Stars** was first published in French in 1939 as **Terre des Hommes,** and this beautifully written, thoughtful account of the author's love affair with flight has become a classic. Saint-Exupéry is best known for his beloved children's book **The Little Prince,** but **Wind, Sand and Stars** and its sequels, **Night Flight** and **Southern Mail,** really showcase his talents.

Although it's difficult to forgive Charles Lindbergh for his views of the events of World War II, that shouldn't prevent us from giving **The Spirit of St. Louis,** his Pulitzer Prize–winning memoir of his historic 1927 solo flight over the Atlantic, its due as one of the outstanding memoirs of the twentieth century. If you absolutely can't bear to read Lindy's own words, there's a beautiful and moving chapter on his flight in A. Scott Berg's **Lindbergh,** an estimable biography of the great pilot and flawed man.

Ernest Gann's whole life was extraordinary—he produced movies as a teenager, was movie-star handsome, spent years as a pilot, both in war and for a commercial airline, and then became a best-selling writer whose two best-known adventure novels are **The High and the Mighty** and **Fate Is the Hunter.** How could his memoir, **A Hostage to Fortune,** be anything but entertaining?

Robert N. Buck was a contemporary of Charles Lindbergh—less famous but no less talented and brave. His **North Star Over My Shoulder: A Flying Life** gives nonpilot readers insight into what drew him in and kept him flying throughout his life.

Beryl Markham's **West With the Night** is the story of her varied and eventful life, but fans of aviation will be drawn to her years as an African bush pilot and her account of her groundbreaking 1936 solo flight across the Atlantic from east to west.

One of the most breathtaking descriptions of what it's like to be a fighter pilot in wartime is found in James Salter's **Burning the Days: Recollection.**

William Langewiesche's father, Wolfgang, wrote **Stick and Rudder,** a book that's still probably read by everyone who pilots a plane. William learned to fly as a child and went on to write **Inside the Sky: A Meditation on Flight,** which looks at many different aspects of the experience, including what makes a plane fly and what the pilot does, as well as many of his own adventures as pilot and passenger.

FOOD FOR THOUGHT

For the pure pleasure of reading about food—even aside from the recipes—try these charmers:

In her many influential books, the British food writer Elizabeth David not only shares her love of food and cooking but writes so evocatively that you can smell and taste the ingredients and dishes as she describes them. She was one of the early popularizers of regional cooking and had enormous influence on the generation of chefs that came of age in the 1960s and 1970s. Two posthumous collections (she died in 1992) serve as appetizers: **South Wind Through the Kitchen: The Best of Elizabeth David** and **Is There a Nutmeg in the House?: Essays on Practical Cooking with More than 150 Recipes** can be fine appetizers, but don't miss **An Omelette and a Glass of Wine; French Provincial Cooking; Italian Food;** and **A Book of Mediterranean Food,** as well as **English Bread and Yeast Cookery** (which will make you hungry, since the delicious smell of bread rising emanates from every page).

M(ary) F(rances) K(ennedy) Fisher expressed her love of good food and its importance in the lives of families and communities in books like **How to Cook a Wolf; With Bold Knife and Fork;** and **The Gastronomical Me.**

Calvin Trillin approaches food with humor and much gusto in the three books that make up **The Tummy Trilogy: American Fried; Alice, Let's Eat;** and **Third Helpings.** These essays, which appeared originally in *The New Yorker,* are treasures.

Jeffrey Steingarten began as the food critic of *Vogue* in 1989. His wide-ranging and entertaining columns are collected in **The Man Who Ate Everything: And Other Gastronomic Feats, Disputes, and Pleasurable Pursuits** and **It Must Have Been Something I Ate: The Return of the Man Who Ate Everything.**

Food played a major role in the lives of both Ruth Reichl (longtime *New York Times* restaurant critic and editor-in-chief of *Gourmet,* who wrote about her lifelong interest in food in two memoirs, the best of which is the first, **Tender at the Bone: Growing Up at the Table**) and Patricia Volk (who wrote about her life in **Stuffed: Adventures of a Restaurant Family**).

Laurie Colwin, a wonderful novelist and columnist for *Gourmet,* died much too early (and unexpectedly) at age forty-eight, leaving behind two collections of writing on food, **Home Cooking** and **More Home Cooking.** (But don't miss her fiction, either: **The Lone Pilgrim** and **Shine On, Bright and Dangerous Object**, especially.)

GEORGE MACDONALD FRASER: TOO GOOD TO MISS

Fraser took a minor character—and an insufferable bully at that—in Thomas Hughes's **Tom Brown's Schooldays** and winkled him into the outrageous Victorian soldier/adventurer/rake extraordinaire Sir Harry Paget Flashman, who somehow manages to be at the forefront of every major British military disaster, on every continent, through most of the nineteenth century. Though he's a coward and a cad, he rises through the ranks of the British army all the way to brigadier general. While the Flashman novels are meticulously researched (which will please the fans of historical fiction), their great appeal lies in the rollicking adventures of our antihero who, though he might lose the battle, always gets his woman. Start with the first and work your way through almost a century of British history. (Don't miss my particular favorite, **Flashman in the Great Game.**) The novels, in order, are:

> **Flashman**
> **Royal Flash**
> **Flash for Freedom!**
> **Flash at the Charge**
> **Flashman in the Great Game**
> **Flashman's Lady**
> **Flashman and the Redskins**
> **Flashman and the Dragon**
> **Flashman and the Mountain of Light**
> **Flashman and the Angel of the Lord**
> **Flashman and the Tiger**

GAY AND LESBIAN FICTION: OUT OF THE CLOSET

Gay novels often tell the story of the protagonist's coming-out to family, friends, or him- or herself (and usually these coming-out novels are autobiographical), or else they describe the complications of relationships in which one of the main characters just happens to be gay.

There's a sharp split in gay fiction between works written prior to 1970 and those written in succeeding decades. The dividing line seems to be, in fact, June 27, 1969, when drag queens and other gay patrons of the Stonewall Inn in Manhattan fought police harassment and asserted their rights to live as they wished, no matter what their sexual orientation was. After Stonewall, especially in novels written closer to the 1980s, the characters display a sense of freedom that was notably lacking in the earlier time period.

Another split in gay fiction occurred with the awareness of AIDS. I think it's safe to say that following the 1987 publication of Randy Shilts's **And the Band Played On: Politics, People, and the AIDS Epidemic,** all gay fiction has as either a major plot element or as a subtext the specter of AIDS.

Coming-out novels tend to be serious and sometimes painful to read (although there are notably wonderful exceptions, like the somewhat humorous story told in **Nothing Is Terrible,** by Matthew Sharpe, in which Mary White, an orphan, falls in love with her sixth-grade teacher and decamps to New York City with her). They, too, can be divided into time periods: those set before and after June 27, 1969, when the Gay Liberation Movement was in full bloom.

Merle Miller's **What Happened** and Edmund White's **A Boy's Own Story** are both set prior to Stonewall. White followed up **A Boy's Own Story** with **The Beautiful Room Is Empty** and **The Farewell Symphony.**

Perhaps the first novel to tackle the issue of homophobia in society was Radclyffe Hall's 1928 novel **The Well of Loneliness,** which depicted the struggle of a lesbian couple to gain acceptance by society. It's interesting to compare Hall's novel with the much later (1969) **Patience and Sarah,** by Isabel Miller.

Here are some other notable coming-out novels:

> *Jim Grimsley's* Comfort and Joy
> *Jane Hamilton's* The Short History of a Prince

Shyam Selvadurai's	Funny Boy *(set in Sri Lanka in the 1970s and '80s)*
Barbara Gowdy's	Mister Sandman
Reynolds Price's	The Promise of Rest
Martin Schecter's	Two Halves of New Haven
Matthew Sharpe's	Nothing Is Terrible
Jeanette Winterson's	Oranges Are Not the Only Fruit
Blanche McCrary Boyd's	Terminal Velocity
David Leavitt's	The Lost Language of Cranes

Books with characters who are gay or lesbian:

John Bowen's	The Girls: A Story of Village Life
Mark O'Donnell's	Getting Over Homer
Stephen McCauley's	The Easy Way Out; The Object of My Affection; *and* The Man of the House
Carol Anshaw's	Lucky in the Corner
Paul Monette's	Afterlife
Vance Bourjaily's	Old Soldier
Michael Cunningham's	A Home at the End of the World
Allan Gurganus's	Plays Well with Others
Dale Peck's	Martin and John
Christopher Isherwood's	The World in the Evening

GEAR UP FOR GARDENING

A life devoted to reading does not leave much time for other hobbies, especially not those activities that could potentially fill up vast amounts of time. Therefore, I am not a gardener (I feel oppressed by even owning houseplants), although I love reading books by gardeners. My favorites include:

Eleanor Perenyi's	Green Thoughts: A Writer in the Garden
Anne Raver's	Deep in the Green: An Exploration of Country Pleasures
Katharine S. White's	Onward and Upward in the Garden
Emily Herring Wilson's	Two Gardeners: Katharine S. White and Elizabeth Lawrence—A Friendship in Letters

GENUINE GENES

A ll the information that trickled down via newspaper and magazine articles in the 1990s from the scientific heights to the readers interested in the human genome project, as well as the very real possibility of cloning animals (and people), made genes and genetics a popular subject. Among the large number of books available now on the topic, here are those I've enjoyed most—all readable, even for nonscience types like me, yet not simplistic in the least.

The best place to begin is at the beginning, with James D. Watson's classic **The Double Helix,** the story of his and Francis Crick's discovery of the structure of DNA, for which they won the Nobel Prize.

(One of the scientists Watson mentions almost in passing is a cranky biologist named Rosalind Franklin, who died in her thirties but still managed to contribute enormously to the field of molecular biology. She's the subject of Brenda Maddox's biography, **Rosalind Franklin: The Dark Lady of DNA**.)

In his very influential **The Selfish Gene**, Richard Dawkins offers a contrarian view of the process of natural selection and evolutionary biology, arguing that the primary explanation for gene behavior is the desire for its own replication.

Matt Ridley's **Genome: The Autobiography of a Species in 23 Chapters** takes an up-close and personal look at each gene in our chromosomes to explain its role in our genetic makeup.

Mapping Human History: Discovering the Past Through Our Genes by Steve Olson uses new developments in the science of genetics, as well as archaeology and history, to describe how genetics has helped us understand where we came from and why we behave the way we do.

A GEOGRAPHY OF FAMILY AND PLACE

Any list of good books about the geography of family and place should begin with the naturalist Terry Tempest Williams's sad and lovely **Refuge: An Unnatural History of Family and Place,** in which she describes the changes in the ecology of Utah's Great Salt Lake as well as the high incidence of cancer in the women in her family.

Williams links the personal and the public in a way that few other writers can do, but here are a few who come close:

In **The Anthropology of Turquoise: Meditations on Landscape, Art, and Spirit,** Ellen Meloy not only shares her love of the Southwestern landscape in which she lives but also describes the history and myths surrounding turquoise, known as the "stone of the desert."

Like Meloy, who also wrote about the American desert landscapes in **Raven's Exile** and **The Last Cheater's Waltz,** Richard Shelton, in **Going Back to Bisbee,** celebrates the mysterious beauty of Arizona's Sonoran desert, as he drives the eighty miles from his home in Tucson to Bisbee, the small mining town where he grew up. Reading Shelton and Meloy will banish forever any perceptions you may have of the desert as being simply a hot and uninteresting place.

Gregory Martin's **Mountain City,** which describes a small community (thirty-three inhabitants when the book opens, thirty-one when it ends) in the mountains of Nevada, is not only a tender and evocative portrait of a place, but also a loving description of Martin's own extended family, who are descended from Cornish miners and Basque sheepherders.

Poet and writer Peter Balakian's elegiac memoir **Black Dog of Fate** relates his experiences growing up in an Armenian American family, with the ghost of the Turkish-Armenian conflict always lurking in the background of his ordinary middle-class life in a typical American city.

GHOST STORIES

In general, I am not a fan of horror fiction. I find real life sufficiently scary, so the thought of adding the supernatural to the mix is enough to send me, quaking with fear, to my bed with my head under a pillow. But for some reason, I rather enjoy ghost stories, which seem to me to be more subtly frightening and therefore easier to take. Ambrose Bierce, who wrote his fair share of ghost stories, believed that a ghost was an "outward manifestation of an inner fear," a belief that's almost universally accepted by both writers and readers. Ghost-stories have an enduring worldwide appeal (you can count on finding ghost stories in the literature of every country, from Ireland to Japan and beyond). The best writers manage to draw horror out of the most innocent activities of ordinary life, so that you're unaware of what awaits you until you're sucked in beyond saving and compelled to read on until the last page.

While there are many excellent contemporary ghost stories, of course, some of the finest were written during the late nineteenth and early twentieth centuries, by some surprisingly literary writers.

Must-reads for the true-blue aficionado of the genre are the works of M. R. James. His collection **Ghost-Stories of an Antiquary** was originally published in 1904. James is worth reading not only for his ability to get under your skin, but also because his stories have been incredibly influential to later writers in the genre. Other must-reads include Henry James's **The Turn of the Screw,** and **The Ghost Stories of Edith Wharton,** which offer yet more proof, if any is needed, that Wharton is a grand mistress of the short story as well as novels.

In Charles Williams's lost classic **All Hallow's Eve,** Lester and her friend

Evelyn find themselves bodiless and wandering the vacant twilit streets of the City, a ghostly echo of London haunted by memories of the living, and visited by the charismatic magus Simon LeClerk, a dark intruder bent on mastery of both worlds. Williams's own spiritual beliefs lend a spellbinding conviction to the ensuing struggle between good and evil, magic and art.

The range of Shirley Jackson's interests can be seen in the variety of books she has written. From her two very funny memoirs of her family, **Raising Demons** and **Life Among the Savages,** to the endlessly anthologized **The Lottery,** to her domestic horror/mystery **We Have Always Lived in the Castle,** Jackson demonstrates a somewhat twisted sensibility, always seeing the bizarre in the quotidian. But it's **The Haunting of Hill House** that has cemented her reputation, despite the two bad movies based on it. This classic ghost story, in which a scientist of the supernatural invites three people to come to Hill House to study and record the occult incidents that occur there, has been scaring people since its publication in 1959.

The ghost story as romance has no better example than Elswyth Thane's **Tryst,** in which Hilary, a soldier who was killed in battle, falls in love with Sabrina, the young bookish woman who comes to live in his house in the British countryside with her professor father and spinster aunt. Get out your hankies when you come close to the end.

For a great introduction to and overview of the ghost story genre, put **The Mammoth Book of 20th-Century Ghost Stories,** edited by Peter Haining, high on your to-read list. The thirty writers included are wonderfully diverse, and include many you'd never dream would have written supernatural tales: Muriel Spark, Agatha Christie, Jack London, Fay Weldon, John Steinbeck, William Trevor, John Mortimer, J. B. Priestley, and Mary Higgins Clark among them.

And don't miss out on discovering or reacquainting yourself with **Topper** and **Topper Takes a Trip** by Thorne Smith, the inspiration for both a television series and films. Topper, a rather uptight banker, finds his life infinitely more difficult when he somewhat uncharacteristically buys a sports car and discovers that it's haunted by its former owners, who died in it while driving home from a party. This ghostly couple is right out of a Noël Coward play, and their appearance in Topper's life leads him into hilarious situations.

GIRLS GROWING UP

To paraphrase an old Neil Sedaka song, "Growing up is har-rd to do," a truth that can be seen in the coming-of-age novel. Because these novels are often the writers' first, and because they are so often a thinly veiled account of the authors' own lives, it makes sense to include both memoirs and novels here.

Some of the classic girls-coming-of-age novels include Betty Smith's **A Tree Grows in Brooklyn,** Harper Lee's **To Kill a Mockingbird,** and Carson McCullers's **The Member of the Wedding.**

When you read Haven Kimmel's **A Girl Named Zippy: Growing Up Small in Mooreland, Indiana,** her memoir of growing up in a very small Midwest town in the 1970s, it's as though you are immediately thrust inside a kid's mind, looking at the world through unjaded eyes, unmediated by an adult's interpretations and perceptions.

If you can imagine Kimmel's Zippy as an upper-middle-class Jewish girl growing up in Brooklyn in the 1930s and '40s, you will recognize **Allegra Maud Goldman,** the main character in Edith Konecky's wonderful novel of that name. We first meet Allegra at the age of three, and leave her, sadly, when she's entering adolescence. Like Kimmel, Konecky manages to write from a child's viewpoint without ending up sounding silly or condescending or false.

There are two great girls-coming-of-age stories from Australia: Jill Ker Conway's **The Road from Coorain,** her memoir of childhood and adolescence on a sheep farm in New South Wales, and Miles Franklin's turn-of-the-twentieth-century first novel **My Brilliant Career,** an autobiographical account of a spirited and rebellious young woman determined not to live the conventional life her family imagines for her.

Doris Lessing's **Martha Quest** is the first volume in her Children of Violence series of highly autobiographical novels published in the 1950s. It's the tale of a young girl growing up in Rhodesia (now Zimbabwe).

Daddy Was a Numbers Runner by Louise Meriwether is the story of Francie Coffin, who is growing up in the spirit-deadening ghettos of Harlem in the 1930s, in a family struggling to survive intact.

Snowy learns about love and sex in **The Cheerleader,** Ruth Doan MacDougall's novel about high school life in New Hampshire in the late 1950s.

Sylvia Plath's painful autobiographical novel **The Bell Jar** is about a young woman's journey to adulthood leading up to and following her psychological breakdown and subsequent incarceration in a mental hospital.

In her quest to discover her brother's killer in a small Mississippi town in the 1970s, twelve-year-old Harriet discovers extremes of both good and evil, in Donna Tartt's riveting **The Little Friend.**

GRAPHIC NOVELS

Perhaps the fastest-growing segment of the literary scene, graphic novels have a popularity which proves that comics are not just for kids anymore. Growing out of the underground comics scene of the 1960s and '70s, graphic novels extended their reach into the regular reading public, a process that culminated in a Pulitzer Prize for the iconic graphic novel by Art Spiegelman, **Maus: A Survivor's Tale: My Father Bleeds History** and its sequel **Maus II: And Here My Troubles Began.** The books tell the story of Spiegelman's father's experiences in the Holocaust, with the different characters cast as animals (the Jews are mice, the Germans are cats, the Americans are dogs).

In a graphic novel, the illustrations are equal in importance to the text, not, unlike an illustrated book, where the text is merely an adjunct to the prose, or a comic book, where the text is supplementary to the illustrations.

Although there are, of course, still plenty of adventure and action comics around, there are also some graphic novels that touch on the great themes of literature and life: surviving hardships, parent-child relationships, and coming of age. And, as you can see from the books described here, the best graphic novels meld illustrations and text to the enhancement of each.

In **The Jew of New York,** Ben Katchor draws on a historical event—the early-nineteenth-century plan to set up a Jewish homeland in upstate New York—to create a weirdly real world of make-believe. Or is it? If you like the strangeness of Katchor's imagination, try **Julius Knipl, Real Estate Photographer: The Beauty Supply District.**

Chris Ware's **Jimmy Corrigan: The Smartest Kid on Earth** shows the eponymous hero (depressive and fearful, he fantasizes that he is the smartest kid on earth) at age thirty-six, with the opportunity to meet his father for the first time.

For those who have the heart for coming face-to-face with the details of a painful childhood and adolescence, **A Child's Life** by Phoebe Gloeckner is essential reading. There's not much here that we haven't read about in other novels, but the illustrations bring the pain home in a deeply disturbing way.

Lynda Barry touches on many of these same themes in her illustrated (though not graphic) novel **Cruddy**, as well as in **The Good Times Are Killing Me**, and **One! Hundred! Demons!.**

Raymond Briggs recounts the touching story of his parents' lives in **Ethel & Ernest,** about a lady's maid and a milkman who meet in 1928, marry, and have one son—for whom they have great hopes. (The author writes amusingly of their reaction when they learned he wanted to be an artist—not exactly the career they had in mind for him!)

GREAT DOGS IN FICTION

Sometimes one of the best characters in a novel happens to be a dog. Not that the other characters aren't interesting, too, and not that the novel isn't entertaining or thought-provoking or enlightening; it's just that when you think about the book, you can't help remembering, for example, Mr. Bones, Lucky, or Soldier. When they're happy, you're happy. When they're mistreated or malnourished or—heaven forbid—dying, you're not exactly on top of your game, either.

This focus on fiction's canine characters most likely results from my having heavily ingested such children's books as F. E. Rechnitzer's **Bonny's Boy,**

Old Yeller by Fred Gipson, **The Dog Next Door** by Keith Robertson, and undoubtedly James Street's **Good-bye, My Lady**, a sad, sad, but engrossing story. Before you begin these novels, get yourself in the mood by reading Mark Doty's wonderful poem "Golden Retrievals."

Carol Anshaw's	Lucky in the Corner
Elizabeth Arthur's	Binding Spell
Paul Auster's	Timbuktu *(narrated by the aforementioned Mr. Bones)*
Kirstin Bakis's	Lives of the Monster Dogs
John Berger's	King *(another novel told from the point of view of a dog)*
Jon Cohen's	The Man in the Window
Joe Coomer's	Apologizing to Dogs *(it's Himself, the canine hero, who sets events in motion here)*
Joan Kaufman's	Dogs, Dreams, and Men
Thomas King's	Truth & Bright Water
Donald McCaig's	Nop's Trials *and* Nop's Hope
Stephen McCauley's	The Man of the House
Clifford Simak's	City *(when humans leave Earth behind as they reach for the stars, only the dogs are left to keep the memory of humankind alive)*

GRIT LIT

Grit lit can be best appreciated as a subcategory of Southern fiction. Grit-lit novels are kissin' cousins to Erskine Caldwell's stories of rural poverty (**Tobacco Road**) and Flannery O'Connor's grotesque fantasies of alienation (**A Good Man Is Hard to Find, and Other Stories**). These books, which might best be described as Southern-fried Greek tragedies, are filled with angry, deranged, and generally desperate characters who are fueled by alcohol and sex. Jane Austen fans might want to steer clear of these books.

For more than thirty years, Harry Crews has published what are arguably some of the finest examples of pure grit lit. In **A Feast of Snakes**, Joe Lon Mackey, adulterer, illiterate, and a champion drinker, resents the hell out of the fact that his days of glory as a high school sports star are long behind him.

Dorothy Allison's **Bastard Out of Carolina** is a coming-of-age novel about Ruth Ann (Bone) Boatwright and a difficult childhood made even harder by her violent and predatory stepfather.

In his dark story collection **Poachers**, Tom Franklin, who once worked in a grit factory, offers the sad and sorry lives of people stuck in the back-waters of the Alabama River, who tend to subsist on a steady diet of moonshine and stale crackers.

Barry Hannah's **Geronimo Rex** is about Harry Monroe, a would-be writer who takes the famous Apache warrior Geronimo as his role model for living.

Any list of grit-lit practitioners worth its whiskey would also include Larry Brown, whose best novels include **Fay** and **Joe**. Fay, who is also a minor character in **Joe**, is a young woman who drifts through her life serenely and seems almost untouched by the violence, death, and bloodshed all around her.

GROWING WRITERS

I think it's safe to say that no writing program has ever been (or continues to be) as influential as the Graduate Program in Creative Writing—informally known as the Iowa Writers' Workshop—located in Iowa City, Iowa, on the University of Iowa campus, which was begun in 1922. Many people would say, though, that it's been entirely too influential; that late twentieth- and early twenty-first-century literature has been unfairly (and unwisely) hijacked by the streaming hordes of graduates who write prolifically and publish widely. Actually, you could do far worse than spend a reading life perusing books by Iowa's distinguished MFA alumni, as the following partial list demonstrates:

T. C. Boyle's	After the Plague and Other Stories *and* The Tortilla Curtain
Ethan Canin's	The Palace Thief *and* Blue River
John Casey's	Spartina
James Hynes's	Publish and Perish: Three Tales of Tenure and Terror *and* The Lecturer's Tale
John Irving's	The World According to Garp
W. P. Kinsella's	Shoeless Joe
Elizabeth McCracken's	Here's Your Hat What's Your Hurry
Flannery O'Connor's	Everything That Rises Must Converge
Susan Power's	The Grass Dancer
Jane Smiley's	Moo *and* A Thousand Acres
Wallace Stegner's	Angle of Repose *and* Crossing to Safety
Charles Wright's	Chickamauga *and* Black Zodiac

For more writers who spent time in Iowa, check out these three books:

The Workshop: Seven Decades of the Iowa Writers' Workshop: 43 Stories, Recollections & Essays on Iowa's Place in Twentieth-Century American Literature, edited by Tom Grimes; A Community of Writers: Paul Engle and the Iowa Writers' Workshop, edited by Robert Dana; and The Eleventh Draft: Craft and the Writing Life from the Iowa Writers' Workshop, edited and with an introduction by Frank Conroy.

ROBERT HEINLEIN: TOO GOOD TO MISS

Robert Heinlein is one of the classic writers of science fiction; many people began their science fiction reading with a Heinlein novel. (I did—with Space Cadet, a book I picked out at the library when I was about ten.) Probably Heinlein is best known for his 1960s cult-classic Stranger in a Strange Land, which brought the term "grok"—a kind of intuitive understanding that had a spiritual-sexual dimension—into common usage, but I still think his best books are those adventure novels that he wrote for young adults. Even now, when someone asks me to recommend a good book for a twelve- to fifteen-year-old boy who doesn't especially like to read, I tell them about these, and once I mention them I find myself going back and rereading them myself.

I'll never forget Willis, the unlikely hero of Red Planet, who looks like a basketball and has all sorts of well-hidden abilities that come in handy while he and his human pal Jim are dodging various problems at Jim's boarding school and at the same time trying to save the humans on Mars.

Space Cadet tells the story of a group of boys who become men during the rigors of their first year of training in the Interplanetary Patrol. Heinlein's portrayal of Venus is imaginative and surprisingly believable.

Along with Willis, my favorite alien is Lummox, the main (nonhuman) character in **Star Beast.** The Stuart family's pet, Lummox, was smuggled to Earth following a deep-space mission many years ago by one of John Thomas's ancestors, and has now grown into an unmanageable metal-eating, rapidly growing but still friendly, very large beast. But whoever thought that Lummox's own family would someday come looking for its missing relative?

In **Time for the Stars,** Heinlein deals with space travel and the way it distorts time, as it plays out in the lives of telepathic twins Pat and Tom, who learn that humankind's forays into outer space are dangerously unpredictable.

Thorby, the main character in **Citizen of the Galaxy,** was kidnapped as a child and sold into slavery; as a teenager he winds up as the adopted son of a legless beggar who is not what he seems.

HELP YOURSELF

One of the very best books (self-help or not) that I ever read was Harriet Lerner's **The Dance of Anger: A Woman's Guide to Changing the Patterns of Intimate Relationships.** Although Lerner has somewhat diluted her message in the many books that followed this one (among them **The Dance of Deception; Life Preservers: Staying Afloat in Love and Life;** and **The Mother Dance**), **The Dance of Anger,** which was originally published in 1985, remains as readable and helpful as it was back then, when I first read it.

Maggie Scarf's insightful and richly detailed **Intimate Partners: Patterns in Love and Marriage** offers some compelling answers to the question: "What is intimacy and what happens in intimate relationships?," based on her in-depth interviews with married couples and a thorough examination of the professional literature on the topic. This is a valuable book for anyone who's engaged in an intimate relationship as well as good preparation for those anticipating beginning one. (Scarf preceded this book with **Unfinished Business** and followed it with **Intimate Worlds: How Families Thrive and Why They Fail.**)

David Reynolds is the foremost American expert on Morita psychotherapy, which is widely practiced in Japan and is based on meditation-like mental discipline. **Playing Ball on Running Water: Living Morita Psychotherapy, the Japanese Way to Building a Better Life** is nontechnical, practical, and wholly compelling. If you're sufficiently intrigued with Reynolds's theories, try **Even in Summer the Ice Doesn't Melt: Constructive Living the Japanese Way Through Morita & Naikan Therapies.**

In Jon Kabat-Zinn's **Full Catastrophe Living: Using the Wisdom of Your Body and Mind to Face Stress, Pain, and Illness; Wherever You Go, There You Are;** and **Mindfulness Meditation: Cultivating the Wisdom of Your Body and Mind,** he advocates the techniques of Vipassana meditation to help lower stress, reduce anxiety, and deal less frantically with the everyday world.

HERE BE DRAGONS: THE GREAT EXPLORERS AND EXPEDITIONS

The urge to explore the unknown is as old as humankind—surely Adam and Eve felt a little bit of excitement when they departed Eden for places strange to them. The need to fill in those blank spaces on maps (those places frequently marked "Here be dragons"), to add to humanity's knowledge of what, exactly, lay beyond the boundaries of the known world, was compelling for a certain type of person. To read about these brave—and often very eccentric—men and women is to enter a heartstopping world of excitement and danger. (One of the requirements for reading these books is to have a good atlas close at hand, so you can actually follow along the routes.)

One of the earliest explorers was Pytheas the Greek, who, in the fourth century B.C.E., traveled from the Mediterranean to as far north as Iceland, and back. Although his own account of his travels, **On the Ocean,** is no longer extant—Barry Cunliffe believes that it was destroyed along with the rest of the volumes in the burning of the great library at Alexandria in the first century A.D.—ancient writers and historians refer to it in their accounts. In **The Extraordinary Voyage of Pytheas the Greek,** Cunliffe makes use of archaeology, history, and geographical studies to recreate the great adventure of the first European to visit the British Isles and write about it.

Pierre Berton based much of his research for **The Arctic Grail: The Quest for the Northwest Passage and the North Pole, 1818–1909,** on letters and diaries of the people involved (and it was a time, thankfully, when most people did keep journals and write letters home during their journeys). In the minds of many, this book is quite simply the best and most definitive work on the topic of Arctic exploration. Both **Barrow's Boys: A Stirring Story of Daring, Fortitude, and Outright Lunacy** and **Ninety Degrees North: The Quest for the North Pole** by Fergus Fleming relate the stories of the explorers who set forth in the nineteenth century under the leadership of John Barrow. In his role as Second Secretary to the British Admiralty, Barrow used the peacetime that followed the Napoleonic Wars to extend the reach of British dominion into Africa, Antarctica, and the Arctic.

The exploration of Tibet is Peter Hopkirk's subject in his tale of secrecy and derring-do, **Trespassers on the Roof of the World: The Secret Exploration** of Tibet. He begins with the earliest foreign visitors in the nineteenth century, who hoped to make a name for themselves by being among the first to enter the mysterious city of Lhasa.

Sven Hedin's **My Life as an Explorer,** his stirring account of his adventures in Asia in the early decades of the twentieth century, when he was one of the first Europeans to visit this unmapped, little-known land, has remained a wonderful read ever since it was published in 1925.

Travels with a Tangerine: A Journey in the Footnotes of Ibn Battutah by Tim Mackintosh-Smith is the story of the author's fascination with a little-known (perhaps publicity-shy) medieval explorer, Ibn Battutah, who at the age of twenty-one in 1325, began a trip from his home in Tangier to Mecca, and basically spent the next thirty years on his travels.

Tony Horwitz's **Blue Latitudes: Boldly Going Where Captain Cook Has Gone Before** brings to life the great eighteenth-century British explorer, who was responsible for Westerners' initial contact with the natives of the South Sea Islands. Horwitz's infectious enthusiasm and irrepressible humor make for exhilarating reading.

In no small way, the contemporary interest in the great explorers can be laid at the feet of Caroline Alexander, whose book **The Endurance: Shackleton's Legendary Antarctic Expedition,** written to accompany a museum exhibit, showed readers just how exciting true adventures of the past can be.

HISTORICAL FICTION
AROUND THE WORLD

The best historical fiction serves two purposes: to entertain and enlighten, and to inspire readers to search out histories, biographies, and other nonfiction books to learn what's real and what the novelist has imagined. Here are some particularly well-researched, well-written historical novels, many set in places far from the United States:

English Passengers, a first novel by Matthew Kneale, relates what follows when a group of Englishmen arrive in mid-nineteenth-century Tasmania with different purposes: to find the Garden of Eden, to prove the natives are less intelligent than the British, and to escape from British law. Kneale also describes the tragic life of a young Aboriginal whose experiences are shaped by the arrival of the British.

Indu Sundaresan, in her debut novel **The Twentieth Wife,** tells the fictionalized saga of Mehrunnisa, the beautiful daughter of a Persian refugee, who becomes the twentieth and most beloved wife of the emperor Jahangir of seventeenth-century Mughal India.

Cousins Isabel and Amal piece together the story of Anna Winterbourne, Isabel's English great-grandmother, who traveled to Egypt one hundred years ago and fell in love with an Egyptian nationalist, in **The Map of Love,** by Ahdaf Soueif.

Amitav Ghosh's multigenerational saga **The Glass Palace,** set in colonial Burma, India, and Malaya, tells the story of Rajkumar, once a poor Indian boy, who becomes a wealthy teak trader in Burma, and lovely Dolly, former child-maid to the queen and second princess of Burma.

In the Time of the Butterflies by Julia Alvarez is based on the true story of the political killing of three sisters—Minerva, Patria, and Maria Teresa Mirabal, known by their political pseudonym *Las Mariposas* ("The Butterflies")—who fought the Trujillo dictatorship in the Dominican Republic.

Wayne Johnston's **The Colony of Unrequited Dreams** is the fictional biography of the first premier of Newfoundland, and his often difficult relationship with his one true love, historian and writer Shelagh Fielding.

Thomas Flanagan's magnificent trilogy—**The Year of the French; The Tenants of Time;** and **The End of the Hunt**—traces the bloody course of Irish history from the eighteenth to the twentieth centuries.

In Andrea Barrett's **The Voyage of the Narwhal,** a search in 1855 for a lost Arctic expedition leads the naturalist Erasmus Darwin Wells on a journey of self-discovery.

HISTORICAL FICTION
FOR KIDS OF ALL AGES

I think I love history because I grew up reading historical fiction. (Certainly that's the reason I got a graduate degree in it.) I still believe that often the best way to understand and appreciate history is to read good children's historical fiction. These books were written originally for children and young adults, but they continue to resonate with adult readers—just try them:

Esther Forbes wrote **Johnny Tremain** after finishing her Pulitzer Prize–winning biography **Paul Revere and the World He Lived In** in 1943, making good use of all the research she'd done for that book. The result is a wonderful novel (winner of the 1944 Newbery Award) about a young man who comes of age during the Revolutionary War.

Harold Keith's 1958 Newbery Award–winning **Rifles for Watie** explores one of the least well-known aspects of the Civil War, the fighting in Kansas and Oklahoma, and a young Union soldier's unexpected meeting with Cherokee Indian Stand Watie, who fought with the Confederacy against the Union army.

Another Newbery Award–winning historical novel (1956) is Jean Latham's **Carry On, Mr. Bowditch,** a fictionalized biography of Nathaniel Bowditch, born into poverty in Salem, Massachusetts, in 1795, apprenticed to a ship's chandler and longing to go to sea. He taught himself science and astronomy, and wrote **The American Practical Navigator,** a manual for sailors that remains in use to this day.

Latham also wrote **This Dear-Bought Land,** the story of the difficult and ultimately tragic settling of Richmond, Virginia, in 1607, as told by a fifteen-year-old English boy, part of the group of ill-fated colonists.

Marylois Dunn published the harrowing and sad **The Man in the Box: A Story from Vietnam** in 1968, and, regrettably, this novel about a young Montagnard Vietnamese who befriends an American prisoner of war has long been out of print. It's definitely worth tracking down.

Although Howard Fast's **Tony and the Wonderful Door** (sometimes called **The Magic Door**) is probably more fantasy than history, it offers some interesting insights into the relationship between the Dutch settlers and the Native Americans in New York City in the early seventeenth century as it tells the story of a boy growing up on the Lower East Side of Manhattan in the 1920s.

HUMOR

Humor, like beauty, is in the eye of the beholder. What's uproariously funny to one person may leave another cold. What's funny today may seem insensitive tomorrow. This is certainly the case with Leo Rosten's 1937 book **The Education of H★Y★M★A★N K★A★P★L★A★N**, which describes the (to my mind) very funny struggles of a group of adult immigrants learning English. Many readers may find Rosten's book patronizing at best and offensive at worst, and issues of political correctness (which often toll the death knell for humor) arise, too. The following books, however, should bring at least a smile to every reader and likely offend only dogs, bears, academics, and cavemen. (And they need to learn to take themselves less seriously!)

Farley Mowat's **The Dog Who Wouldn't Be** is the deliciously entertaining story of Mutt, who entered Mowat's life and heart during his boyhood on the Canadian prairies in the 1930s and '40s.

Hal Jam, the protagonist of **The Bear Went Over the Mountain** by William Kotzwinkle, experiences fame and fortune when a book manuscript he unexpectedly finds becomes a best-seller—oh, did I forget to tell you that Hal's a bear from the woods of Maine?

In **The Evolution Man, Or, How I Ate My Father,** Roy Lewis describes the eventful life of a Pleistocene-era cave family, as seen through the eyes of young Ernest, who has a questioning and inventive mind.

A midlife crisis engulfs Hank Devereaux, acting head of the English department at a third-rate university, in **Straight Man** by Richard Russo.

Leonard Wibberley lampooned the Cold War era in **The Mouse That Roared,** in which a small bankrupt country declares war on the United

States. (The book is much better than the movie.)

Cheaper by the Dozen by Frank B. Gilbreth, Jr. and Ernestine Gilbreth Carey, the story of a family of twelve children and two parents (who were world-famous efficiency experts), remains one of the funniest books ever. Who can forget the way Frank Sr. taught his children to type, or the best way to wash yourself in the bath?

Donald Westlake's comic spy novel, **A Spy in the Ointment**, relates the experiences of J. Eugene Raxford who, as a result of a typographical error, is recruited against his will (bribed, really) to infiltrate a group of terrorists for the FBI.

I LOVE A MYSTERY

Mysteries are probably the most popular of all the fiction genres, and there are mystery novels to satisfy every taste, from the tame to the grotesque. You'll find some of my favorite books here, but keep in mind that mystery writers are, in general, incredibly prolific, so take these suggestions as just a place to start.

A subgenre of mysteries has an amateur detective as its main character, and the biggest challenge for the writer here is to come up with an occupation in which it makes sense that said amateur detective will frequently stumble on (both literally and figuratively) dead bodies. Nancy Pickard had the right idea when she made her heroine, Jenny Cain, the director of a charitable trust, in **Generous Death**. What could be better than to have a profession that brings you into close contact with death and money, both prime movers in the crime business?

You can find amateur detectives involved in occupations ranging from A

(Actor: Charlie Paris, in Simon Brett's **Star Trap** and others) to at least W (Writer: Molly Cates, in Mary Willis Walker's chilling **Under the Beetle's Cellar** and **The Red Scream**), with stops along the way at B (Banker: John Putnam Thatcher, in Emma Lathen's most excellent **Banking on Death; A Place for Murder; Murder to Go; Accounting for Murder;** and many more), and C (Caterer: Goldy Bear, in **Chopping Spree** and other humorous mysteries by Diane Mott Davidson), to a major pileup at L (for Lawyers and Little old ladies). Here are some of my favorites, in these and other occupations:

> *Sarah Caudwell's* **Thus Was Adonis Murdered** *(lawyers)*
>
> *Edmund Crispin's Gervase Fen series, especially* The Moving Toyshop; The Case of the Gilded Fly; *and* The Glimpses of the Moon *(Oxford don)*
>
> *Agatha Christie's* **Nemesis,** *a mystery featuring Miss Marple, written quite late in Christie's career, but up to her high standards (little old lady)*
>
> *Dorothy Sayers's* **Gaudy Night,** *the best of the Lord Peter Wimsey and Harriet Vane series (wealthy dilettante and writer)*
>
> *Nevada Barr's* **Blind Descent; Flashback;** *and* **Hunting Season** *(park ranger)*
>
> *M. C. Beaton's* **Agatha Raisin and the Quiche of Death** *(the first in the series featuring a public relations flak)*
>
> *Ayelet Waldman's* **The Big Nap** *(stay-at-home mom, ex–public defender)*
>
> *Susan Conant's* **Bloodlines** *(dog fanatic)*
>
> *Earlene Fowler's* **Mariner's Compass** *(museum curator)*

Joan Hess's Out on a Limb *(bookstore owner)*

Jonathan Kellerman's When the Bough Breaks *(psychologist)*

Sharyn McCrumb's Paying the Piper *(anthropologist)*

Barbara Neely's Blanche on the Lam *(cleaning woman)*

Rick Boyer's Billingsgate Shoal *(doctor)*

Michael Nava's Rag and Bone *(lawyer)*

Lia Matera's Face Value *(lawyer)*

John Mortimer's Rumpole of the Bailey *(British lawyer)*

Veronica Black's A Vow of Compassion *(nun)*

G. K. Chesterton's The Best of Father Brown *(priest)*

Harry Kemelman's Friday the Rabbi Slept Late *(rabbi)*

Ellis Peters's A Morbid Taste for Bones *(medieval monk)*

Amanda Cross's The Theban Mysteries *(college professor)*

Carolyn Hart's The Christie Caper *(bookstore owner)*

Elizabeth Peters's Crocodile on the Sandbank *(Victorian explorer and fan of all things Egyptian)*

Another sort of mystery is the police procedural (or *romans policiers*, as they are known in France). These mysteries with a police-detective hero are an enduring favorite. Fans of the subgenre can find good series set in Scotland Yard and the French Sûreté, as well as in the police forces of cities large and small around the world, including Los Angeles, Oxford, Amsterdam, New York, and Hong Kong.

The best part about the best police procedurals series is that readers come to know a diverse cast of characters who grow and develop from book to book. Two grand masters of the procedural are Georges Simenon and Ed McBain. I find that readers either love or hate the Maigret novels by Simenon. If you're interested in a classic psychological mystery, **Maigret and the Madwoman** is a good one to begin with. The Maigret novels are much less action-oriented than most of the other police procedurals; you spend a lot of time inside Maigret's head as he thinks about his aches and pains, boredom and hunger, even as he's working at his job.

Cop Hater, Ed McBain's first mystery set in the Eighty-seventh Precinct of the New York City Police Department (a locale, I'd wager, that's become more familiar to most people than their own local police station), was published in 1956, and McBain hasn't looked back since, continuing to write high-quality mysteries like **The Big Bad City** and **Fuzz**. (Incidentally, McBain was the first writer to feature a deaf person as a recurring character in his books—Teddy, the wife of featured policeman Steve Carella.)

Nicolas Freeling's psychological mysteries featuring Dutch police inspector Peter Van der Valk remain classics of the genre. His first book was **Love in Amsterdam**, published in 1962, but I think the best one is **Because of the Cats**. (Many years after first reading this novel I still remember how creeped-out I felt when I finished it.)

Swedish writers Maj Sjöwall and Per Wahlöö continued the tradition of Simenon's psychological mysteries with their Martin Beck novels. Try **The Laughing Policeman**, a particularly fine story.

Inspector Ghote Breaks an Egg is my favorite in H. R. F. Keating's series featuring an East Indian policeman, Inspector Ganesh Ghote, who works for the Bombay police department.

I recommend that only those readers with strong stomachs take on ex-cop Joseph Wambaugh's crackling page-turners. **The Choirboys** (the title is ironic), like Wambaugh's other novels, is gritty and realistic, filled with dark and dirty humor and not a little pain. Although it was written more than thirty years ago, it remains one of the best depictions of the lives of policemen.

Two good recent series are those by Elizabeth Gunn, set in a small Minnesota police department in a town not far from the Twin Cities, featuring chief of detectives Jake Hines and his fellow cops (a particularly good one is **Seventh-Inning Stretch**), and Peter Turnbull's stark and dark procedurals set in Glasgow, Scotland; try **Long Day Monday** for a taste of this author's potent brews.

Some other good police procedurals include:

Catherine Aird's	Henrietta Who?
Robert Barnard's	Bodies
K. C. Constantine's	Always a Body to Trade
Colin Dexter's	The Daughters of Cain
Elizabeth George's	A Great Deliverance *(the first book in a series that needs to be read in order)*
Martha Grimes's	The Anodyne Necklace
Jamie Harrison's	The Edge of the Crazies
Tony Hillerman's	The Blessing Way
P. D. James's	Devices and Desires *(or any of the Adam Dalgliesh books)*
J. A. Jance's	Until Proven Guilty
Henning Mankell's	One Step Behind
Ian Rankin's	Knots and Crosses

Ruth Rendell's	Some Lie and Some Die
Martin Cruz Smith's	Gorky Park
Arthur Upfield's	Death of a Swagman
	(the series, which is set in Australia, features a half-Aboriginal detective)

In the 1990s women detectives (and women authors) seemed to take over the whole subgenre of mysteries featuring private detectives, with a few notable exceptions like Robert Parker's Spenser series, Bill Pronzini's "Nameless Detective" books, and Lawrence Block's Matt Scudder novels. This trend is perhaps reversing with the addition of recent male private eyes like Charlie "Bird" Parker, the PI in John Connolly's **The Killing Kind** and Stephen Greenleaf's mysteries featuring John Marshall Tanner. But when I have a hankering for a good book with a private eye, I always reread two classic writers: Raymond Chandler and Ross Macdonald. Despite the fact that their external settings might seem a bit fusty and the pay scale is all wrong, the novels of these two authors have worn remarkably well.

In the late 1930s, Chandler extolled the virtues of Dashiell Hammett (who, he felt, took murder out of the library and put it back on the streets where it belonged) and defined the hard-boiled detective genre in an essay for the *Atlantic Monthly* entitled "The Simple Art of Murder." He might have been writing a justification of his own work as well: uncluttered prose, lots of metaphors, a wisecracking detective (Philip Marlowe), and the mean streets of a tough and uncaring city. Although my favorite remains **The Big Sleep,** a close second is **Farewell, My Lovely.**

Ross MacDonald's novels are heavily Freudian in their exploration of how events in the past cast long and entangled tendrils into the present, and how the sins of the father (or mother) are forever visited on the child. Lew Archer, a spiritual descendant of Philip Marlowe's, is at his best in **The**

Galton Case; The Goodbye Look; and The Zebra-Striped Hearse.

The leader of the pack of women private eyes is Kinsey Millhone, Sue Grafton's inspired invention, who has had a multiplicity of imitators. **A Is for Alibi,** which introduces Kinsey, is a good place to start, of course, but try **F Is for Fugitive** or **Q Is for Quarry,** other equally good puzzles.

Other private detectives include the team of Lydia Chin and Bill Smith in the wonderful series by S. J. Rozan, which began with **China Trade,** and Precious Ramotswe, a wonderful invention of Alexander McCall Smith's, in the series beginning with **The No. 1 Ladies' Detective Agency,** about Botswana's only female detective.

Here are some more private-eye novels:

Arthur Conan Doyle's	**The Complete Sherlock Holmes**
Dana Stabenow's	**A Fine and Bitter Snow**
Robert Crais's	**The Monkey's Raincoat**
Stuart Kaminsky's	**To Catch a Spy**
Karen Kijewski's	**Kat's Cradle**
Marcia Muller's	**Edwin of the Iron Shoes**
Rex Burns's	**Ground Money**
Sara Paretsky's	**Burn Marks**
Linda Barnes's	**Cold Case**
Dennis Lehane's	**Prayers for Rain**
James Crumley's	**The Last Good Kiss**
Larry Beinhart's	**You Get What You Pay For**
Sandra Scoppettone's	**My Sweet Untraceable You**
Earl Emerson's	**The Portland Laugher**
G. M. Ford's	**Who in Hell is Wanda Fuca?**

INTRIGUING NOVELS

It's most intriguing to read spy novels set in the years between what's known as "the Great Game"—Britain's struggle with Tsarist Russia for supremacy over Central Asia—and the beginning of World War II, when disillusion began to set in and the nature of spycraft became ever more deadly. Some of my favorite spy novels are from this time period.

I always recommend Rudyard Kipling's **Kim** to people who (a) love India, (b) think they dislike Kipling because of his political views; he's seen as a racist and strong supporter of the British empire, (c) think Kipling is just for kids, and (d) want to read a good adventure yarn. I find myself rereading it every two or three years.

Erskine Childers's chilling **The Riddle of the Sands,** published in 1903, concerns a German plot to invade England via the English Channel, and the two young Englishmen who must foil the plotters. I've always found it sadly ironic that Childers was executed as a traitor to England and Ireland in 1922, despite the fact that his novel did much to alert the British government and public to the early threat of German aggression.

E. Phillips Oppenheim's **The Great Impersonation** involves identity theft— or does it? This classic novel was filmed three times before World War II.

Manning Coles (the pseudonym for Adelaide Manning and C. Henry Coles) wrote several novels featuring British schoolteacher and master spy Tommy Hambledon, the best of which are **Drink to Yesterday** (a young Brit is sent behind the German lines in 1914 as a spy) and **A Toast to Tomorrow** (a high official in the Nazi bureaucracy discovers to his amazement that he is actually British, and a spy to boot).

IRISH FICTION

Irish novelists have two major influences: the writer James Joyce (**Dubliners, A Portrait of the Artist as a Young Man, Finnegans Wake,** and, of course, **Ulysses**) and the bloody political and religious history of Ireland, with all its attendant tragedies. Northern Ireland and its struggle between Catholics and Protestants, known as The Troubles, is an ongoing theme of contemporary Irish fiction. It's somewhat rare to find an Irish novel whose plot doesn't turn on betrayal or deceit, and the reach of the past is strong and deadly.

Although there are some humorous Irish novels (Roddy Doyle's "Barrytown Trilogy"—**The Commitments, The Snapper, The Van**—immediately comes to mind), on the whole, and realizing that I'm making a huge overgeneralization, I find Irish fiction to be a whole lot sadder than most American fiction, or even than works by other Western European writers. (Eastern European fiction is a different story.)

J. G. Farrell's **Troubles,** set at a resort hotel on the Irish coast in 1919, is one of a loose trilogy of novels that deal fictionally with England's colonialist policies, along with **The Singapore Grip** and **The Siege of Krishnapur.**

William Trevor is probably the best-known contemporary Irish writer. Whether he writes better short stories (**The Collected Stories**) than novels (**Felicia's Journey** is especially good) is worth a debate. Suffice it to say that he does both remarkably well.

In **Reading in the Dark** by Seamus Deane (which reads more like a memoir than a novel, so real are the characters and setting), the unnamed narrator, growing up in Ireland in the 1940s and '50s, attempts to understand not only his family's tragic past, but the tragic history of his country.

From the first sentence of Roddy Doyle's **A Star Called Henry,** you know you're in for a real treat. This is the story of the first eighteen years in the life of young Henry Smart, who grows up in the Dublin slums, takes part in the Easter Uprising of 1916, and becomes an assassin for the Irish Republican Army.

Deirdre Madden's **One by One in the Darkness** is the story of three sisters looking back over a childhood filled with violence, both personal and political.

The Virgin Mary appears in contemporary Ireland, showing up in sites as diverse as a pub, a garage, and a Protestant's kitchen, in Mary Breasted's satirical **Why Should You Doubt Me Now?**

Other good novels set in Ireland include Nuala O'Faolain's **My Dream of You,** Katharine Weber's **The Music Lesson,** James Hynes's **The Wild Colonial Boy, Breakfast on Pluto** by Patrick McCabe, Colm Tóibín's **The Blackwater Lightship,** Thomas Flanagan's **The End of the Hunt,** and Sebastian Barry's **The Whereabouts of Eneas McNulty.**

THE ISLAMIC WORLD

The events of September 11, 2001, made it pretty clear that for most Americans the Islamic world in general, and militant Islam in particular, remain a mystery. Here are some good books that provide a much-needed context for our thoughts about this region of the world.

Perhaps the best book to begin with is Karen Armstrong's relatively short, accessible, clear, and intelligently written **Islam: A Short History.** Here you'll find a brief biography of Muhammad (much expanded in the author's fulllength book **Muhammad: A Biography of the Prophet**), the development of the schism between Sunni and Shi'ite Muslims, and an explanation for the rise of militant Islam.

Jason Elliot's perceptive and exciting **An Unexpected Light: Travels in Afghanistan** should also be high on everyone's must-read list. Part history lesson and part travelogue, it's the work of a British writer who first traveled to Afghanistan in the 1980s and returned ten years later, reconnecting with old friends and meeting many members of the Northern Alliance, which was then engaged in a losing guerrilla war with the Taliban. Elliot's sympathies lie with the Afghan people, and he makes us painfully aware of their complicated history and unspeakable present.

Two other good books about militant Islam are Robert D. Kaplan's **Soldiers of God: With Islamic Warriors in Afghanistan and Pakistan** and Mary Anne Weaver's **A Portrait of Egypt: A Journey Through the World of Militant Islam**. Although Kaplan's book was originally published in 1990, a new edition has a new introduction and final chapter, which bring it up-to-date. Weaver, a writer for *The New Yorker*, presents a convincing case for her theory that Egypt is bound to fall under the sway of its most militant Islamic fundamentalists.

For an insider's view of Afghanistan, I recommend the first fascinating chapters of Tamim Ansary's **West of Kabul, East of New York: An Afghan American Story**, in which Ansary describes growing up as the son of a Pashtun Afghan father and Finnish-American mother in the 1960s in a village outside Kabul—a world few Westerners have any idea about.

ISLANDS, DESERT AND OTHERWISE

Who hasn't thought longingly, at one time or another, of escaping from the noisy, crowded world and settling down on a secluded island, dislodging what Philip Larkin called "that toad work" and the demands of family and friends, and heading off somewhere quiet and far away? And the island doesn't even have to be tropical, although long days of sunshine, blue skies, and warm water are hard to resist. There's no better time to read about the island experiences of others than when you're dreaming about your own.

Two classic accounts of island life (read these consecutively) are Robert Dean Frisbie's **The Book of Puka-Puka: A Lone Trader on a South Sea Atoll** and Tom Neale's **An Island to Oneself.** Frisbie's is one of the earliest tales we have of the life of a trader on a remote island in the Pacific. Originally published in 1928, Frisbie's book influenced several generations of adventurous young men, including Tom Neale, whose own book describes his decision to leave his job as a shopkeeper in the Cook Islands and head out to Suvarov, a Pacific atoll, where he spent six years alone.

Of course, when you think about long stays on deserted or semideserted islands, Robinson Crusoe inevitably comes to mind. Both Tim Severin's **In Search of Robinson Crusoe** and Diana Souhami's **Selkirk's Island** explore the real-life sailor who was the model for the protagonist of Daniel Defoe's classic tale. Severin also offers up some fascinating tales of other castaways.

ITALIAN AMERICAN WRITERS

I asked some of my reading friends to name all the books by Italian Americans they could think of. Each started off confidently, naming the same book—Mario Puzo's **The Godfather.** Then they wavered, mumbled a bit, and gave up. (One asked me if I thought that Tony Soprano had written or would write a novel.) And although this was nowhere near a scientific sampling, I think it's probably safe to assume that there's still a lot of work to be done introducing some wonderful Italian American writers to a wider audience.

Of course, Mario Puzo's **The Godfather** *is* the novel that most people associate with Italian American fiction. (Rereading this action-packed epic, as I did recently, filled as it is with violence, love, betrayal, and deception, it's easy to see the parallels between Puzo's novel and the HBO series *The Sopranos.*)

Another important and influential Italian American writer well worth reading is John Fante, a favorite of the Beat Generation writers. Charles Bukowski wrote an introduction to **Ask the Dust,** Fante's best-known novel, which is part of his series of autobiographical novels that centers around a young man growing up in difficult circumstances in Colorado who then goes to California to realize his dream of becoming a writer.

Rita Ciresi's sparkling novels and short stories take place far from the worlds of Puzo and Fante. **Pink Slip** and **Blue Italian** are set squarely in the province of middle-class Italian Americans.

Laughter is never far from the surface during a reading of **The Black Madonna** by Louisa Ermelino, a novel that takes place in New York's Little Italy and focuses on the experiences of a quartet of Italian American women from the 1930s to the 1960s.

Revere Beach, a small city just north of Boston, is the setting for Roland

Merullo's **Revere Beach Boulevard,** a story of difficult family dynamics and the awful power of untold secrets, told from the point of view of each member of the Imbesalacqua family, each of whom offers his or her own interpretation of events over four days: the patriarch, Vito, whose guilt over his long-ago infidelity has not diminished; his dying wife, Lucy; and their two children. Merullo is also the author of **Revere Beach Elegy: A Memoir of Home and Beyond,** which is a collection of personal essays, as well as **In Revere, in Those Days,** another family saga of growing up Italian American.

One of my favorite memoirs of growing up Italian in America is **Were You Always an Italian? Ancestors and Other Icons of Italian America,** in which Maria Laurino describes her life from childhood in New Jersey to her marriage. (The title comes from a question that Governor Mario Cuomo asked the author.)

Two excellent collections are **The Milk of Almonds: Italian American Women Writers on Food and Culture,** edited by Louise DeSalvo and Edvige Giunta, which introduces readers to a wonderful assortment of writers in a wide variety of genres, including fiction, memoir, and poetry; and a collection of essays, **Don't Tell Mama!: The Penguin Book of Italian American Writing,** edited by Regina Barreca, which includes works by writers as diverse as Don DeLillo and Evan Hunter.

JAPANESE FICTION

Whenever the subject of Japanese fiction comes up, often the first author mentioned is Yukio Mishima, whose writing and graphically filmed suicide symbolized the militaristic culture that led Japan to enter World War II. His most famous work is the four-volume **The Sea of Fertility,** which chronicles the decay of traditional Buddhist and Japanese culture and values through the course of the twentieth century.

In **Snow Country,** Yasunari Kawabata, the first of Japan's two Nobel laureates, describes the sad and sorry love affair of a geisha from the country and an intellectual from the city. It's interesting to compare this doomed affair with the romantic portrait of geisha life in such Western novels as Arthur Golden's **Memoirs of a Geisha.**

The lens through which the second Nobel laureate, Kenzaburō Ōe, looks at the world is that of a father of a severely disturbed son. He explores this situation in **Teach Us to Outgrow Our Madness,** a collection of four novellas. Ōe's novels are not pretty, not comforting, and not easy to forget. One reads to experience "layers of sorrow and pain," he has said. A novel which offers that experience is his **An Echo of Heaven.**

In its descriptions of a family trying to find suitable mates for three sisters, **The Makioka Sisters** by Junichirō Tanizaki brings to mind the novels of Jane Austen and Anton Chekhov.

Haruki Murakami writes unclassifiable novels and short stories that more or less describe contemporary Japan through a scrim of postmodernism. My two favorites are **A Wild Sheep Chase** (think of a Japanese Philip Marlowe on the hunt for a power-hungry sheep) and **The Wind-Up Bird Chronicle** (in which the disappearance of his wife and cat sets Toru Okada on a search complicated by a bizarre group of people and events, all linked by the remembrance of the Soviet army massacre of Japanese troops on the Manchurian border in 1939.

Other good reading from Japan includes Banana Yoshimoto's **Kitchen,** with its heroine who finds whatever comfort she can in food; Miyuki Miyabe's **All She Was Worth,** about identity theft and out-of-control consumerism; Kōbō Abe's existential **The Woman in the Dunes;** Yoshikichi Furui's dark **Child of Darkness: Yōko and Other Stories;** and Akimitsu Takagi's hardboiled mystery **Honeymoon to Nowhere,** which exposes the seamy underbelly of contemporary Japan.

THE JEWISH AMERICAN EXPERIENCE

Over the past one hundred years or so, Jewish American writers have created a rich, varied, and significant body of work that chronicles the immigrant experience and its various components: the problem of assimilation, the impact of the Holocaust, the relationship between blacks and Jews, the tug-of-war between faith and secularism, and the search for self-identity. Two Jewish American authors have been awarded the Nobel Prize for literature: Isaac Bashevis Singer and Saul Bellow.

Although a dedicated reader could spend several lifetimes reading through the works of Jewish American writers, here are some of my favorite authors—in rough chronological order—and the book of each that I've enjoyed the most.

Abraham Cahan was the founder of the influential *Jewish Daily Forward* newspaper, and many critics believe that his 1917 novel, **The Rise of David**

Levinsky, remains the best novel about the immigrant Jewish experience. It's the story of a young Russian immigrant who fights his way out of the New York ghetto to become a garment industry tycoon. (To get an idea of the importance of Cahan's newspaper, take a look at **Bintel Brief: Sixty Years of Letters from the Lower East Side to the Jewish Daily Forward,** edited by Isaac Metzker.)

Also set during the same time period on New York's Lower East Side is Michael Gold's **Jews Without Money,** a political novel that goes a long way toward explaining the radicalism of the first and second generation of immigrant families.

Henry Roth's **Call It Sleep,** originally published in 1934 and written in stream-of-consciousness style, takes the reader inside the mind of a young boy grappling with adulthood—intellectually, emotionally, and psychologically.

One of the iconic novels exploring Jewish American life—and a book that gave new life to the now stereotypical view of Jews striving at all cost to reach the top—is Budd Schulberg's **What Makes Sammy Run?**

During the 1960s and '70s, a group of writers chronicled the lives of the children of immigrant Jews. Although little read today, the novels of Jerome Weidman (**I Can Get It For You Wholesale; The Sound of Bow Bells**), Zelda Popkin (**Herman Had Two Daughters; Dear Once;** and **Quiet Street,** a particularly interesting novel about the founding of Israel), and Herman Wouk (**Marjorie Morningstar**) are still good for readers who are fond of solid and well-plotted novels.

Wouk's **Marjorie Morningstar,** a coming-of-age love story about a Jewish girl who wants to be an actress, was probably the favorite novel of many a teenage girl growing up in the 1950s and '60s. I know it was mine.

Although **The Fixer,** Bernard Malamud's tale of anti-Semitism (which is based on a historical event and won both the Pulitzer Prize and the National Book Award in 1967), is not about the Jewish American experience, his other novels and many of his short stories are, including **The Assistant** and **A New Life.**

In novels like **Herzog,** Saul Bellow chronicles the lives of second-generation Jews coming to adulthood in the first half of the twentieth century.

Philip Roth is probably best known for **Portnoy's Complaint,** the cri de coeur of Jewish young men all over America, but my favorite is **My Life as a Man,** which seems to me to have all of the themes (obsessions?) of Roth's later novels, but approaches its material—male-female relationships, the blurring between fact and fiction—in a fresh and compelling way.

Cynthia Ozick's brilliance and wit shines through in all her writing, but nowhere more so than in the linked short stories of **The Puttermesser Papers,** a fictional biography of the life (and death and afterlife) of a Jewish woman in Manhattan. Attorney and dedicated reader Ruth Puttermesser's existence includes a stint as mayor of New York, several love affairs, and the creation of a golem. Not to be missed.

Chaim Potok wrote two novels that I think are indispensable to understanding the Hasidic and Orthodox American Jewish communities following the Holocaust: **The Chosen** and **My Name Is Asher Lev.**

And don't forget the wonderful short stories of Grace Paley, including the collections **The Little Disturbances of Man** and **Enormous Changes at the Last Minute,** which were revolutionary in their day.

A whole new generation of writers continues to explore Jewish identity in America. Among the finest are Allegra Goodman (**Kaaterskill Falls**), Elizabeth Rosner (**The Speed of Light**), Katie Singer (**The Wholeness of a Broken Heart**), Rebecca Goldstein (**The Mind-Body Problem**), Nathan Englander (**For the Relief of Unbearable Urges**), Myla Goldberg (**Bee**

Season), Pearl Abraham (**The Romance Reader**), and Joshua Henkin (**Swimming Across the Hudson**).

WARD JUST: TOO GOOD TO MISS

Too few readers of fiction know the novels of Ward Just, which is a real shame, since he is a master craftsman, unafraid to tackle deep and difficult topics. In many ways he seems to be the American Graham Greene, concerned always with the morality of human behavior. His novels are thoughtful, beautifully written, and often bleak bleak bleak. I sometimes think that Just never met a happy ending that he liked.

A Dangerous Friend, set in Vietnam just before American troops descend en masse, has echoes of Greene's **The Quiet American** but is at the same time entirely original. It shows how even the best-intentioned actions can go badly awry. (Just was a reporter in Vietnam and wrote **To What End: Report from Vietnam,** an account of his experiences there.)

You always expect government to be spelled with a capital G in a Ward Just novel; his personal hero (and the hero of many of his characters) is Abraham Lincoln, who tried to save the Union at any cost. This is nowhere plainer than in **Echo House,** the story of the Behl family, who have played a major role in American politics through three generations, from before the New Deal to the present. People come and go, Just tells us, but the government is forever, and much more than the sum of the men and women who carry out its mandates at any particular time. In **Echo House,** nothing particular happens: Deals are made, vows are broken, backs are stabbed and handshakes nullified, but the work goes on and everything matters.

The American Ambassador is the story of the challenging relationship between a father and his son, set during the period of the Iranian revolution and the taking of American hostages. It has one of the most devastating endings of any novel I've ever read, and even given Ward Just's propensity for unhappy endings, this is a doozy.

Other books by Just include **A Soldier of the Revolution; The Translator; Stringer; Jack Gance; The Congressman Who Loved Flaubert, and Other Washington Stories; A Family Trust; Honor, Power, Riches, Fame, and the Love of Women; Ambition and Love; Lowell Limpett: and Two Stories; The Weather in Berlin;** and **In the City of Fear.**

KING ARTHUR

Ever since Thomas Malory wrote his fourteenth-century epic **Le Morte d'Arthur,** the legend of King Arthur has been a powerful draw for readers of all ages, so it's no surprise that writers, too, have found it to be a rich lode of inspiration and subject matter. Authors have taken a wide variety of approaches to the legend, from the traditional view of Arthur and his men of the Round Table as exemplars of medieval life and chivalric customs, to interpretations of the historical Arthur, to fantastical novels of witchcraft and white and black magic. In other words, there's an Arthur for every age and taste.

Once you read Rosemary Sutcliff's romantic and well-researched **Sword at Sunset** (one of my very favorite novels), in which an all-too-human Arthur leads his fellow Britons in a fight to the death against the invading Saxon armies, knowing full well that a loss will mean the coming of the dark and the end of civilization, you'll never be able to picture Arthur in any other way.

T. H. White's quartet of Arthurian novels, collectively entitled **The Once and Future King,** inspired the Broadway musical *Camelot.* **The Sword in the**

Stone—aimed at young readers and filled with sly humor—opens the series. It introduces the young orphan Wart, who innocently pulls the famous sword Excalibur from a stone in a churchyard and becomes the High King. In **The Queen of Air and Darkness;The Ill-Made Knight;** and **The Candle in the Wind,** the tone grows darker, as White depicts a world in which even the most chivalrous knights and powerful wizards are unable to change their fates.

Close behind Sutcliff and White on my list of favorites is Mary Stewart's **Merlin Trilogy,** composed of **The Crystal Cave; The Last Enchantment;** and **The Hollow Hills.** Here the focus is on the great wizard Merlin, as he attempts to help Arthur navigate through a world complicated by human emotions, fate, and magic.

The Arthur legend is also the basis for other historical series, such as Jack Whyte's **Camulod Chronicles,** including **The Skystone; The Fort at River's Bend; Uther;** and others; Sharan Newman's **Guinevere; The Chessboard Queen;** and others; and Rosalind Miles's **Guenevere: Queen of the Summer Country;** and Bernard Cornwell's darkly realistic series of men at war during the Dark Ages, **The Warlord Chronicles,** including **The Winter King; Enemy of God;** and **Excalibur.**

The Mists of Avalon by Marion Zimmer Bradley is one of the most enduringly popular novels about King Arthur. Bradley retells the legend from the viewpoint of the major female characters: Arthur's mother Igraine and his half-sister Morgaine, his wife Gwenhwyfer, and the Lady of the Lake, Vivian. The central conflict here is religious—between the matriarchal Druidic beliefs and the more patriarchal, newly influential Christianity.

Although Stephen R. Lawhead's **Pendragon Cycle** was set in Camelot during the Middle Ages, his **Avalon: The Return of King Arthur** posits a rebirth and return of Arthur in the modern world.

KITCHEN-SINK POETRY

In talking to my friends who are both poets and teachers of poetry, I learned that there's no official name for the loose confederation of poets that I've dubbed "the kitchen-sink [as in everything-but-the-kitchen-sink] gang of five." (I have no idea if these men even know one another in any other than a hail-fellow-poet-well-met sort of way, or what they would think of being grouped with one another, although I hope they'd be pleased.) David Kirby, Billy Collins, James Tate, Campbell McGrath, and Dean Young aren't formalists, lyricists, language poets, or any of the other "ists" and "isms" by which we tend to categorize poets. What the gang of five share is their conversational, seemingly stream-of-consciousness approach to their subjects (which are wacky in their own right) and the ability to make readers feel that they're about to become involved in often complicated and convoluted stories. Their poems are filled with specific details ("words but more than words," as James Tate says), and there's no way of predicting from the opening lines where the poem is going to end up. The kitchen-sink gang of five's poetry is punctuated with humor, to be sure, but it is not light verse. To anyone who feels baffled and put off by contemporary poetry, let me recommend these five poets and some of their specific poems:

David Kirby's **The House of Blue Light** is probably his best-known book. Some of my favorite poems in it are "The Exorcist of Notre-Dame," "Strip Poker," "Dear Derrida," and the title poem (in fact, just go ahead and read the whole book!). Other Kirby poems I adore are "The Search for Baby Combover" and "The Elephant of the Sea."

In James Tate's **Shroud of the Gnome,** try "The Blind Heron" or "Days of Pie and Coffee."

I think perhaps the Billy Collins poems I most enjoy reading and reread-ing are "Forgetfulness," "Workshop" (from **The Art of Drowning**), the very witty (and oh-so-true) "Introduction to Poetry" (which appeared in **The Apple That Astonished Paris**), and "By a Swimming Pool outside Syracusa."

Don't miss Campbell McGrath's "The Golden Angel Pancake House" and Dean Young's "Blue Garden" and "Goodbye, Place I Lived Nearly 23 Years / Almost Everyone Left Before Me."

P. F. KLUGE: TOO GOOD TO MISS

P. F. Kluge's **Biggest Elvis** is one of those friend-defining novels that come along every so often. If you meet someone and discover in the first ten minutes of conversation that you've both read and loved Kluge's quirky first novel, why then you've probably made a friend for life.

American imperialism in the Philippines is the subtext of this well-written and highly entertaining novel. Former college professor Ward Wiggins, along with the Lane brothers, does two shows a night at Graceland, a crummy bar in Olongapo, Philippines. The three impersonate Elvis at the various stages of his life for an enthusiastic audience of sailors on shore leave and their "dates," the bar girls who make a meager living sat-isfying the desires of Americans at the nearby naval base. Chester plays "Baby" Elvis (the handsome, sexy Presley), Albert is "Dude" Elvis (during the movie years), while Wiggins portrays "Biggest" Elvis (Presley during his last, sad, drug-addled years). While Chester and Albert regard this gig as tem-porary, Biggest Elvis takes his role more seriously and involves himself in bettering the lives of the bar girls. This trio of sympathetic, three-dimensional characters takes turns telling the story, each responding differently to the redeeming possibilities of love and the opportunities for betrayal that life offers them.

Others novels by Kluge include **MacArthur's Ghost, Season for War, Eddie and the Cruisers,** and **The Day That I Die.** His nonfiction titles are **Alma Mater** and **The Edge of Paradise.**

ERIC KRAFT: TOO GOOD TO MISS

E ric Kraft has spent his writing career creating a series of comic masterpieces under the general rubric of "The Personal History, Adventures, Experiences & Observations of Peter Leroy," and am I ever glad he did. In this series of autobiographical tales and writings, Peter Leroy constructs an alternative history of his own life, from birth to adulthood. Beginning with **Little Follies,** Leroy recalls the many incidents that make up his life and the lives of his friends and extended family, and muses on philosophical issues, large and small. Most of the novels take place in Babbington, "the clam capital of America" (which is a problem for Peter, since an accident he suffered as a young child has left him with an enduring fear of bivalves), a small town on the southern end of Long Island, during the middle years of the twentieth century. The meaning of memory and the meaning of self are these novels' themes. Think of Proust with a sense of humor, or on drugs.

Kraft talks about these books as being part of a soup, say a clam chowder, in which all the ingredients are good by themselves (yum! the clams; goody! the potatoes; wow! the onions—sweet as sugar!) but together they're even better. The books can be read in any order, but be warned: Once you start the series, you won't want to read anything else until you finish them all.

The Peter Leroy saga includes:

MARK KURLANSKY: TOO GOOD TO MISS

There are few people I'd rather be with at a dinner party than Mark Kurlansky. (Unfortunately, this is unlikely, as I know no one who knows him.) Not only is he seemingly interested in everything under the sun, but his enthusiasm—conveyed in a series of well-written, good-humored books—for even the most arcane subjects is infectious. Plus, he loves good food.

I certainly never imagined what importance a simple fish could have in the course of human history, but in **Cod: A Biography of the Fish That Changed the World** (which won the James Beard Award for Excellence in Food Writing), Kurlansky convinced me I had overlooked a major influence on world events, especially events in the North Atlantic area related to the fishing industry and conservation (cod nearly became extinct because of overfishing).

After reading **Salt: A World History** you'll never take that not-so-simple condiment for granted again. In fact, you could devote a whole game of trivia to salt: Did you know it was the root of the word "salacious"? Or that salt was used as currency in some countries? Or that the Egyptians used salt to preserve bodies? Or that Homer called it "the divine substance"? Kurlansky leaves no salt cellar unturned as he fills us in on salt's piquant history.

While **The Basque History of the World** is basically a straightforward analysis of the history and culture of a small area in the Pyrenees that overlaps the border between France and Spain and has been the scene of an ongoing independence struggle for what seems to be centuries, Kurlansky offers so many digressions and side trips (including recipes) that you barely realize how much you're learning.

Kurlansky also edited a delightful compendium: **Choice Cuts: A Savory Selection of Food Writing from Around the World and Throughout History.**

LADY TRAVELERS

The Victorian era was prime time for intrepid women travelers. I often think of them, dressed in their drab ankle-length dresses with long sleeves and high collars, their sensible shoes, their hair pinned up, setting off into the great unknown carrying reticules and calling cards, venturing out from England in the second half of the nineteenth century to all points of the compass. Their stories are fascinating, whether they tell them themselves or we see them through the eyes of later biographers.

One of the best overviews of the topic is Dorothy Middleton's **Victorian Lady Travellers,** which covers the well-known travelers (Mary Kingsley and Isabella Bird) as well as the relatively unknown (May French Sheldon and Annie Taylor). In **Unsuitable for Ladies: An Anthology of Women Travellers,** Jane Robinson assembles women's writings from various time periods about their great and mundane experiences far from home.

Isabella Bird was one of the more dashing and irresistible travelers. She left her native England to go adventuring in America (as she relates in **A Lady's Life in the Rocky Mountains**), Japan (**Unbeaten Tracks in Japan**), Tibet (**Among the Tibetans**), and the South Seas (**Six Months in the Sandwich Islands**), among other exotic locales.

Another of the famous adventurers was Mary Kingsley, whose **Travels in West Africa** remains as fascinating to read now as when it was first published in 1895 (and it's been in print continuously since then). The best biography of this woman who climbed Mount Cameroon (and left her calling card on the summit) is Katherine Frank's **A Voyager Out: The Life of Mary Kingsley**. Caroline Alexander describes her experiences replicating Kingsley's journey in **One Dry Season: In the Footsteps of Mary Kingsley**.

Freya Stark (1893–1993), the subject of **Passionate Nomad: The Life of Freya Stark** by Jane Fletcher Geniesse, carried on the tradition of the Victorian adventurers, visiting and writing insightfully about the Middle East in books such as **Traveller's Prelude: Autobiography 1893–1927; Beyond Euphrates; The Valleys of the Assassins** (the one to read if you read only one by Stark); and **The Coast of Incense**.

Other notable lady travelers of the twentieth century (and their best books) include Emily Hahn (**China to Me**), Ella Maillart (**Forbidden Journey**), Rebecca West (**Black Lamb and Grey Falcon**), and Martha Gellhorn (**Travels with Myself and Another**).

LATIN AMERICAN FICTION

Writers from the many nations that make up Latin America offer readers a stunning array of plots, characters, and writing styles from which to choose. Here are some good places to start:

From Spain comes Soledad Puértolas, whose novel **Bordeaux** conveys her three main characters' struggle with isolation, melancholy, and disappointment in love.

Rosario Ferré's **The House on the Lagoon** incorporates almost a century of Puerto Rican history in her story of the Mendizabal family.

You can read Julio Cortázar's **Hopscotch** in a conventional fashion, from first page to last, but the Argentinean author offers an alternative approach as well, listing chapters in a suggested (new) reading order.

Alicia Yánez Cossío's novel **Bruna and Her Sisters in the Sleeping City,** which is set in a small town in the author's native Ecuador, is the story of a family plagued by ghosts and their own eccentricities.

My favorite novel by Mario Vargas Llosa, Peru's most famous novelist, is the partly autobiographical **Aunt Julia and the Scriptwriter.**

Manuel Puig's **Kiss of the Spider Woman** is set in an Argentinean prison, where a political prisoner and a self-centered gay window dresser become unlikely friends.

The life, death, and rebirth of a small town in the midst of the cacao plantations in Brazil is the subject of Jorge Amado's **Show Down.**

Innocent games turn nightmarish during the summer holidays at the magnificent Chilean country estate of the Ventura family when the children—thirty-three cousins ranging in age from six to sixteen—are left to their own devices while their parents pursue their pleasures and pastimes in José Donoso's **A House in the Country.**

Other writers from Latin America include:

Humberto Costantini's	The Long Night of Francisco Sanctis
Nélida Piñon's	Caetana's Sweet Song
Jorge Luis Borges's	Collected Fictions
José Saramago's	Blindness
Gabriel García Márquez's	Love in the Time of Cholera
Isabel Allende's	Eva Luna
Paulo Coelho's	By the River Piedra I Sat Down and Wept

JONATHAN LETHEM: TOO GOOD TO MISS

Jonathan Lethem is one of those rare novelists who refuse to write the same book twice, except that all of his books are exquisitely written and wildly original retakes on traditional themes. Since he can't be categorized precisely, his novels don't fit comfortably in any "ist" or "ism." You can't even assign them to particular genres, since each novel takes a particular genre and then tweaks and contorts it into something entirely original: a mystery for those who don't care for mysteries, science fiction for non-sci-fi fans, and so on. A close reading of Lethem's novels will turn up signs of the influence of writers as diverse as David Lodge, Don DeLillo, and Isaac Asimov. Great combination, isn't it? You might as well add Katherine Dunn and Lewis Carroll to the list, too. Loving one Lethem book is no guarantee that you'll even moderately like the next one. Here are some of my favorites:

Gun, with Occasional Music (Philip Marlowe–like hero meets a talking kangaroo in a dystopian Oakland); **Amnesia Moon** (a road trip undertaken by Chaos, of Hatfork, Wyoming); **The Wall of the Sky, the Wall of the Eye** (a collection of short stories); **Girl in Landscape** (coming of age on another planet); **As She Climbed Across the Table** (a physicist falls in love with Lack, a Black Hole, to the consternation of her boyfriend); and **Motherless Brooklyn** (a young man with Tourette's syndrome tries to track down the murderer of his foster father).

ELINOR LIPMAN: TOO GOOD TO MISS

You can always count on Elinor Lipman for an inviting and sprightly work of fiction, marked by a deep affection for her all-too-human characters and her delight in introducing them to us, so we can adore them, too. Lipman's novels are all about relationships—those between men and women, of course, but also between mothers and daughters and good and bad friends. I think of Lipman's novels as being the perfect comfort food for the mind, and I go back to them again and again. My two favorites are **The Way Men Act** and **The Inn at Lake Devine**, both of which are slightly more serious than her other novels (but still thoroughly enjoyable, trust me); the former touches on issues of race, and the latter on the issue of anti-Semitism.

Lipman's other books are **Then She Found Me; Into Love and Out Again; Isabel's Bed; The Ladies' Man; The Dearly Departed;** and **The Pursuit of Alice Thrift.**

LOST WEEKENDS

The English poet A. E. Housman once wrote, "Malt does more than Milton can / To justify God's ways to Man," and many a writer has written—in fiction or in memoir—about their close, not to say intimate, relationship with grape and grain. Perhaps none has better expressed the attraction of alcohol—and by extension the nature of addiction in general—than Caroline Knapp, in her memoir **Drinking: A Love Story.**

Pete Hamill combines a memoir of his coming-of-age in Brooklyn in the 1930s and '40s with an account of his many years of serious boozing in **A Drinking Life: A Memoir.**

When Jack London published his memoir **John Barleycorn** in 1913, he was writing about and trying to recover from his experiences with the demon rum (and other varieties of liquor) during a tumultuous year (1912) that he spent in New York.

A best-seller in 1944 (when attitudes toward alcohol and alcoholism were far different from today's; we now look at alcoholism as a disease and not as a sign of weak character), Charles Jackson's autobiographical novel **The Lost Weekend** relates the downward spiral of wannabe-writer Don Birnam over four days of uncontrollable drinking.

Lawrence Block's series of mysteries featuring ex-cop Matt Scudder always have drinking as their subtext, since Scudder is a recovering alcoholic. In **When the Sacred Ginmill Closes,** Scudder looks back (unsentimentally) on his drinking days and a series of crimes that took place in various Manhattan bars. (The title for this novel comes from a song by Dave Van Ronk: "And so we've had another night / of poetry and poses / And each man knows he'll be alone / when the sacred gin mill closes.")

MAGICAL REALISM

Although the term "magical realism" has become almost synonymous with Latin American fiction, writers from around the world make use of the conventions of the form. A German art critic named Franz Roh first used the term in the late 1920s to describe painters who were portraying reality in a new way. Although the first person to apply it to Latin American literature seems to have been Arturo Uslar Pietri, a Venezuelan literary critic, the term became known around the world when the Guatemalan poet and novelist Miguel Angel Asturias used it to describe his novels when he won the Nobel Prize in 1967.

But what is magical realism, really? Science-fiction writer Gene Wolfe believes that "magical realism is fantasy written in Spanish," but we might add that it is usually fantasy without any of the magic folk (elves, witches, orcs) that are regularly present in fantasy novels. magical realism is, rather, more a style of writing that allows authors to look at our own world through the lens of another world, an imagined yet very familiar one in which past, present, and future are often intertwined.

Some good examples of magical realism include:

Gabriel García Márquez's	One Hundred Years of Solitude
Tim Winton's	Cloudstreet
Alice Hoffman's	Illumination Night
Lawrence Thornton's	Imagining Argentina
Sherman Alexie's	Reservation Blues
Ana Castillo's	So Far from God
Patrick Chamoiseau's	Texaco
Angela Carter's	Nights at the Circus
Milan Kundera's	Immortality

IAN MCEWAN: TOO GOOD TO MISS

Ian McEwan is the author of two collections of short stories (**First Love, Last Rites** and **In Between the Sheets**) and nine novels: **The Cement Garden; The Comfort of Strangers; The Child in Time; The Innocent; Black Dogs; The Daydreamer; Enduring Love; Amsterdam** (which won the Booker Prize in 1998); and **Atonement** (which won the National Book Critics' Circle Award in 2003).

You need a strong stomach for some of his early novels, which are drenched in elegantly well-written violence (think about the early novels of Cormac McCarthy for a good comparison). He is wonderful at portraying the complexities of human relationships, including those between husbands and wives, parents and children, siblings, lovers, and the past and present. Although many readers believe that **Atonement** is his masterpiece, my favorite McEwan novel is **Black Dogs,** which describes the stormy marriage between June and Bernard Tremaine. Their fraught relationship begins during their honeymoon, when June is nearly attacked by two large, vicious black dogs. Or is she?

MECHANICAL MEN, ROBOTS, AUTOMATONS, AND DEEP BLUE

From the court of Maria Theresa of Austria to the artificial intelligence laboratory at the Massachusetts Institute of Technology, from the ancient Greeks to the present time, we've been enthralled with the possibility of creating a machine that thinks like a human. This idea has been explored in fiction and nonfiction, by authors as diverse as Mary Shelley (whose **Frankenstein** was originally published in 1818) and Karel Capek, who coined the term "robot" in his 1921 play *R.U.R.* to describe mechanical beings who perform dehumanizing work.

Gaby Wood's **Edison's Eve: A Magical History of the Quest for Mechanical Life** is an especially interesting and instructive look at the attempts to build machines that act like humans.

The Turk: The Life and Times of the Famous Eighteenth-Century Chess-Playing Machine by Tom Standage is a most entertaining account of a marvelous invention: a life-size chess-playing mannequin "dressed in exotic Oriental garb," invented by Wolfgang von Kempelen for Maria Theresa, empress of Austria-Hungary, in 1770. Was it a hoax? Standage doesn't reveal the truth until the very last page.

Feng-Hsiung Hsu led the team that designed the computer that defeated Garry Kasparov. Hsu tells the story behind the invention in **Behind Deep Blue: Building the Computer That Defeated the World Chess Champion**, which, although somewhat scholarly, is a less daunting book than I had anticipated.

Rodney A. Brooks speculates on the future relationship between men and machines in **Flesh and Machines: How Robots Will Change Us.**

Of course, when it comes to fiction and robots the best place to begin is with Isaac Asimov's classic **I, Robot,** a collection of short stories in which the author developed the three basic laws of robotics that have been adopted by all subsequent sci-fi writers as though they were fact and not fiction.

In **Galatea 2.2,** Richard Powers retells the myth of Pygmalion in a novel about a young professor of English who helps a cognitive neurologist create a thinking machine that can pass a comprehensive master's exam in literature, and in the process discovers that Helen has developed a mind of her own.

As in his novel **The Grand Complication,** Allen Kurzweil fills his delightful first novel **A Case of Curiosities** with puns and wordplay, historical facts, and wonderful characters. Set just before the French Revolution, this is the story of a young boy, his fascination with the mechanics of movement, and his design of the ultimate mechanical being.

MEMOIRS

In the fourth century, St. Augustine penned his **Confessions,** the first tell-all memoir. (It makes fascinating reading even today, more than sixteen hundred years later.) Augustine writes of his overwhelming desire to serve God and his seeming inability (or unwillingness) to give up the pleasures of the flesh. Everyone's favorite sentence in the book is probably his plaintive prayer, which goes something like this: "Lord, give me chastity, but not yet."

Of course, most contemporary memoirists are more focused on understanding themselves and their families, no doubt following the dictum of Socrates about the unexamined life not being worth living.

The Liars' Club by Mary Karr is a funny yet painful-to-read account of the author's life growing up in a small town in East Texas with a mercurial mother, a larger-than-life father, and a perfectly brilliant sister.

In **Another Life: A Memoir of Other People**, Michael Korda describes— in a wonderfully affectionate, nondishy, nonegocentric manner—the authors he worked with and the office politics in which he played a role throughout his long career as an editor at Simon & Schuster.

Nora Sayre's **On the Wing: A Young American Abroad** recounts the author's early twenties, when she traveled to London to live and work, and hobnobbed with such luminaries as Arthur Koestler, A. J. Liebling, Mai Zetterling, and Tyrone Power.

Terry Ryan's **The Prize Winner of Defiance, Ohio: How My Mother Raised 10 Kids on 25 Words or Less** is a hymn of love to a large family and a small town, and especially the author's mother, Evelyn, who endured a difficult marriage and penury by using her abundant sense of humor and her ability to turn a phrase to win hundreds of jingle contests.

In **Time to Be in Earnest: A Fragment of Autobiography**, mystery writer P. D. James offers a tastefully done and blessedly nonconfessional memoir of her seventy-seventh year. (Samuel Johnson advised that at seventy-seven it was "time to be in earnest.")

Dave Eggers's postmodern memoir **A Heartbreaking Work of Staggering Genius: Based on a True Story** is the heady, surprising, funny, and ultimately moving story of his experiences raising his younger brother, Christopher, after their parents die within a few weeks of one another, when Dave was in his early twenties.

MEXICAN FICTION

By far the best known Mexican writer is Carlos Fuentes. Of his many books, my favorite remains **The Old Gringo,** an imaginative retelling of the fate of Ambrose Bierce, who has come to Mexico to die.

Montserrat Fontes's disturbing novel of a family trying to survive the brutal Porfirio Díaz regime at the turn of the twentieth century, **Dreams of the Centaur,** is followed by **First Confession.**

The False Years, by Josefina Vicens, is the story of a young man trying to live up to the memory of his dead father—so much so that eventually he begins to feel that perhaps he has died while his father has gone on living.

The heroine of Laura Esquivel's charming **Like Water for Chocolate** is predestined to spend her life unmarried; she can communicate her love for Pedro, her brother-in-law, only through culinary magic that wreaks havoc on her family.

In **Macho!** by Victor Villaseñor, a seventeen-year-old illegal alien who has left his home in Mexico to work the California harvests learns important lessons about love, loyalty, and death.

Francisco Hinojosa's **Hectic Ethics: Stories** is a great introduction to the work of a young Mexican writer whose books are just starting to be translated and available in the United States.

Juan Rulfo's **Pedro Páramo,** the tale of a son's search for his father, is an early (1955) example of Latin American magical realism.

David Toscana's postmodern **Tula Station,** with its three separate narratives that are woven inextricably together, demands much of the reader, but offers a great deal of pleasure in return.

THE MIDDLE EAST

Each of these books does what the best history and political science books can do: provides a context and background that make the present more understandable. (I always feel so much smarter—not just better informed—when I read the newspaper if I've read an outstanding book on the topic, too.) These particular books are indispensable for understanding the terrible complexities of the Middle East:

Thomas Friedman's now-classic **From Beirut to Jerusalem** was first published in 1989 and updated in 1995. It remains an eminently readable, vital, and engaging account of the history and politics of the region, by the *New York Times* reporter who covered it. (Worth reading, too, is Friedman's **The Lexus and the Olive Tree.**)

Six Days of War: June 1967 and the Making of the Modern Middle East by Michael B. Oren is a massively thorough and equally readable history of the events leading up to the conflict and what resulted from it.

In **The Middle East: A Brief History of the Last 2,000 Years,** Bernard Lewis, one of the leading Middle Eastern scholars, delivers a cogent, well-written chronology of people, places, and events (even if the book is over 400 pages!).

In **War Without End: Israelis, Palestinians, and the Struggle for a Promised Land,** Anton La Guardia offers a balanced account of the tragedy of Middle Eastern politics today.

David Shipler interviewed many people—Arabs, Israelis, and Americans—while he was a *New York Times* reporter in Jerusalem from 1979 to 1984. The result of those interviews can be seen in **Arab and Jew: Wounded Spirits in a Promised Land,** which won the Pulitzer Prize for nonfiction in 1987. It should still be required reading for anyone interested in the early days (especially) of the Intifada and Israeli occupation of the West Bank.

MERLE MILLER: TOO GOOD TO MISS

If people know Merle Miller's name at all, it's most likely because they're familiar with his presidential biographies, including **Ike the Soldier: As They Knew Him** and **Lyndon: An Oral Biography,** but especially **Plain Speaking: An Oral Biography of Harry S. Truman.** (Miller always said that he felt a special kinship with Truman because he, too, had been called a sissy as a child.) But Miller also wrote a number of moving and often painful novels. He was born in 1919 in a small Iowa town, and grew up homosexual long before the freedoms that Stonewall began to open up for the gay community; he lived for most of his life in the closet. He wrote about his coming out in a nonfiction book called **On Being Different,** which first appeared as an article in *The New York Times* magazine and addressed the same issues as did his novel **What Happened.** All of Miller's books have as their basic theme alienation and the pain of living a lie.

My three favorite Miller novels are **A Gay and Melancholy Sound,** a heartbreaking coming-of-age novel, which just might be my all-time favorite book; **Reunion;** and **A Secret Understanding,** a semimystery novel. But I also love Miller's comic masterpiece, **Only You, Dick Daring,** written with Evan Rhodes, about their experiences writing a television pilot for Jackie Cooper. Other Miller books include **The Judges and the Judged; The Sure Thing; That Winter; We Dropped the A-Bomb** (written with Abe Spitzer); and **Island 49.**

MONTANA: IN BIG SKY COUNTRY

Something about the Montana sky provides a powerful incentive to writers. Outside of California and New York, it's hard to think of another state that's produced such a range of fine fiction, poetry, and memoirs. Probably the best place to begin a reading of Montana's literary treasure is **The Last Best Place: A Montana Anthology,** which includes poetry, fiction, and essays. Among the authors represented are Norman Maclean (**A River Runs Through It, and Other Stories**), D'Arcy McNickle (**Wind from an Enemy Sky**), James Welch (**Winter in the Blood**), A. B. Guthrie (**The Big Sky**), Mary Clearman Blew (**Balsamroot: A Memoir**), and Thomas McGuane (**Ninety-Two in the Shade**), as well as poetry by William Stafford, John Meade Haines, Patricia Goedicke, and Richard Hugo. To someone like me, who grew up in Detroit always believing that I was really supposed to be living in Cut Bank, Montana, it was (and remains) a wonderful treat.

Some of my favorite contemporary Montana writers and their books include Annick Smith's **Homestead,** a memoir of her experiences, along with her husband and four children, homesteading in the Blackfoot Valley on 163 acres in the 1960s; Deirdre McNamer (most people mention her **Rima in the Weeds** as their favorite, but I much prefer **One Sweet Quarrel**); and Elizabeth Savage's **The Girls from the Five Great Valleys,** a wonderful novel about the coming-of-age of five girls in Missoula, Montana, in 1934. (Originally published in 1977, this book is little known and now rarely read, but worth seeking out.)

And of course Montana mysteries are their own subset: James Crumley's **The Last Good Kiss** (the title comes from a Richard Hugo poem), Jamie Harrison's **The Edge of the Crazies,** and Peter Bowen's **Wolf, No Wolf.**

For an update of **The Last Best Place,** take a look at **Writing Montana:**

Literature Under the Big Sky, edited by Rick Newby and Suzanne Hunger.

The best book about Montana by a non-Montanan is **Bad Land: An American Romance**, by Jonathan Raban, a transplanted Brit now living in Seattle.

THE MOON'S MY DESTINATION

The best book about America's race for the moon remains one of the first books ever written about the manned space program and the men who focused on getting there first. **The Right Stuff** is the account of the original seven American astronauts, but Tom Wolfe begins his story back in the 1940s, when test pilots were trying to break the sound barrier, and moves forward, giving each astronaut his place in the sun (or the moon) as he brings the story up to the 1970s, when the book appeared. Incredibly moving, and a prime example of what became known as "New Journalism."

What sets **Apollo: The Epic Journey to the Moon** by the classical archaeologist David West Reynolds apart from other histories of the space race are the numerous high-quality illustrations in the book, including both photos and drawings, and Reynolds's ability to explain complex information in terms that an interested though not particularly educated-in-science reader can understand.

The editors of *Air & Space* and *Smithsonian* magazines have put together a beautiful pictorial history of the space shuttle program in **Space Shuttle: The First 20 Years—The Astronauts' Experiences in Their Own Words**, edited by Tony Reichhardt, complemented by a text that includes the astronauts' words on all aspects (from the sublime to the practical) of all the missions, including a moving section on the *Challenger* disaster.

Many of the astronauts themselves wrote about their lives and their experiences in space. Some good examples are **We Seven** by Scott Carpenter (a good companion read with Wolfe's **The Right Stuff**); Edwin (Buzz) Aldrin's **Return to Earth**; and **Apollo: An Eyewitness Account** by the astronaut, explorer, artist, and moonwalker Alan Bean.

Science writer Jeffrey Kluger coauthored **Lost Moon: The Perilous Voyage of Apollo 13**, along with astronaut Jim Lovell, the flight's commander. Though you may have seen and enjoyed the movie, don't miss the book, which brings a new dimension to the now familiar account of the heroism of the three-man crew.

Even before humankind reached the moon, unmanned space probes sent from Earth were there first. And they've moved on to deeper and darker space, as Kluger's **Journey Beyond Selēnē: Remarkable Expeditions Past Our Moon and to the Ends of the Solar System** makes clear, taking a long look at the work of the heroic scientists from the Jet Propulsion Laboratories in California who are planning and implementing these space probes.

The purpose of Andrew Chaikin's **A Man on the Moon: The Voyages of the Apollo Astronauts** is to make real for us the almost unbelievable fact that twenty-four men have actually walked on the moon. In-depth interviews with each of the twenty-four, as well as with the people who remained behind but contributed mightily to the success of the endeavors, are the basis of the book.

MOTHERS AND DAUGHTERS

As I read these books I thought of that old saying, "A son is a son 'til he takes him a wife, but a daughter's a daughter for all of her life." What could ever be more complicated and filled with potential for a disastrous outcome than the relationship between a mother and daughter? Many writers have tackled this theme (both in fiction and nonfiction), but each of the novels listed below offers an especially sensitive and nuanced portrait of mothers and their daughters.

Many of Gail Godwin's early novels touch on the mother-daughter relationship, either as an important subplot, as in the wonderful **The Odd Woman** (which I reread with pleasure every year or so) and the later **A Mother and Two Daughters,** which is in many ways the same book, with the subplot moved into the forefront of the story about how the wife and daughters of the Southern gentleman Leonard Strickland come to terms with his sudden death.

Amy and Isabelle by Elizabeth Strout tells the story of a turbulent year in the life of a single mother and her teenage daughter, who falls in love with her high school math teacher, one of the most loathsome men in contemporary fiction.

Mona Simpson's **Anywhere but Here** is the story of Adele August, a strong-willed mother who moves with her daughter, Ann, to Hollywood in order to make Ann into a movie star.

Three generations of mothers and daughters interact in **Charms for the Easy Life,** my favorite novel by Kaye Gibbons, set around World War II in small-town North Carolina. Charlie Kate, midwife and healer, her daughter Sophia, and Sophia's daughter, Margaret, have made a comfortable life for themselves, sans men, until Margaret falls in love. You don't often run across a strong elderly heroine, but Charlie Kate is one terrific senior citizen.

The mother-daughter relationship in Mary Bringle's **True Confessions** is really a minor part of this gem of a novel, but I loved the idea of a daughter pretending that she has gone to London for an extended period simply to avoid spending time with her mother—and making fake long-distance calls in order to keep up the charade.

MOTHERS AND SONS

Mothers of adoring pre-kindergarten sons will relate to the description given by Kate Reddy, the heroine of Allison Pearson's **I Don't Know How She Does It: The Life of Kate Reddy, Working Mother**. She says that being the mother of a young son is like being a movie star in a world without any critics, a situation in which you are universally (and uncritically) admired. The operative word is, of course, "young." The opposing view is usually found in novels about mothers and their (non-adoring) older sons.

There are certainly some novels that depict good relationships between mothers and their adolescent (or older) sons (Eric Kraft's **Inflating a Dog**, for one), but in general, mother-son novels describe difficult relationships, surely complicated by the whole Oedipal shtick. The books that follow are all good reads, if not necessarily instructive on What Mothers Ought Not to Do:

Maxine Chernoff's	**A Boy in Winter**
Pat Conroy's	**The Prince of Tides**
Helen DeWitt's	**The Last Samurai**
Robert C. S. Downs's	**The Fifth Season**
David James Duncan's	**The Brothers K**

IRIS MURDOCH: TOO GOOD TO MISS

I was introduced to Iris Murdoch's novels in the early 1980s, and I read them, in no particular order, in a flurry of delight and awe, thoroughly convinced that she was among the most brilliant writers I had ever encountered, an opinion I still hold. Even when I read a novel of hers that didn't quite click with me, I knew I was in the presence of a major twentieth-century writer. In fact, one of the major regrets of my reading life is that I don't think I will have enough time to reread her twenty-six novels, which were written over the course of nearly forty years.

From her first novel, **Under the Net,** published in 1954, to her final novel, **Jackson's Dilemma,** written in 1995, when she was in the early stages of Alzheimer's disease, Murdoch's works always deal with ideas: the role of love and power in the lives of her characters, the workings of fate, nature versus nurture, the meaning of life, good versus evil (her characters frequently struggle to be good in the face of evil, or slide into evil even in the presence of good). In her early novels, especially, you can see the influence of the philosophy of Jean-Paul Sartre. Yet even with their philosophical underpinning, Murdoch's novels are intensely rooted in the real world, filled with intricate plots and an intense attention to detail. Her writing is so meticulous that even throwaway sentences conjure up vivid pictures in readers' minds. Among the many wonderful Murdoch quotes, my all-time favorite is this one from **An Accidental Man:**

> *Matthew held in his hand something which was for him one of the most beautiful things in the world. It was a shallow Sung bowl with a design of peonies cut under the glaze. Its color was a sort of milky ivory, what an angel might conceive of if asked to conceive of white.*

Here's a list of Murdoch's novels, with asterisks by my very favorites:
Under the Net
The Flight from the Enchanter
The Sandcastle
The Bell
A Severed Head
An Unofficial Rose
The Unicorn
The Italian Girl

The Red and the Green

The Time of the Angels

The Nice and the Good

★Bruno's Dream

★A Fairly Honourable Defeat

★An Accidental Man

★The Black Prince

★A Word Child

The Sacred and Profane Love Machine

Henry and Cato

★The Sea, the Sea
(Murdoch's only Booker Prize–winning novel)

Nuns and Soldiers

★The Philosopher's Pupil

★The Good Apprentice

★The Book and the Brotherhood

The Message to the Planet

The Green Knight

Jackson's Dilemma

MUSIC AND MUSICIANS

The stressful, mercurial, emotionally and physically exhausting lives of professional musicians are explored sensitively in several good novels. Some are thinly fictionalized biographies, while others take the real person and place him in an unlikely situation, as in Bill Moody's **Looking for Chet Baker: An Evan Horne Mystery,** in which the jazz-pianist detective looks into the events surrounding the mysterious death of Baker, who fell, or was pushed, from an Amsterdam hotel window in 1988.

Dorothy Baker's great novel **Young Man with a Horn** is probably the classic novel of its type. Loosely based on the life of the jazz great Bix Beiderbecke, it is a tale of a trumpet player, Rick Martin, cursed by too much talent, too much ambition, and not quite enough self-discipline.

Richard Currey's **Lost Highway** is the tale of three country music singers, trying to make it big in the years between World War II and the war in Vietnam.

Say Goodbye by Lewis Shiner tells the story of the swift rise—and equally swift fall—of (fictional) pop singer and songwriter Laurie Moss, as related by her (fictional) biographer, who is more than half in love with her himself.

Salman Rushdie retells the myth of Orpheus and Eurydice in **The Ground Beneath Her Feet,** making the main characters two rock-and-roll idols from Bombay.

For a slightly different take on music in fiction, try Rafi Zabor's **The Bear Comes Home,** in which a saxophone-playing bear with mystical inclinations finally gets his big break as a jazz musician.

MY OWN PRIVATE DUI

In the beginning, Melville Dewey wanted to change his name to Melvil Dui. He was forever in a rush—places to go, books to read, libraries to reorganize. Spelling needed to be simplified so that words would take a shorter time to write as well as to read. The Melvil stuck, the Dui did not, so we know him today as Melvil Dewey, the father of the decimal classification system that nearly all public libraries still use.

Dewey's divisions make a certain amount of sense for libraries, but I find them next to useless when it comes to organizing my own book collection. Herewith, then, are seven eccentric categories that I propose for those of us who live the reading life, along with personal examples of what books belong where.

Books that are better remembered than reread:

Most children's books cannot be reread by an adult without her feeling disappointed, betrayed, and embarrassed. And this includes all of Betty Cavanna's teenage novels (except **Going on Sixteen**) and Beverly Cleary's **Fifteen**. Kit Reed's **At War As Children** and Lee Colgate's **Oh, Be Careful** are two children's novels I found impossible to reread, although I loved them the first time around.

Books that are simply treasures and ought not to go unread:

John O'Hara's	**Sermons and Soda-Water**
Martin Quigley's	**Winners and Losers**
Dick Francis	**Nerve** *and* **Odds Against**
James Morris	**Heaven's Command; Pax Britannica;** *and* **Farewell the Trumpets**
P. J. Kavanagh's	**The Perfect Stranger**
Sara Jeanette Duncan's	**The Pool in the Desert**

Wonderful books that are too emotionally devastating to read a second time:

Merle Miller	A Gay and Melancholy Sound
Rosemary Sutcliff	Sword at Sunset
Stephanie Plowman	The Road to Sardis

Books I wish I had not read yet so I could have the joy of reading them for the first time:

Paul Scott's	The Raj Quartet
Salman Rushdie's	Midnight's Children
J. R. R. Tolkien's	The Lord of the Rings
	All of Iris Murdoch's novels
	All of Eudora Welty's short stories

Books I reread when I'm feeling blue:

Carol Shields	The Republic of Love
Stephen McCauley's	The Easy Way Out
Elinor Lipman's	The Way Men Act
Muriel Spark's	A Far Cry from Kensington
Roy Lewis's	The Evolution Man, Or, How I Ate My Father
William Kotzwinkle's	The Bear Went Over the Mountain

Guilty pleasures that I reread any old time:

All the novels of Elswyth Thane, D. E. Stevenson, and Elizabeth Cadell.

Books that people always assume I've read but I haven't:

Come on, you don't really think I'm going to let you know what's on these shelves, do you?

NEW MEXICO

The spare, dusty landscape of New Mexico, our forty-seventh state, and the ongoing collision between Anglo and Hispanic cultures often make for good plots and a nicely evoked setting.

Some classics of New Mexico fiction include Conrad Richter's **The Sea of Grass,** originally published in 1936, which takes place high on the shaggy prairie of New Mexico at a time when sod-busting "nesters" clashed with hard-nosed ranchers to tame a violent land; Willa Cather's story of a French missionary priest in nineteenth-century New Mexico, **Death Comes for the Archbishop;** and John Nichols's comic **The Milagro Beanfield War.**

One of the best-known Hispanic writers is Rudolfo A. Anaya, and **Bless Me, Ultima** is probably his best-known novel. In it, six-year-old Antonio learns about the ways of the world from the magical healer Ultima, who comes to live with him and his family. Some readers may prefer the somewhat darker **Alburquerque,** in which a young man searches for his biological father in the economically and ethnically divided city of Albuquerque. (Incidentally, that extra "r" in Anaya's title is correct: it's the way the city's name was originally spelled.)

All of Rick Collignon's novels are well worth reading, but my favorite is his second book, **Perdido,** a moving story of the racial divide as it plays out in the life of an Anglo carpenter in a small northern New Mexico town, when his innocent questions regarding the death (more than two decades before) of a young woman lead to an eruption of violence among the townspeople.

Denise Chávez's antic and energetic second novel **Loving Pedro Infante** also takes place in a small New Mexico town, where Tere Avila, a teacher's aide, is obsessed with the dead Mexican movie star Pedro Infante as well as her married boyfriend (who just can't seem to leave his wife).

The insularity of small-town life is a frequent topic in contemporary fiction, but when that small town is in New Mexico, no one writes it better than Laura Hendrie in **Remember Me,** the story of a young woman—shunned and disliked by her neighbors—who is forced to reassess her life and her memories when her only friend, an elderly man, has a stroke.

NEW ORLEANS

Jazz and good food inevitably come to mind when you think about the city known as the Big Easy, but you'd be well advised to make a mental note to add "fiction" when you're thinking of New Orleans, as it's the setting for some great reads.

The Awakening, Kate Chopin's short and tragic story of Edna Pontellier's attempt to break away from the constrictions imposed on her as a woman by her Creole society, remains as moving today as when it was published in 1899, and it's impossible to read without asking yourself just how much—really—has changed for women today who dare to be different.

My two favorite New Orleans–set novels are **The Moviegoer,** Walker Percy's National Book Award–winning novel of disconnectedness, and Nancy Lemann's elegiac novel of family dysfunction, **Lives of the Saints.** But the best known and probably best beloved (as well as the novel with the most interesting publishing history) is John Kennedy Toole's raucous tragicomedy **A Confederacy of Dunces,** the adventures (often mis-) of Ignatius J. Reilly.

Two (very different) historical novels set in 1830s New Orleans are Edna Ferber's **Saratoga Trunk** (the main character must decide between marrying for love or money) and Barbara Hambly's **A Free Man of Color,** the first in a series of historical mysteries featuring Benjamin January, a Creole physician and music teacher who returns home to New Orleans after many years of living abroad and takes on the job of investigating the death of a high-class octoroon prostitute.

Other mysteries set in New Orleans include Julie Smith's series about detective Skip Langdon (**New Orleans Mourning** is the best) and James Lee Burke's series about Cajun detective Dave Robichaux (my favorite is **A Morning for Flamingos**).

In John Gregory Brown's **Decorations in a Ruined Cemetery,** the collapse of a bridge is the catalyst for the unveiling of the Eagen family's long-suppressed secrets.

Only parts of **Burning Marguerite** by Elizabeth Inness-Brown and **Hello to the Cannibals** by Richard Bausch take place in New Orleans, but the authors evoke the sense of the city remarkably well.

NEW YORK, NEW YORK

There are some wonderful novels about New York—books in which the city, in all its contradictions, complexities, and compelling energy, functions as another character and not merely the setting. Try these:

Cheryl Mendelson's **Morningside Heights**

Jonathan Lethem's **Motherless Brooklyn**

Jack Finney's contemporary time-travel classic **Time and Again**

Jay McInerney's brat-pack novel of hip urban transplants **Bright Lights, Big City**

Edith Wharton's portraits of upper-class society life in turn-of-the-twentieth-century Manhattan, including **The Age of Innocence** *and* **The House of Mirth**

Kate Christensen's **In the Drink** *and* **Jeremy Thrane**

E. L. Doctorow's **World's Fair**

Steven Millhauser's **Martin Dressler: The Tale of an American Dreamer**

Thomas Beller's **The Sleep-Over Artist**

Colum McCann's **This Side of Brightness**

And don't miss the wonderful memoir: **Manhattan, When I Was Young** by Mary Cantwell.

9/11

In years to come, September 11 may well be seen as a day, not unlike the day of the Japanese attack on Pearl Harbor, when the world changed. The wide range of books that were published in response to the terrible events of that day give us an opportunity not only to read first-person accounts of what happened, but also to step back and take a look at why it happened.

What happened:

Out of the Blue: The Story of September 11, 2001, From Jihad to Ground Zero, *by Richard Bernstein and the staff of* The New York Times.

David Halberstam's Firehouse

Jere Longman's Among the Heroes: United Flight 93 and the Passengers and Crew Who Fought Back

Portraits 9/11/01 *(the complete "Portraits of Grief," brief profiles written by* New York Times *reporters about the victims of the September 11 attacks)*

Dennis Smith's Report From Ground Zero: The Story of the Rescue Efforts at the World Trade Center

Thomas Von Essen's Strong of Heart: Life and Death in the Fire Department of New York

James B. Stewart's Heart of a Soldier: A Story of Love, Heroism, and September 11

William Langewiesche's American Ground: Unbuilding the World Trade Center

Required background reading:

Judith Miller's God Has Ninety-Nine Names:

Reporting from a Militant Middle East

Peter L. Bergen's Holy War, Inc.: Inside the Secret World of Osama bin Laden

Allan Gerson and Jerry Adler's The Price of Terror: One Bomb, One Plane, 270 Lives: The History-Making Struggle for Justice After Pan Am 103

Anthony Lake's 6 Nightmares: Real Threats in a Dangerous World and How America Can Meet Them

Daniel Benjamin and Steven Simon's The Age of Sacred Terror

John Miller and Michael Stone's The Cell: Inside the 9/11 Plot, and Why the FBI and CIA Failed to Stop It

Mark Riebling's Wedge: From Pearl Harbor to 9/11 How the Secret War Between the FBI and CIA Has Endangered National Security

You might also want to look at the books discussed in "The Islamic World" and "The Middle East" sections of this book.

LEWIS NORDAN: TOO GOOD TO MISS

Lewis Nordan is probably the best writer you've never heard of. His novels, all set in Arrow Catcher, Mississippi, deep in the heart of the Dixie delta, are quirky, dark, hilarious, heartfelt, and richly rewarding, filled with pleasures large and small—timeless themes, an array of three-dimensional characters, and wonderfully evocative writing.

Nordan's fiction (as well as his memoir, **Boy with Loaded Gun**) exemplifies his deep belief that humor and tragedy spring from the same source—he says that "all comedy is underpinned by loss." This can be seen especially in **Wolf Whistle,** a novel loosely based on the lynching of young black Emmett Till in Mississippi in 1955, in which all the citizens of Arrow Catcher struggle with their differing levels of complicity in the crime and wrestle with the true meaning of evil. In **The Sharpshooter Blues,** Nordan tells the story of sweet and simple Hydro Raney, especially how his life changes after "two lovely children" are killed during their robbery of the William Tell Grocery. **Boy with Loaded Gun,** Nordan's memoir of growing up in the 1950s in itty-bitty Itta Bena, Mississippi, with his widowed mother, includes a chapter on his sojourn in New York (the best chapter in the book, which I dare you to read without laughing out loud).

Nordan's books include:

> **Welcome to the Arrow-Catcher Fair**
> **The All-Girl Football Team**
> **Music of the Swamp**
> **Wolf Whistle**
> **The Sharpshooter Blues**
> **Sugar Among the Freaks**
> **Lightning Song**
> **Boy with Loaded Gun**

NOT ONLY FOR KIDS:
FANTASIES FOR GROWN-UPS

The popularity of J. K. Rowling's Harry Potter series with both adults and children proves that what kids look for in a good fantasy is the same as what grownups enjoy: a good plot, an unusual setting, and fascinating characters. So it's no surprise that grown-ups will enjoy the best children's fantasies as much as children do. Although most of the books I list here have never achieved the widespread recognition of the Harry Potter books, they sure should have:

Eoin Colfer's **Artemis Fowl** is a romp through a very different fantasy world from the one we're accustomed to: an inept group of fairies and a hero who seems awfully—well, unheroic doesn't seem too strong a term.

Lemony Snicket's series called "A Series of Unfortunate Events" begins with the warning that if the reader is looking for a book with a happy ending, look elsewhere! The three Baudelaire children, beleaguered by one misfortune after another, endure through wonderful book after book, including, among many others, **The Bad Beginning; The Reptile Room; The Wide Window;** and **The Vile Village.**

Nancy Farmer's **The Ear, the Eye, and the Arm** is set in 2194, in Harare, Zimbabwe, where three children are captured by the wicked servants of the city's seamy underworld and sent into slavery. Their father hires a trio of very unusual detectives to rescue them.

Which Witch? by Eva Ibbotson is the story of Arriman, a bachelor wizard who, desperate to have a child to carry on the family wizarding business, seeks to marry the wickedest of wicked witches—which brings us to Belladonna, the sweetest, smallest, and prettiest witch in the coven, who is determined to marry Arriman and needs only to convince him of her sinister character.

Norton Juster's **The Phantom Tollbooth** has delighted readers old and young ever since its publication over forty years ago. In fact, it's likely that adults enjoy the wordplay and adventures more than children do. It's possible that James Thurber's **The 13 Clocks** also appeals to adults more than kids. A wicked duke, determined not to let his niece marry, is ultimately defeated by a ragamuffin prince.

Natalie Babbitt's **Tuck Everlasting** is a moving fantasy that addresses the issue of the value of life, the meaning of death, and the choices that everyone must ultimately make.

100 GOOD READS, DECADE BY DECADE

1900s:

Henry James's	The Golden Bowl
Mark Twain's	The Man That Corrupted Hadleyburg
G. K. Chesterton's	The Man Who Was Thursday
Joseph Conrad's	Heart of Darkness
Miles Franklin's	My Brilliant Career
E. M. Forster's	A Room with a View
Rudyard Kipling's	Kim
Edith Wharton's	The House of Mirth
Thomas Mann's	Buddenbrooks
Upton Sinclair's	The Jungle

1910s:

James Joyce's	A Portrait of the Artist as a Young Man
Willa Cather's	My Ántonia

Sherwood Anderson's	Winesburg, Ohio
D. H. Lawrence's	Sons and Lovers
Franz Kafka's	The Metamorphosis
P. G. Wodehouse's	Psmith in the City
Somerset Maugham's	Of Human Bondage
John Buchan's	The Thirty-Nine Steps
E. O. Somerville's	The Irish R.M.
E. C. Bentley's	Trent's Last Case

1920s:

Erich Maria Remarque's	All Quiet on the Western Front
F. Scott Fitzgerald's	The Great Gatsby
E. M. Forster's	A Passage to India
Theodore Dreiser's	An American Tragedy
Anita Loos's	Gentlemen Prefer Blondes
A. A. Milne's	Winnie-the-Pooh
Virginia Woolf's	Mrs. Dalloway
Margaret Mead's	Coming of Age in Samoa
Carl Sandburg's	Abraham Lincoln: The Prairie Years
Thomas Mann's	The Magic Mountain

1930s:

Pearl Buck's	The Good Earth
John Dos Passos's	1919
Dashiell Hammett's	The Maltese Falcon
John Steinbeck's	The Grapes of Wrath
James Hilton's	Goodbye, Mr. Chips
Nathanael West's	Miss Lonelyhearts
A. J. Cronin's	The Citadel
C. S. Forester's	Captain Horatio Hornblower

William Faulkner's	Light in August
Margaret Mitchell's	Gone With the Wind

1940s:

John Hersey's	Hiroshima
Evelyn Waugh's	Brideshead Revisited
Edmund Crispin's	The Moving Toyshop
Laura Hobson's	Gentleman's Agreement
Jack Schaefer's	Shane
Marjorie Kinnan Rawlings's	Cross Creek
Albert Camus's	The Plague
Christopher Isherwood's	The Berlin Stories
Ernest Hemingway's	For Whom the Bell Tolls
Richard Wright's	Native Son

1950s:

Anne Morrow Lindbergh's	Gift from the Sea
J. D. Salinger's	The Catcher in the Rye
Ralph Ellison's	Invisible Man
James Agee's	A Death in the Family
William Golding's	Lord of the Flies
Anne Frank's	The Diary of a Young Girl
Ray Bradbury's	Fahrenheit 451
Sloan Wilson's	The Man in the Gray Flannel Suit
J. R. R. Tolkien's	The Fellowship of the Ring
Simone de Beauvoir's	The Mandarins

1960s:

John le Carré's	The Spy Who Came in from the Cold
Vladimir Nabokov's	Pale Fire
Paul Scott's	The Jewel in the Crown
Roy Lewis's	The Evolution Man, Or, How I Ate My Father
Doris Lessing's	The Golden Notebook
Chaim Potok's	The Chosen
Thornton Wilder's	The Eighth Day
Olivia Manning's	The Balkan Trilogy
Harper Lee's	To Kill a Mockingbird
William Styron's	The Confessions of Nat Turner

1970s:

Toni Morrison's	Song of Solomon
Elizabeth Taylor's	Mrs. Palfrey at the Claremont
Eudora Welty's	The Optimist's Daughter
J. G. Farrell's	The Siege of Krishnapur
Clair Huffaker's	The Cowboy and the Cossack
Judith Guest's	Ordinary People
Steven Millhauser's	Edwin Mullhouse: The Life and Death of an American Writer, 1943–1954
Stephen King's	The Shining
Jack Finney's	Time and Again
Ella Leffland's	Rumors of Peace

1980s:

Salman Rushdie's Midnight's Children
Don DeLillo's Libra
Kazuo Ishiguro's The Remains of the Day
Anne Tyler's Dinner at the Homesick Restaurant
Tom Wolfe's The Bonfire of the Vanities
Ellen Gilchrist's Victory Over Japan
Pat Conroy's The Prince of Tides
Graham Swift's Waterland
Muriel Spark's A Far Cry from Kensington
Martin Cruz Smith's Gorky Park

1990s:

Mary Doria Russell's The Sparrow
Beryl Bainbridge's The Birthday Boys
Jeffrey Eugenides's The Virgin Suicides
Leah Hager Cohen's Train Go Sorry
Jacquelyn Mitchard's The Deep End of the Ocean
Chang-rae Lee's Native Speaker
Howard Norman's The Bird Artist
Rohinton Mistry's A Fine Balance
Cormac McCarthy's All the Pretty Horses
Mark Helprin's Memoir from Antproof Case

OUR PRIMATES, OURSELVES

The relationship between humans and those other primates like chimpanzees, baboons, monkeys, and gorillas has captured the imagination of scientists from the Victorian period to the present, resulting in books both scholarly and popular. When you read their books, you can see how much respect and admiration these scientists have for their subjects.

I loved **A Primate's Memoir: A Neuroscientist's Unconventional Life Among the Baboons,** Robert Sapolsky's memoir of the years he spent as a member of a tribe of baboons in Africa. Sapolsky comes across here as a warm and humane researcher, conscious of, and all for, the bond between humans and animals.

Frans de Waal has written many fascinating and accessible books about primates, especially the great apes, including **Bonobo: The Forgotten Ape.** (For the intellectually curious, there's a great discussion here about the comparative sex lives of humans and bonobos.) In **The Ape and the Sushi Master: Cultural Reflections of a Primatologist,** in which de Waal answers his critics and defends his belief that man is not the only species that has culture.

Jane Goodall is the foremother of ethology, the study of animals in the wild, and she describes her work with chimpanzees in **In the Shadow of Man,** which has become a classic since its original publication in 1971.

Dian Fossey made a heartfelt plea for protection of the mountain gorilla in the now-classic **Gorillas in the Mist,** an account of her experiences among the gorillas in Rwanda.

Yet another woman primatologist is Birute Galdikas, who describes her work with orangutans in the rain forests of Borneo in **Reflections of Eden.**

Like Sapolsky, especially, Galdikas introduces the reader to her particular favorites among the animals she studied.

PASSAGE TO INDIA

One of these days, I'm sure I'll make it to India, but in the meantime I'm content to travel there in books. Here are a few of my favorite Indian novels:

In Khushwant Singh's **Train to Pakistan,** the bloody violence sweeping India after partition has not yet touched Mano Majra, a small village of Muslims and Sikhs on the India-Pakistan border. But in the summer of 1947, the murder of a Hindu moneylender and the arrival of a trainful of dead Sikhs set off a tragic chain of events.

Cracking India by Bapsi Sidhwa reveals the upheaval of partition through the eyes of a child, "Lame Lenny," a young Parsi girl crippled from polio. Lenny's world is her beloved and beautiful Hindu ayah and her ayah's many Muslim admirers, the cook Imam Din, and the Untouchable gardener.

In Salman Rushdie's **Midnight's Children,** narrator Saleem Sinai is born at the stroke of midnight on August 15, 1947, the moment India receives her independence from Britain. Saleem's life, along with the lives of 1,001 other children born at the same time, are bound up with his country's fate as an independent nation.

The setting for Rohinton Mistry's **A Fine Balance** is an Indian city in 1975 during Indira Gandhi's state of emergency. A young Parsi widow, forced to find ways to make ends meet, takes in a student boarder and two lower-caste tailors. For a time, the four strangers move past their differences, but the fragile bond breaks against the sharp politics of India.

Shashi Tharoor's **The Great Indian Novel** is a retelling of the history of modern India through the ancient Hindu epic, **Mahabharata**. This entertaining, clever work of fiction includes real historical events and characters.

PAWNS OF HISTORY

J ames Buchan's **The Persian Bride** combines a moving love story, a political thriller, and a history of modern Iran in a beautiful novel about the relationship of two people caught up in the Iranian revolution: John Pitt, a young man from England who arrives in Isfahan, Iran, in 1974, and seventeen-year-old Shirin, one of John's students, whose father is a general in the shah's army.

During her work in Central America, nurse-midwife Kate Banner, the main character in **Hummingbird House** by Patricia Henley, finds her life turned upside down when she meets Marta, an eight-year-old whose brother is one of the many "disappeared," and Father Dixie Ryan, a radicalized Catholic priest helping the victims of the ongoing violence.

A Gesture Life by Chang-rae Lee tells the story of a repressed and melancholy man whose life in a New York suburb was shaped by his experiences as a medic in the Japanese army during World War II.

Amy Wilentz's **Martyrs' Crossing** is set against the ongoing tension of Israeli-Palestinian relations. When a Palestinian woman is turned back at the checkpoint at Ramallah as she attempts to take her sick child to an Israeli hospital, she and the young Israeli soldier who's guarding the crossing find their lives altered forever.

When we use the phrase "pawns of history," we usually refer to individuals or groups of people caught up in political turmoil, but the characters in Marilyn French's **The Women's Room** are caught up in the whirlwind of social change at the birth of the women's movement. Considered shocking when it first appeared in 1977, the novel is remembered today by many women in their forties and older as one of the most influential novels they've ever read.

PEOPLE YOU OUGHT TO MEET

Feeling isolated? Need to be distracted from your problems? Bored? In a rut? Want to see how other people have shaped their lives to get some hints on how (or how not) to mold yours? Want to meet some very interesting people who just happen to be real? Don't miss these fascinating biographies:

The subtitle of **Banvard's Folly** by Paul Collins says it all: **Thirteen Tales of Renowned Obscurity, Famous Anonymity, and Rotten Luck.** This is a good introduction to a variety of people, most of whom have fallen from the public eye.

Mr. Wilson's Cabinet of Wonder: Pronged Ants, Horned Humans, Mice on Toast, and Other Marvels of Jurassic Technology, by Lawrence Weschler, greatly deserved its nomination as a finalist for nonfiction in both the National Book Critics Circle Award and the Pulitzer Prize contests. It's the story of a very unusual museum in Los Angeles, and the man behind it.

Zelda Fitzgerald's plight, both as a woman and, more specifically, as the wife of the renowned F. Scott, is most compellingly told in **Zelda: A Biography,** by Nancy Milford.

Nicholas Shakespeare's **Bruce Chatwin** chronicles the short but intensely lived life of the great travel writer, novelist, and sexual adventurer.

Scott Anderson's **The Man Who Tried to Save the World: The Dangerous**

Life & Mysterious Disappearance of Fred Cuny is the story of a man whose descriptive nickname was "The Master of Disaster," and whose life was spent devising plans for what to do when disasters (either natural or man-made) occurred.

The wife of another writer—but one far different from Zelda Fitzgerald—is introduced in Stacy Schiff's graceful, informative, and entertaining **Vera (Mrs. Vladimir Nabokov)**; it's most definitely not aimed only at fans of her husband's writing.

Susan Orlean's brilliantly written **The Orchid Thief** is, on the surface, the story of a man named John Laroche, as well as other men and women infected with what the Victorians called "orchidelirium," but underneath it's the study of monomaniacal attachments to things.

Among the biographies of Benjamin Franklin, one of the best is by the Yale historian Edmund S. Morgan, whose **Benjamin Franklin** places great stress on Franklin's years of public service, much of it spent across the Atlantic in England and France.

The finest biography of the well-biographied Eleanor Roosevelt is Blanche Wiesen Cook's **Eleanor Roosevelt**. Volume I, which covers the years 1884–1933, is not to be missed, especially if Roosevelt is one of your heroines.

Three excellent group biographies are Eileen Simpson's memoir **Poets in Their Youth,** which includes some of the finest poets of the 1940s and '50s, including John Berryman (to whom Simpson was married for a time), Randall Jarrell, Robert Lowell, and Delmore Schwartz; Phyllis Rose's **Parallel Lives: Five Victorian Marriages,** which describes the iffy marital relationships of five stalwarts of the Victorian period—Charles Dickens, George Eliot, John Stuart Mill, John Ruskin, and Thomas Carlyle; and Francine

Prose's **The Lives of the Muses: Nine Women & the Artists They Inspired,** which looks at the role of women such as Yoko Ono, Alice Liddell, and Gala Dalí in the lives of the men whom they inspired to artistic brilliance.

PHYSICIANS WRITING MORE THAN PRESCRIPTIONS

While I was reading these books I kept thinking that if these authors ever tired of doctoring, they might well consider a writing career. That is to say, these books are all eloquent, perceptive, honest, and sobering. I have one caveat for potential readers: Don't read any of them if you're suffering from any illness, from headache to muscle pain to the flu. And it would help to be in a reasonably good mood, too.

Jamie Weisman explores her dual role as doctor and patient (she suffers from a congenital autoimmune deficiency disorder that predisposes her to continual infections) in **As I Live and Breathe: Notes of a Patient Doctor,** a memoir exceptional in the beauty of its writing.

Atul Gawande, who majored in philosophy and ethics as an undergraduate, is both a surgeon and a staff writer for *The New Yorker* magazine, where many of the essays in **Complications: A Surgeon's Notes on an Imperfect Science** first appeared. Gawande details what can go wrong in almost any medical procedure (which is scary enough to make me want to avoid hospitals at almost any cost). He discusses the problems inherent in medical education, and the role of physicians in making life-and-death decisions, but above all he reminds us that doctors are only human. It is easy for even the best-trained, most well-meaning physicians to make mistakes.

Other physicians who write about their personal and professional lives include **A Taste of My Own Medicine** by Ed Rosenbaum (which was made into the movie *The Doctor*), Perri Klass's **Baby Doctor** (and her other nonfiction), David Biro's **One Hundred Days: My Unexpected Journey from Doctor to Patient,** Robert Pensack's **Raising Lazarus,** and Abraham Verghese's **My Own Country.**

POETRY: A NOVEL IDEA

It could easily be argued that the first novels in Western literature were poetry: Homer's **Iliad** and **Odyssey,** Virgil's **Aeneid,** and **Beowulf,** newly (and beautifully) translated by Nobel Prize–winning poet Seamus Heaney. Still, when we think about novels we generally think prose. Take a look at these, though, and you just might change your mind:

Eugene Onegin, Aleksandr Pushkin's classic story of the lives of six men and women set in Russia in the 1820s still offers many pleasures—literary, philosophical, and historical.

Jana Harris is a poet and teacher (try her book **Oh How Can I Keep on Singing? Voices of Pioneer Women**), and she draws on her interest in and appreciation for the pioneer experience as well as her literary skills in **The Dust of Everyday Life: An Epic Poem of the Pacific Northwest.**

Vikram Seth's best-known novel is **A Suitable Boy,** but before that was written he had already published **The Golden Gate: A Novel in Verse,** a funny, warm story told in sonnets, of yuppies looking for love in 1980s San Francisco.

Brad Leithauser is a poet and novelist who never writes the same book twice. Take a look at **Friends of Freeland** and **A Few Corrections** for a sample of his wide-ranging interests. In **Darlington's Fall: A Novel in Verse,** he describes the life story of a lepidopterist, from his birth in 1888 to his death in the 1930s, covering his childhood in rural Indiana, his unfortunate marriage, and finally the accident he suffered while butterfly-hunting on a South Sea island.

The Australian Les Murray's rousing eight-line stanzas in **Fredy Neptune** describe the wide-ranging adventures and wanderings of Friedrich Boettcher, from his engagement as a German soldier in World War I, to his lifetime of travels throughout the rest of the world, including the Middle East, Africa, America, and finally back to Australia.

POLISH POEMS AND PROSE

Poland has had four Nobel laureates in literature—Henryk Sienkiewicz in 1905, Wladyslaw Stanislaw Reymont in 1924, Czeslaw Milosz in 1980, and Wislawa Szymborska in 1996. Not bad for such a small country, and one that has been violently tossed and turned by the vicissitudes of history.

In recent years it's been the poets, not the novelists, who are the most prominent in the English-speaking world. Any country that can count Czeslaw Milosz, Wislawa Szymborska, Zbigniew Herbert, and Adam Zagajewski among the brightest stars in its literary firmament is incredibly lucky—as are we, who are able to read them in English.

Although Milosz, who has been in exile from Poland since 1950, is best known to American readers as a poet (and his **New and Collected Poems, 1931–2001** is a splendid introduction to those who don't know his work), Milosz is also a fine prose writer. Try **To Begin Where I Am: Selected Essays** for an entrée into the mind of an extraordinarily thoughtful thinker.

Wislawa Szymborska's **New and Collected Poems, 1957–1997** is a wonderful introduction to her writing—sad, sly, pointed, and lyrical. Some of my favorite poems include "True Love," "Tortures," and "The End and the Beginning."

Herbert Zbigniew's poetry reflects both his country's history and his own political views, while incorporating aspects of classical mythology. His last collection (he died in 1998) is the well-titled **Elegy for the Departure and Other Poems.**

Born more than a generation later than the other three poets, Adam Zagajewski came of age in Poland in the 1960s and '70s. Those previously unfamiliar with his work most likely discovered him after September 11, 2001, when his poem "Try to Praise the Mutilated World" appeared on the back page of *The New Yorker*. Although written well before the terrorist attacks, it spoke eloquently about sorrow and its place in the world. Like Milosz, Zagajewski writes both poetry and prose. Try **Without End: New and Selected Poems** and **Another Beauty,** a memoir of his life as a young dissident in his native country and his experiences as an exile in various European capitals.

Two of my favorite contemporary novels from Poland are Antoni Libera's **Madame,** a coming-of-age story set in Soviet-dominated Poland, and **The Beautiful Mrs. Seidenman** by Andrzej Szczypiorski.

POLITICS OF FICTION

Probably the greatest American novel about politics is Robert Penn Warren's 1947 Pulitzer Prize–winning **All the King's Men**, loosely based on the life of the infamous Louisiana politician Governor Huey Long. Despite its age, the novel hasn't an ounce of mustiness.

Another very popular (and Pulitzer Prize–winning) novel that does seem a bit dated (mostly due to the diminished role of the U.S. Senate in deciding American policy these days) is Allen Drury's **Advise and Consent**. Its story of a nominee for secretary of state who runs into confirmation problems is still riveting.

Charles McCarry's **Shelley's Heart** tells the story of a presidential election that is stolen by computer fraud, and the winning and losing candidates whose lives are changed by the outcome. Eerily familiar, this is a perfect novel for today's paranoia-filled world.

Ward Just has chronicled American political life for many decades, combining the moral complexities of Graham Greene or John le Carré with some low-key but powerful writing. **Echo House** is the story of three generations—from before the New Deal to the present—of a quintessentially political family.

Novels of political satire are legion, including the best-known **Primary Colors** by Anonymous (Joe Klein), but for a really dark romp through the excesses of politics try Larry Beinhart's **American Hero,** with its nastily ingenious proposition that the 1991 Gulf War was developed and staged for television by Hollywood filmmakers. Made into the movie *Wag the Dog,* this is a rare treat. (My favorite Beinhart novel is **You Get What You Pay For,** the first mystery featuring private eye Tony Cassella.)

THE POSTMODERN CONDITION

In general, the pomo designation for a work of fiction refers to works published in the last forty years or so of the twentieth century (there'll surely be a new term for the writings of the twenty-first, perhaps post-postmodern, or popomo), books that are global in their scope and settings and take as their themes issues such as the threat of nuclear annihilation, the assault on natural resources, rampant consumerism, and general uncertainty about the possibility, or value, of survival. These issues are viewed through a thick lens of irony, skepticism, and paranoia, and the novels themselves are filled with references to popular culture, real products, and real people. Other descriptions of pomo fiction include an elliptical style and a self-consciousness on the part of the author-narrator. The growth industry of hypertexts, in which the writer and reader collaborate on a work of fiction, shows the influence of postmodernism. (The series of children's books called **Choose Your Own Adventure** are another sign of pomo's reach.)

All of Don DeLillo's novels have postmodern themes and concerns, but **White Noise** and **Libra** are two of his best; Thomas Pynchon's **Gravity's Rainbow** is one of the best-known pomo novels, but for a less intense introduction to his work try **The Crying of Lot 49**. Other excellent pomo books and authors include Italo Calvino's **If On a Winter's Night a Traveler;** Ishmael Reed's **Mumbo Jumbo; Big If** by Mark Costello; **Pale Fire** by Vladimir Nabokov; Kathy Acker's books, including **Empire of the Senseless;** David Foster Wallace's **Infinite Jest;** John Barth's **Lost in the Funhouse; A Wild Sheep Chase** by Haruki Murakami; William Gaddis's **The Recognitions;** Bruce Sterling's **Zeitgeist;** and **The Twenty-Seventh City; Strong Motion;** and **The Corrections** by Jonathan Franzen (which melds the conventions of the pomo novel with the more domestic concerns of writers like Anne Tyler).

If we accept that Dave Eggers's **A Heartbreaking Work of Staggering Genius** is a memoir (although there are many who would argue that it is fiction), it's one of the first examples of pomo nonfiction.

For some good examples of how science fiction has embraced postmodernism, take a look at the section "Cyberspace.com."

RICHARD POWERS: TOO GOOD TO MISS

Powers brings a fierce intelligence and a passionate (and well-informed) interest in the sciences and humanities to all of his books, which tend to be dense, challenging, and ultimately rewarding to the reader who is willing to work rather than coast through a novel. In an article in *Tikkun*, Melvin Bukiet has described Powers (along with novelists Thomas Pynchon and Jonathan Franzen), using a phrase from Powers's novel **Prisoners' Dilemma**, as a "crackpot realist": a contemporary writer who defines existence as having physical, emotional, and political dimensions. (I would suggest that Mark Costello with his **Big If** and Don DeLillo with his **White Noise** and **Libra** also meet this definition.) Whether their theme revolves around genetics, virtual reality, industrial pollution, or artificial intelligence, Powers's novels, which are big in scope and (amply fulfilled) ambition, are filled with characters who are intensely human—not always likeable, deeply flawed, conflicted in their relationships with those closest to them—and you'll find they remain in your mind long after you turn over the last page of the book. (I don't think it's possible ever to forget Helen, the computer in **Galatea 2.2**.)

Other novels by Powers include **Three Farmers on Their Way to a Dance; The Gold Bug Variations; Operation Wandering Soul; Gain; Plowing the Dark; and The Time of Our Singing.**

PRESIDENTIAL BIOGRAPHIES

A mong the myriad presidential biographies available to us, here are some classics, old and new:

David McCullough has gained a wide readership both for his works of history (**Path Between the Seas: The Creation of the Panama Canal, 1870–1914** is the best of those) and biography. Although **John Adams** and **Truman** are probably his best-known presidential biographies, my favorite remains **Mornings on Horseback: The Story of an Extraordinary Family, a Vanished Way of Life, and the Unique Child Who Became Theodore Roosevelt,** which covers the president's early life, from his sickly childhood through his first marriage, the birth of his child, and the death of his wife when he was twenty-seven. You might follow this up with Edmund Morris's **The Rise of Theodore Roosevelt** and **Theodore Rex.**

There are hundreds, if not thousands, of biographies of Thomas Jefferson, each reflecting one aspect or another of Jefferson's complicated character and his centrality to the most important issues in American history and culture. Given that huge number, you can hardly do better than to read Joseph Ellis's **American Sphinx: The Character of Thomas Jefferson,** but it would be a mistake not to take a long look at the multivolume biographies by Claude Bowers (**The Young Jefferson, 1743–1789; Jefferson and Hamilton: The Struggle for Democracy;** and **Jefferson in Power: The Death Struggle of the Federalists**) and Dumas Malone (his multivolume **Jefferson and His Time** includes Jefferson, the Virginian; Jefferson and the Rights of Man; Jefferson and the Ordeal of Liberty; Jefferson the President, First Term, 1801–1805; Jefferson the President, Second Term, 1805–1809; and The Sage of Monticello). Claude Bowers's books, written over the first forty years of the twentieth century, are the work of a man who believed with all his heart in democracy and the rights of man, who supported Franklin Roosevelt's New Deal programs, and who served as American ambassador to Spain during the Spanish Civil War. He saw Jefferson in terms of mid-twentieth-century values and took great pains to link the beliefs of two great presidents: Jefferson and Roosevelt. The standard Jefferson biography is Malone's, but it sees Jefferson as flawless, or nearly so.

Robert Caro's life work is his multivolume The Years of Lyndon Johnson; which includes The Path to Power; Means of Ascent; and Master of the Senate. And what a brilliant, wide-ranging, thought-provoking work it is. The scope of each volume befits the largeness and complexity of its subject, and Caro takes a long and honest look at a difficult man who unexpectedly became president at a most difficult time in America's history.

Outstanding one-volume biographies include Doris Kearns Goodwin's No Ordinary Time: Franklin and Eleanor Roosevelt: The Home Front in World War II and Grant by Jean Edward Smith.

PROSE BY POETS

These beautiful and moving memoirs by poets shed light on the experiences, events, and relationships that have shaped their poetry.

A civilian conscientious objector working with war-injured children in Vietnam, John Balaban was wounded during the 1968 Tet Offensive. He later returned to Vietnam, traveling the countryside to record folk poetry in the oral tradition. **Remembering Heaven's Face: A Moral Witness in Vietnam** is Balaban's memoir of that period. A good selection of his poetry can be found in **Locusts at the Edge of Summer: New and Selected Poems**.

Although he was legally blind at birth, Stephen Kuusisto's parents' disavowal of his blindness, combined with his own self-delusion, led him to spend years pretending to be able to see much more than he could. Kuusisto's **Planet of the Blind** tells of his gradual acceptance of a white cane and then Corky, a guide dog who changed his life. Some of the same themes are explored in **Only Bread, Only Light: Poems**.

Maxine Kumin won the Pulitzer Prize for poetry for her 1972 **Up Country: Poems of New England** (but also don't miss **The Long Marriage: Poems**). In **Inside the Halo and Beyond: The Anatomy of a Recovery**, she writes of her miraculous recovery from a near-fatal riding accident and the time spent "inside the halo," a device that kept her head immobile.

The accidental, fatal shooting of his brother Peter at age twelve profoundly changed Gregory Orr's life and that of his family. In **The Blessing**, Orr, in his fifties, looks back and tries to answer the question, "Why was I spared?" His poetry can be found in **The Caged Owl: New and Selected Poems**.

In **Heaven's Coast**, Mark Doty writes eloquently and lovingly of the illness and subsequent death from AIDS of his long-term partner, a theme he also explored in **Sweet Machine: Poems.**

PYM'S CUP RUNNETH OVER

Barbara Pym's novels are the closest you can come to reading the sorts of books Jane Austen might have written, had she lived in the middle of the twentieth century. Pym's books are witty and stylish, filled with unforgettable, gently quirky characters, and marked by insidiously charming opening lines. Many of the protagonists are single women of a certain age, inching past their prime, whose major activity seems to be supporting their local church (there are many references to obscure hymns in these novels) and doting on the young curates who move in and out of the parish. Pym had a roller coaster of a writing career. Her first six books, published between 1950 and 1961, were quite popular although never blockbusters. When Pym submitted her seventh novel to her longtime publisher, he declined to publish it, believing it would never recoup the company's investment. When another novel was also rejected, Pym disappeared from the literary scene for almost a decade and a half. Then in 1974 the *Times Literary Supplement* asked a number of well-known authors to list the most underrated writers of the century; Barbara Pym was the only writer mentioned twice, by the poet Philip Larkin and the politician Lord David Cecil. Her career was reborn and she went on to publish several more books before her death at the age of sixty-seven, in January 1980.

My favorites are among her earliest books: **Excellent Women** (which opens with, "'Ah, you ladies! Always on the spot when there's something happening!' The voice belonged to Mr. Mallett, one of our churchwardens, and its roguish tone made me start guiltily, almost as if I had no right to be discovered outside my own front door."); **Some Tame Gazelle** (which begins with, "The new curate seemed quite a nice young man, but what a pity it was that his combinations showed, tucked carelessly into his socks, when he sat down."); and **No Fond Return of Love** ("There are various ways of mending a broken heart, but perhaps going to a learned conference is one of the more unusual.").

Pym's other books include:

Jane and Prudence

Less Than Angels

A Glass of Blessings

An Unsuitable Attachment

A Few Green Leaves

Quartet in Autumn

The Sweet Dove Died

Crampton Hodnet

An Academic Question

A Very Private Eye:
An Autobiography in Diaries and Letters

Civil to Strangers

REAL CHARACTERS

Sometimes reading's best fun comes from meeting characters whose personality traits range from interesting to quirky to downright weird. Since it's no doubt true that one person's interesting is another's definitely weird, you'll have to decide for yourself where on the scale these characters fall.

One of the strangest people I've ever encountered between the pages of a novel (and it's a novel that people either love or hate) is Karen Joy Fowler's eponymous heroine **Sarah Canary**. This mysterious woman, seemingly unable to speak, wanders into a camp of Chinese railroad workers in the late nineteenth century, and one of the young men there is delegated to travel with her from the Pacific Northwest to San Francisco to see if she can be cured.

Anne Tyler's novels are filled with eccentrics—ordinary people who have one or two tics that set them apart from the run of humanity. My favorite eccentrics appear in **The Accidental Tourist; The Clock Winder;** and **Searching for Caleb.**

Cathie Pelletier's hilarious and sometimes heartbreaking Mattagash, Maine, novels (**The Funeral Makers; Once Upon a Time on the Banks; The Weight of Winter;** and **Beaming Sonny Home**) are filled with stories of the McKinnons, eccentric descendants of the town's founders.

Quintus Horatius Flaccus, the very engaging main character in Frederick Reuss's **Horace Afoot,** wanders through the streets of Oblivion, befriends a dying librarian, and involves the other residents of the small town in Socratic phone dialogues. **Henry of Atlantic City** and **The Wasties** are also peopled by somewhat strange characters.

The two wonderfully odd families who are the focus of Tim Winton's

Cloudstreet—the Pickles and the Lambs—are brought together at first by the hard economic times following World War II in Australia, and then united by a marriage.

In **I'll Take It** by Paul Rudnick, Yale grad Joe Reckler accompanies his mother and her two sisters—shoplifters all—on a journey through New England's outlet malls.

The beginning of a Minnesota radio station, filled with odd employees and owned by a pair of eccentric brothers, is the subject of Garrison Keillor's humorous **WLT: A Radio Romance.**

When a visiting government agent comes to the mining village of Whitey's Falls, New South Wales, the inbred residents put aside their differences for the sake of progress, in Rodney Hall's **Just Relations.**

Lamb in Love by Carrie Brown is the story of what happens when fifty-five-year-old postmaster and lifetime bachelor Norris Lamb falls unexpectedly in love with Vida Stephen, a middle-aged spinster.

VAN REID AND THE MOOSEPATH LEAGUE: TOO GOOD TO MISS

Van Reid's delightfully breezy novels about the Moosepath League (named for an incident involving a moose and long underwear) are perfect for the dog days of summer, but they're equally good if you need some light and humorous reading during the winter months. They're entertaining books to read aloud and are fine family fare.

In the novels, set in and around Portland, Maine, in 1896, the League's charter members are three eccentrics, Matthew Ephram, Christopher Eagleton, and Joseph Thump. Together, these do-gooders stumble upon all manner of adventure, frequently (but not always) involving beautiful young girls in need of assistance.

Although the tone and intent of Reid's novels couldn't be less like that of Charles Dickens, there are many similarities between the two writers. Reid's books, like Dickens's, were originally written to be serialized in the newspaper. And, again like Dickens, Reid's novels are thick with subplots; he clearly adores inventing the names of his characters (Sundry Moss and Maude the Bear are two of my favorites), and he never met a plot twist that he didn't immediately work into his fiction.

In **Cordelia Underwood: Or, The Marvelous Beginnings of the Moosepath League,** Cordelia inherits some property and fends off suitors, and Ephram, Eagleton, and Thump meet (accidental) adventurer Tobias Walton and ask him to lead the Moosepathians in their quest to help Cordelia.

In **Mollie Peer: Or, The Underground Adventures of the Moosepath League,** the Moosepathians become involved with a beautiful young reporter, an orphan, Indians, and some dastardly villains.

In **Daniel Plainway: Or, The Holiday Haunting of the Moosepath League,** the Moosepath League gets involved with a lawyer searching for a kidnapped child, a group of men known as the Dash-It-All Boys, a spinster, and some ancient runes.

RIDING THE RAILS: RAILROAD HISTORY

I love the picture of Irish immigrant workers from the East, and Chinese laborers from the West, coming together in 1869 at Promontory, Utah, to pound in the last spike that finally connected the Union Pacific and the Central Pacific railroads, creating one grand cross-country railroad. The romance and the reality of the railroad in American history, its role in the public imagination and the settling of the West, the men who dreamed it, who gained and lost in this great undertaking—all are the subjects of many interesting books.

I would begin my reading with David Haward Bain's well written, comprehensive, and very long (800-plus pages) **Empire Express: Building the First Transcontinental Railroad,** which captures the hopes and excitement of a nation embarked on a great (and greatly difficult) undertaking. Bain's book is helped by excellent maps and vintage photographs.

Stephen Ambrose offers a slightly less weighty but still detailed account in **Nothing Like It in the World: The Men Who Built the Transcontinental Railroad 1863–1869.**

I always think that a good way to learn about most things is to read a really great children's book on the subject, and in the case of the transcontinental railroad there are two excellent ones, both by well-regarded authors of histories for young adults: Rhoda Blumberg's **Full Steam Ahead: The Race to Build a Transcontinental Railroad,** which is aimed at young adults, and Leonard Everett Fisher's **Tracks Across America: The Story of the American Railroad, 1825–1900: With Photographs, Maps, and Drawings,** which offers a great overview of the history and lore of the railroad.

Although **Last Train to Paradise: Henry Flagler and the Spectacular Rise** and Fall of the Railroad That Crossed an Ocean by Les Standiford is not about the transcontinental railroad, it's a terrific story (written by a man better known for his mysteries than his histories) about the cofounder of Standard Oil, whose dream of a railroad connecting Miami with Key West was triumphantly realized, but only for a very short time.

In Bad Land: An American Romance, Jonathan Raban explores the importance of the railroad in the government's attempts to bring settlers into eastern Montana.

RIVERS OF WORDS

The best books about the world's major rivers discuss not only their discovery and exploration, but also their place in the larger context of history and geopolitics, showing the effects the rivers have had throughout time on a city, a country, a continent, or the world.

Two classic examples of this technique are Alan Moorehead's books about Africa's Nile River, The White Nile and its sequel The Blue Nile, which are filled with names like Livingstone, Speke, and Stanley, as well as insights into the colonization of what was then known as "the dark continent."

In The Nile, Robert Collins also takes a historical approach, but concludes his book with a lively discussion of the technology that's gone into controlling the river, including the building of the Aswan Dam.

The Yangtze River is the subject of many good books, including Deirdre Chetham's Before the Deluge: The Vanishing World of the Upper Yangtze River and Simon Winchester's The River at the Center of the World: A Journey Up the Yangtze River and Back in Chinese Time.

There are two excellent accounts of journeys down the Mississippi

River—Mark Twain's **Life on the Mississippi** and Jonathan Raban's **Old Glory, An American Voyage.**

Most books about the mighty American rivers emphasize the need to protect and conserve these remaining natural resources, and, when it's a Western river, there's always the issue of water rights. Two good examples are Charles Bergman's **Red Delta: Fighting for Life at the End of the Colorado River** and John Graves's book on the Brazos River in Texas, **Goodbye to a River.**

Although Holling C. Holling's magnificent children's book **Paddle-to-the-Sea** is not strictly about rivers, this story of a small boat carved by an Indian boy in the middle of Canada (far from any large body of water) that travels through the Great Lakes on its way to the Atlantic Ocean is a wonderful blend of history and geography.

ROAD NOVELS

Not only was Jack Kerouac's **On the Road** was the bible of the Beat Generation, but his novel about Sal Paradise's travels across America in search of new people, unusual experiences, and self-understanding also launched a new literary genre within contemporary fiction: the road novel. Whether the characters in these novels are on the run from personal problems or life's responsibilities, life on the road often becomes an answer to questions they never knew they had.

Tim Winton's **Dirt Music** takes the road novel to the desert of western Australia in this story of an unlikely pair of lovers trying to escape their pasts and find peace together.

Going Away by Clancy Sigal, a finalist for the 1963 National Book Award, is the story of a man disillusioned with politics, with love, and with himself, and of his car trip from Hollywood to Chicago in search of his radical, truer past.

In **Going to the Sun** by James McManus, the female protagonist bicycles from Chicago to Going to the Sun Road in Montana's Glacier National Park to try to understand what went wrong with her life.

The young woman at the center of Cathryn Alpert's **Rocket City** picks up a hitchhiking dwarf on her travels down New Mexico's bluest highways.

As she follows the rodeo from town to town in 1960s Texas in **Moving On,** Patsy Carpenter tries out various personas—wife, student, vamp, adulterer, and druggie.

Bruce Duffy's **Last Comes the Egg** is the story of a week-long joyride taken in a stolen car by three friends—twelve-year-old Frank (who is grieving for his dead mother), an orphan, and a budding juvenile delinquent.

ROMANCE NOVELS: OUR LOVE IS HERE TO STAY

One of the best pieces of advice I ever read was Betty Rosenberg's assertion in the book **Genreflecting** that no one need apologize for his or her tastes in reading. But somehow, even the most dedicated romance reader sometimes feels a need to qualify her love of the romance genre by saying, "Well, I know it's not good literature, but . . ." or some such. Nonsense. Romance novels, like mysteries, westerns, and science fiction, qualify as perfect escapist brew. If you're tempted to see what all the fuss is about, keep reading.

Romance can generally be broken into five subcategories: historical, Regency, contemporary, action-suspense, and paranormal. Historical romances take place, of course, in the past, include historical details, and usually revolve around a warrior winning his lady or some court-political intrigue. Regency romances pay a great deal of attention to the manners and lifestyle of the very rich and titled (the ton) during the reign of George IV of England (1820–1830). They often include humor, misunderstandings, misadventures, and battles of wits between the main characters. Contemporary romances involve independent women and successful men struggling to find love. Action-suspense romances blend mystery and thriller elements into their plot lines. They range from violent and dark to fast-paced and exciting. Paranormal romances include elements of the fantasy or science fiction genres; space travels, fairy worlds, and time travel are typical elements woven into the story lines.

At a panel on genre fiction that I moderated, well-known romance novelist Jayne Ann Krentz characterized romance fiction as novels in which the answer is always yes. Here are some outstanding examples from each category that animate Krentz's description:

> *Historical*—A Kingdom of Dreams *by Judith McNaught*
>
> *Regency*—More Than a Mistress *by Mary Balogh*
>
> *Contemporary*—The "Dream" Trilogy *by Nora Roberts:* Daring to Dream; Holding the Dream; *and* Finding the Dream
>
> *Action-Suspense*—"The Donovan Series" *by Elizabeth Lowell:* Amber Beach; Jade Island; Pearl Cove; *and* Midnight in Ruby Bayou
>
> *Paranormal*—Outlander *by Diana Gabaldon*

For those readers who want a further romantic fix, here are some more novels that have an important place in the history of romance fiction.

Classic romances:

Two classic romances that are on many school reading lists are **Pride and Prejudice** by Jane Austen and Charlotte Brontë's **Jane Eyre.**

Daphne du Maurier's **Rebecca** is a yearly read for many fans.

The prolific Georgette Heyer is the best known Regency writer—and **The Grand Sophy** (think of the heroine as the Regency period's Auntie Mame) is great.

Victoria Holt (a pseudonym for Eleanor Hibbert) wrote many novels of romantic suspense, of which **The Pride of the Peacock** is one of the best.

Elsie Lee wrote historicals, romantic suspense, Regencies, and mainstream romance novels, including **Diplomatic Lover; The Nabob's Widow;** and **The Spy at the Villa Miranda.**

Baroness Emmuska Orczy's **The Scarlet Pimpernel** portrays the swash-buckling hero at his best, in a story full of intrigue and suspense.

Anya Seton combines historical fact and fiction in many of her novels. For a good sampling of her work, try **Katherine** and **Green Darkness.**

Mary Stewart was a mistress of the romance suspense novel. My particular favorites are **My Brother Michael** and **The Ivy Tree.**

Kathleen Winsor's **Forever Amber** is a true classic, forbidden to many young readers in the 1940s because of its raciness.

Contemporary romances:

Sharon and Tom Curtis (a.k.a. Laura London and Robin James) are no longer writing, and their books are long out of print, but this pair wrote a handful of novels worth tracking down. **Sunshine and Shadow** might be the best-conceived romance novel since the genre began. **The Golden Touch** and **The Testimony** are well-crafted contemporary novels of deeply com-mitted love. **The Windflower** is an iconoclastic romp of a pirate story.

The hallmark of Jayne Ann Krentz (who also writes as Amanda Quick, Jayne Bentley, Jayne Castle, Amanda Class, Amanda Glass, Stephanie James, and Jayne Taylor) is the good humor of her novels and her steadfast resistance to the growing trend of violence and mean-spiritedness that pervades many current romance novels. Try **Trust Me** and **Family Man** for two fun contemporary romances.

Suzanne Brockmann writes military romances that combine action-adventure with romance, giving a female slant to the James Bond ethos. Multiple plots, story lines and sharply drawn characters that extend through all of her books, and lots of military detail make reading her work especially interesting. She's also the frankest and sexiest of the bunch, so if that's what you're looking for, try **The Unsung Hero; The Defiant Hero; Over The Edge; and Out of Control.**

Lee Damon was one of the first to write about spousal abuse in a romance novel, in **Again the Magic.**

Anne McCaffrey's **Ring of Fear** is a love story from a writer usually associated with fantasy rather than romance.

Historicals:

Dorothy Garlock's **Homeplace** is a good example of why her readers love her frontier romances.

Julie Garwood's novels, including **Gentle Warrior; Honor's Splendour; and Saving Grace,** are marked by a sense of humor, adroit plots, and well-drawn characters.

Roberta Gellis writes novels of pageantry and passion, bringing the medieval period to life, as in **A Tapestry of Dreams.**

Maggie Osborne set many of her books in the frontier American West; a good one is **The Seduction of Samantha Kincade.**

Amanda Quick (the pseudonym that Jayne Ann Krentz uses for historical romances) is known for her opening chapters that grab the reader and deliver her into temptation and a well-plotted story—try **Slightly Shady; Wicked Widow; Mistress;** and **Mystique.**

Two of the prolific Lavyrle Spencer's novels are **The Gamble** and **Vows.** Spencer changed the look of romance novels when she negotiated with her publisher to have a flower on the cover instead of a couple in a clinch. She was also the first romance author of the 1980s to be published in hardcover.

Paranormal:

In **Dream Walker,** Jacqueline Marten introduces a reincarnation theme as lovers through the ages finally catch up with each other.

Rita Clay Estrada's **The Ivory Key** is about the relationship between a stressed-out reporter and a ghost.

Dreamcatcher by Dinah McCall shows how love is found in both the spirit and physical worlds.

Among Nora Roberts's many novels are some great historicals including: **The Donovan Legacy,** and the novels that comprise the Three Sisters Island trilogy: **Face the Fire; Heaven and Earth;** and **Dance upon the Air.**

Linda Howard's **Dream Man** is a good example of the romantic, paranormal suspense book.

Regency:

Carla Kelly's **Mrs. Drew Plays Her Hand** is filled with well-developed characters and a gripping plot. Other good examples include Joan Wolf's **His Lordship's Mistress;** Edith Layton's **The Abandoned Bride; Scandal** by Amanda Quick; and Nancy Butler's **The Discarded Duke.**

ROMANS-FLEUVES

The term *roman-fleuve* comes from the French words for novel and river. The fourth edition of the **American Heritage Dictionary of the English Language** defines it as "a long novel, often in many volumes, chronicling the history of several generations of a family, community, or other group and often presenting an overall view of society during a particular epoch."

If you have a lot of reading time available—say you're going to be staying on a desert island for an extended period—you might want to consider taking along a roman-fleuve—a novel that either covers several generations or consists of a number of titles that feature the same characters in ongoing development. In these novels, the sum of the total narrative experience is greater than its individual parts, and no one novel is self-contained. (In contrast, while Martha Grimes's Richard Jury or Elizabeth George's Thomas Lynley mysteries all feature the same set of major characters, the story told within each separate book is more important than the connecting threads between the books.)

Romans-fleuves embrace all kinds of stories, cross all genres, and are driven by character development and tightly controlled plotting. The term was first used to describe books by Marcel Proust (**Remembrance of Things Past**) and Honoré de Balzac (**The Human Comedy**). As the form has expanded and grown, **The Lord of the Rings** by J. R. R. Tolkien has become the classic example of this form of extended narrative. The examples that follow require a certain commitment from readers, as the stories they tell span numerous titles that are often quite long, but to readers who get caught in the intricate weave of the romans-fleuves, the longer they last the better.

Bernard Cornwell's roman-fleuve of the Napoleonic Wars consists of eighteen interrelated novels that paint a broad portrait of the times. Each is distinguished by a strong narrative drive and perceptive character development. **Sharpe's Eagle,** which takes place during the Talevera campaign in July 1809, was the first book published. It establishes the relationships between the main characters, explores the power and price of war, and offers incisive social commentary—all of which are hallmarks of the series.

Philip Pullman's roman-fleuve **His Dark Materials** consists of **The Golden Compass; The Subtle Knife;** and **The Amber Spyglass.** The books cast the reader into an epic battle between good and evil that ranges between our world and a parallel one. Pullman has created a universe that is richly detailed, mysterious, and populated with humans living alongside fighting bears, witch clans, and other magical beings. Pullman's finest invention was the daemon, a spirit-familiar who is paired with a human, perhaps as an outward manifestation of humans' inner souls.

Diana Gabaldon's **Outlander** roman-fleuve consists (to date) of five novels. While none live up to **Outlander,** the first in the series, there's no denying the fact that once a reader becomes involved with Jamie and Claire, he or she never wants to let go. **Outlander** begins at the end of World War II when Claire, on a visit to Scotland, stumbles upon a standing-stone circle and is transported to eighteenth-century Scotland on the eve of the second Jacobite uprising. Claire must figure out what has happened to her, avoid being charged as a spy by both the Scottish and the English, and evade danger while trying to find a way back to her own time. Weaving together Celtic lore and period detail, Gabaldon crafts a richly textured world in which Claire struggles with her growing love for an eighteenth-century Scot, Jamie Fraser, and her weakening memories of her twentieth-century husband.

RUSSIAN HEAVIES

A good part of a reading life can be spent most productively with the great (and well-known) Russian books—among them Leo Tolstoy's **Anna Karenina** and **War and Peace** (or, if you want to spend a little less time, the brilliant **The Death of Ivan Ilych**), Fyodor Dostoyevsky's **The Brothers Karamazov** or **Crime and Punishment**, Aleksandr Solzhenitsyn's **One Day in the Life of Ivan Denisovich** or **The First Circle**, Anton Chekhov's **Forty Stories** (or his plays), and Nobel Prize winner Boris Pasternak's **Dr. Zhivago.**

But there are also some lesser-known Russian writers whose books can provide hours (days, weeks, months, years) of pleasure:

Three of my favorite early-nineteenth-century novels are Mikhail Lermontov's loosely connected series of stories **A Hero of Our Time,** which prefigures the disillusion and despair that would become typical of late-nineteenth-century Russian novels; Nikolai Chernyshevsky's **What Is To Be Done?,** which describes the realities of Russian serfdom; and Aleksandr Pushkin's novel-in-verse **Eugene Onegin.**

And from the twentieth century:

Isaac Babel's **The Collected Stories** shows a masterly practitioner of the minimalist school of writing at his best.

Nina Berberova's best works are **The Tattered Cloak and Other Stories** and the three novellas that make up **The Ladies from St. Petersburg,** both showcasing her talent for incisive characterization and crystalline writing.

Children of the Arbat, the first novel in a trilogy by Anatolii Rybakov (followed by the aptly titled **Fear** and **Dust and Ashes**), takes place in the 1930s, just as Stalin was beginning the reign of terror that would send millions of intellectuals to the Soviet gulag.

Stalin's reign of terror is also the backdrop for Vasily Grossman's **Life and Fate,** a book that should be read right along with Solzhenitsyn's **The First Circle.**

Victor Pelevin's **A Werewolf Problem in Central Russia and Other Stories** is a mind-bending mixture of Kafkaesque surrealism and the hyperrealism of Russian food shortages, censorship, and bureaucracy.

SCIENCE BOOKS (FOR THE INTERESTED BUT APPREHENSIVE LAYPERSON)

Those of us who are interested in, but a little unsure of our ability to understand, books set in the complicated world of science (which probably includes most English majors, but I suspect you know who you are), should take a look at these titles. They cover a variety of subjects, but share the qualities of being thought-provoking yet totally readable.

Reading Dick Teresi's fascinating **Lost Discoveries: The Ancient Roots of Modern Science: From the Babylonians to the Maya** is a wonderful lesson in humility for Westerners, who are raised on the idea that science began with the ancient Greeks and pretty much ended with Einstein and modern physics. Wrong!

Heinz Pagels, who died much too young in a mountain-climbing accident, left as his legacy **The Cosmic Code: Quantum Physics as the Language of Nature,** probably the most accessible book ever written on quantum physics.

The Blind Watchmaker: Why the Evidence of Evolution Reveals a Universe Without Design is one of the scientist Richard Dawkins's many stimulating and controversial books. In this one he makes solid arguments for the correctness of Darwin's theories.

Originally published in 1979, **Gödel, Escher, Bach: An Eternal Golden Braid** by Douglas R. Hofstadter still captures the imagination of readers interested in the melding of the arts and sciences.

About Time: Einstein's Unfinished Revolution by P. C. W. Davies makes a mind-boggling topic as understandable as it can be for nonphysicists. (If you only had time to read it.)

In **Almost Everyone's Guide to Science,** cosmologist John Gribbin expands his repertoire to include discussions of not only astronomy but also chemistry, biology, geology, and almost any other scientific "ology" you can think of, presented in his usual noncondescending yet remarkably clear style. A great beginning.

Jared M. Diamond's **Guns, Germs, and Steel: The Fates of Human Societies** is a very readable look at social evolution, especially how geography and environment caused different societies to develop in different ways, at different rates; one of his important points is that being "civilized" does not necessarily make a society superior.

James Gleick is one of the leading science writers around, and all of his books are worth a try, though none is a truly easy read. **Chaos: Making a New Science** lost me near the end, but it is so worthwhile—elegant writing matched with elegant ideas. His **Faster: The Acceleration of Just About Everything** and **What Just Happened: A Chronicle from the Information Frontier** are more accessible.

SCIENCE FICTION, FANTASY, AND HORROR

I like to think about science fiction, fantasy, and horror as being on a continuum, one genre leading into the other. Science fiction deals with the world of the possible, if not the probable; fantasy deals with another world, one that doesn't conform to the natural laws of the world in which we live; and horror fiction (often referred to as dark fantasy) depicts a world marked by unnatural terrors. A good example of this continuum can be found in C. S. Lewis's trilogy **Out of the Silent Planet,** which is basically science fiction, **Perelandra,** which is basically fantasy, and **That Hideous Strength,** which is horror.

Science Fiction:

The shortest science fiction novel on record, which is always attributed to that most prolific author, Anonymous, is in its entirety: "The last man on Earth sat in a room. There was a knock on the door," which I think has all the hallmarks of a good sci-fi novel: It's very accessible, there's at least one mind-bending idea, it has an interesting character, and don't you want to find out what happens next? As you will in these books, too:

Father Emilio Sandoz, the main character in **The Sparrow** by Mary Doria Russell, is a Jesuit priest and leader of an expedition sent out from Earth to explore the source of music picked up by radio telescopes; he and his team discover, to their sorrow, that a desire to do good sometimes leads to unspeakable evil. The sequel, not nearly as good, is **Children of God.**

A training regime of playing video and other games is how Ender Wiggin, the hero of Orson Scott Card's **Ender's Game,** and his genius classmates are being groomed to someday destroy Earth's enemies, who have already attacked the planet twice. (Sequels to this novel, which each have their own pleasures, are **Speaker for the Dead; Xenocide; Children of the Mind; Ender's Shadow; Shadow of the Hegemon;** and **Shadow Puppets**.)

You really can't call yourself well-read in the area of sci-fi without a thorough grounding in Isaac Asimov's books, particularly his very influential "future history" series, which concerns the fall of the Galactic Empire and the rise of the Foundation (whose work, led by Hari Seldon, is based on psychohistory, a scientific way of predicting the future). The stories of the Foundation's successes and failures should be read in this order: **Foundation; Foundation and Empire; Second Foundation; Prelude to Foundation; Forward the Foundation; Foundation's Edge;** and **Foundation and Earth**. If all that reading seems a bit daunting, the only real must-read is **Foundation**.

Gateway by Frederik Pohl is one of the most inventive novels in a genre filled to the brim with inventiveness. Humans have found preprogrammed starships on a distant planet with which to explore the universe, but since there's no way to control the ships, they don't know what they'll find when they get to wherever the ship is set to go, and there's absolutely no guarantee they'll ever get back from wherever they're going. On the other hand, untold riches await some lucky people, and Robinette Broadhead travels to Gateway to take a flying chance. Pohl went on to write several sequels to **Gateway**, including **Beyond the Blue Event Horizon; Heechee Rendezvous;** and **The Annals of the Heechee,** but none live up to the excellence of the first one.

The novels and short stories of Clifford Simak are indifferently written at best, but since they're so interesting I always include them in any list of great sci-fi. My favorite novels are **Shakespeare's Planet; City; Way Station;** and the very mysterious **Destiny Doll,** but several of his short stories shouldn't be missed: "The Answers" and "Shadow Show" are two of his best.

Other great reads include **Childhood's End** by Arthur C. Clarke, **The Forever War** by Joe Haldeman, Roger Zelazny's **Nine Princes in Amber,** Frank Herbert's **Dune** series, and Ursula Le Guin's **The Left Hand of Darkness** and **The Dispossessed.**

Fantasy:

My favorite quotation about the possibilities of fantasy comes from J. R. R. Tolkien, the author of what is widely regarded as the archetypal fantasy trilogy, **The Lord of the Rings,** in his children's book **Farmer Giles of Ham:** "'So knights are mythical!' said the younger and less experienced dragons. 'We always thought so!'"

It's been said that Tolkien wrote his first book, **The Hobbit,** for his young children, and when they grew up he wrote **The Fellowship of the Ring; The Two Towers;** and **The Return of the King.** While Tolkien is certainly not the first to write fantasy novels, he's probably the best known. Three other early fantasy novelists are E. R. Eddison (**The Worm Ouroboros**), Hope Mirrlees (**Lud-in-the-Mist**), and Mervyn Peake, whose Gormenghast trilogy (**Titus Groan; Gormenghast;** and **Titus Alone**) is regarded by many people as the best fantasy ever written, although I loved John Crowley's **Little, Big** even better.

Some contemporary critically acclaimed fantasy includes:

Guy Gavriel Kay (The Fionavar Tapestry, composed of **The Summer Tree; The Wandering Fire;** and **The Darkest Road**); Robert Jordan's massive Wheel of Time series, which included, when this book went to press, **The Eye of the World; The Great Hunt; The Dragon Reborn; The Shadow Rising; The Fires of Heaven; Lord of Chaos; A Crown of Swords; The Path of Daggers; Winter's Heart;** and **Crossroads of Twilight;** Piers Anthony's very punny Xanth series, including **A Spell for Chameleon; Crewel Lye: A Caustic Yarn; Up in a Heaval;** and countless others; Alan Dean Foster's Spellsinger series, including, among others, **Spellsinger** and **The Day of the Dissonance;** Andre Norton's Witch World series, including **Witch World; The Jargoon Pard;** and **The Warding of Witch World;** Katherine Kurtz's Deryni series, including **Deryni Rising;** and her Legends of Camber of Culdi series, which includes the award-winning **Camber the Heretic.**

Incidentally, the best way to discover the new and hot fantasy writers is to corral any teenage boy and ask him. As a tactic, it's never failed me yet.

Horror:

Of all the genres, I have to say that horror is my least favorite; and I prefer horror novels that stick fairly close to fantasy. However, the horror-novel continuum is larger than the novice reader might realize. The genre encompasses writers as diverse as Henry James (**The Turn of the Screw**), Sheridan LeFanu (**In a Glass Darkly**), John Webster (**The White Devil**), Michael Crichton (**Jurassic Park** and others), Anne Rice (**Interview with the Vampire, The Vampire Lestat,** and so on), and Stephen King (**Carrie, The Stand**). (Even William Shakespeare wrote horror— fits comfortably into this genre.) As can be seen from the books that follow, ghosts, werewolves, ghouls, vampires, the undead, witches, and warlocks are all staples of horror fiction.

I couldn't sleep for days after I read William Hjortsberg's **Falling Angel,** which I'd been lured (by an unscrupulous friend) into thinking was a Raymond Chandleresque private-eye novel. It isn't. It might share all the conventions of the hardboiled mystery genre, but the plot—the search for a missing singer in 1950s New York—is animated by supernatural evil, and the denouement is stunning and disturbing.

Of all the Stephen King books, my favorite is actually the first book of his I ever read, the very subtly frightening first novella in **Hearts in Atlantis.**

Barbara Hambly's **Those Who Hunt the Night** is a perfect vampire novel for people who think they don't like vampire novels.

Shirley Jackson's **We Have Always Lived in the Castle** and **The Haunting of Hill House** are both superb examples of the range of horror fiction.

Richard Matheson's **I am Legend** was the inspiration for the film *Night of the Living Dead* and its sequels.

And although it has none of the classic components of horror fiction, Dalton Trumbo's soul-shaking **Johnny Got His Gun** is an unforgettable and terrifying antiwar novel.

SEA STORIES

For contemporary readers, the archetypal oceangoing adventures are those written by Patrick O'Brian, which feature Jack Aubrey and Steven Maturin. These novels, set in the Napoleonic era, are well loved by both men and women, and by those readers who have spent time on boats as well as those who have never set foot in a seagoing vessel or even stepped into a rowboat, kayak, or canoe. One of the aspects of the novels that readers most appreciate—besides the reliable historical detail and the evocative writing—is how the friendship between Maturin and Aubrey develops over the course of the series. The books are best read in order, from **Master and Commander** on through **Blue at the Mizzen**.

But before O'Brian there was C. S. Forester, still the greatest storyteller of life on the high seas. His classic series follows the career of Horatio Hornblower as he serves in the Royal Navy during the Napoleonic era, and includes such classic novels as **Mr. Midshipman Hornblower; Flying Colours;** and many more, concluding with **Admiral Hornblower in the West Indies.** (Incidentally, Forester also wrote the novel **The African Queen,** on which the great Humphrey Bogart film is based.)

If you've read through the O'Brians and the Foresters and still long for a seaworthy series or three, try these, also set during the Napoleonic era:

Alexander Kent's swashbucklers begin with **Richard Bolitho, Midshipman** and include **Colors Aloft!; Sword of Honour;** and **Second to None,** among many others.

Dudley Pope's Nicholas Ramage, featured in **Ramage; Ramage & the Rebels;** and **Ramage at Trafalgar,** are all fine examples of his adventure series.

The series by Richard Woodman includes such rousing tales as **1805; An Eye of the Fleet** (probably the one to read first); and **A Brig of War.**

SEX AND THE SINGLE READER

Okay. I'll come clean. The four sexiest books I've ever read are Kathleen Woodiwiss's **Shanna,** a heaving-bosom/swollen-manhood sort of romance novel that my high school boyfriend gave me (which is weird in and of itself); **Endless Love** by Scott Spencer, a hymn to overheated teenage love; Terry Southern's **Candy;** and Nicholson Baker's **Vox,** a fine example of literary erotica, especially as it relates to phone sex.

Other stellar examples of literary erotica include James Salter's **A Sport and a Pastime,** the story of an American college student and his passionate affair with a French shopgirl; Milan Kundera's very sexy (the political is *very* personal, it turns out) **The Unbearable Lightness of Being;** Alec Waugh's lesbian romp, **A Spy in the Family: An Erotic Comedy;** D. H. Lawrence's **Lady Chatterley's Lover;** and Mario Vargas Llosa's **The Notebooks of Don Rigoberto.**

Erik Tarloff's **The Man Who Wrote the Book** is a very funny novel about the troubles an author finds himself in following the publication of his porno best-seller, *Every Inch a Lady.*

For a collection of all the really "good" parts of novels, try the selection offered in **The Literary Companion to Sex: An Anthology of Prose and Poetry,** edited by Fiona Pitt-Kethley.

If you're really hot and heavy and want to find some other good books, take a look at those nominated for Britain's annual *Literary Review* Best Bad Sex in Fiction award—former nominees and winners include John Updike, Michael Frayn, and Sebastian Faulks (the 1998 winner for **Charlotte Gray**)—keeping in mind, of course, that one person's bad sex scene is another person's pleasurable encounter with prose.

SHORT STORIES

I'll admit it here: Short stories never really thrilled me; they seemed so meager. I empathized with C. S. Lewis, who once said, "You can't get a cup of tea large enough or a book long enough to suit me." But in recent years I've come to appreciate what the best stories have to offer: clarity of vision, with no wasted words. Or as that master short-story writer V. S. Pritchett wrote: "The novel tends to tell us everything, whereas the short story tells us only one thing, and that intensely."

If you want to read the absolute best, seek out the collected stories of Eudora Welty and John Cheever. But there are some other excellent writers whose work has consistently given me pleasure.

T. C. (Tom, to his friends, and formerly known as T. Coraghessan) Boyle is the kind of writer who lulls you into a state of mind. You think the story is going in one direction, and then, boom! he turns around and punches you (metaphorically) in the stomach. The best stories in his stellar collection **After the Plague and Other Stories** are nervy and disconcerting, and often very funny, leaving you uncomfortable with yourself and the world. Here are my three favorites: "Captured by Indians" (with its powerful last sentence), "My Widow," and the devastating "The Love of My Life."

The shortest stories in Lydia Davis's **Samuel Johnson Is Indignant** are a sentence long. (Your reaction to the title story, which is: "Samuel Johnson is indignant: that Scotland has so few trees" will probably determine whether you want to continue on.) I especially loved "The Thyroid Diaries." Think of Davis as an amalgam of Laurie Colwin and Grace Paley, yet entirely original.

The Lone Pilgrim is a collection of Laurie Colwin's sparkly and engaging stories. Though published way back in 1981, they are without a whiff of staleness. My favorite story is "The Achieve of, the Mastery of, the Thing," but the title story is a close second.

Amy Bloom's **A Blind Man Can See How Much I Love You** is marked by her empathy for her flawed (and therefore all-too-human) characters. The title story, about a woman whose daughter is having a sex-change operation, is unforgettable.

I love the voice of the main character in Julie Hecht's **Do the Windows Open?**, a collection of humorous linked stories about a very neurotic young woman.

The stories in Dan Chaon's **Among the Missing** explore loss: of people, of places, of possibilities, and of the various ways we try to fill the loneliness at the heart of our lives. The two stories that I reread frequently are "Big Me," in which a twelve-year-old boy believes that a new arrival in the neighborhood is him—all grown up, and "Here's a Little Something to Remember Me By," in which the disappearance of a fifteen-year-old boy reverberates throughout his best friend's life.

SHRINKS AND SHRINKEES

Psychiatrists, psychologists, psychoanalysts, therapists, witch doctors, juju men, social workers ... the list of emotional-care providers goes on, as does the list of novels that focus on the relationship between doctor (or M.A.) and patient (or client). Who knows? You may recognize your own problems or solutions herein.

The warmly competent psychiatrist in the highly autobiographical **I Never Promised You a Rose Garden** by Joanne Greenberg (originally written under the name Hannah Green, in order to spare her family embarrassment) sets a high standard for both fictional and real therapists, as does Dr. Berger in Judith Guest's moving (and critically underrated) **Ordinary People** and Dr. Rachel Lindholm in **The Good Patient** by Kristin Waterfield Duisberg.

For a very funny portrayal of the world of psychiatric hospitals and the patients and doctors therein, read Samuel Shem's **Mount Misery,** which is told from the point of view of Dr. Roy Basch, a young psychiatrist in training.

In the humorous style of **Mount Misery,** Paul Buttenwieser's **Free Association** is the story of psychiatrist Roger Liebman, who discovers that his own problems with life and love are awfully similar to those he hears about from his patients.

The tone is notably different in Pat Barker's **Regeneration,** set during the carnage of World War I, psychiatrist William Rivers, after trying with little success to "cure" the very sane poet Siegfried Sassoon, starts to doubt the wisdom of sending shell-shocked soldiers back to their battalions.

There are interesting portraits of therapists of all stripes in these novels as well: Pat Conroy's **The Prince of Tides;** Timothy Findley's **Pilgrim;** Wally Lamb's **I Know This Much Is True;** Judith Rossner's **August;** Eric Swanson's **The Boy in the Lake;** and Irving Yalom's **Lying on the Couch.**

SOUTHERN FICTION

The South has a long history of great fiction-writing and includes among its ranks many of the classic authors of the last century, writers like William Faulkner (**The Reivers** and **As I Lay Dying**), Eudora Welty (**The Optimist's Daughter** and **The Collected Stories**), Harper Lee (**To Kill a Mockingbird**), Flannery O'Connor (**Everything That Rises Must Converge**), Carson McCullers (**The Member of the Wedding** and **The Ballad of the Sad Café**), and Thomas Wolfe (**You Can't Go Home Again** and **Look Homeward, Angel**), to name just a few. (I've put my favorites by each of these authors in parentheses after their names.)

But you'd do yourself a grave disservice if you failed to look at these authors, too. Their novels range from the very funny (**Handling Sin**) to the tragic (**The Sharpshooter Blues**), from chronicles of dysfunctional families (**The Prince of Tides**) to coming-of-age tales (**Edisto** and **Jim the Boy**), and everything in between:

Dorothy Allison's	**Bastard Out of Carolina**
William Baldwin's	**The Hard to Catch Mercy**
Hamilton Basso's	**The View from Pompey's Head** *and* **The Light Infantry Ball**
Doris Betts's	**Souls Raised from the Dead**
Larry Brown's	**Joe**
Pat Conroy's	**The Prince of Tides**
Tony Earley's	**Jim the Boy**
Clyde Edgerton's	**Raney**
Kaye Gibbons's	**Charms for the Easy Life**
Josephine Humphreys's	**Dreams of Sleep**
Michael Malone's	**Handling Sin; Foolscap;** *and* **Dingley Falls**
Lewis Nordan's	**The Sharpshooter Blues** *and* **Wolf Whistle**

Walker Percy's	The Moviegoer
Padgett Powell's	Edisto
Reynolds Price's	Kate Vaiden
Lee Smith's	Fair and Tender Ladies *and* Black Mountain Breakdown
Peter Taylor's	A Summons to Memphis
Ken Wells's	Meely LaBauve

SPIES AND SPYMASTERS: THE REALLY REAL UNREAL WORLD OF INTELLIGENCE

Books about spies and spying are addictive. You can begin anywhere—with novels like Len Deighton's **Berlin Game** or John le Carré's **The Spy Who Came in from the Cold,** or with nonfiction books like master spy Kim Philby's **My Silent War** or David Wise's biography **Spy: The Inside Story of How the FBI's Robert Hanssen Betrayed America,** or Mark Riebling's **Wedge: From Pearl Harbor to 9/11 How the Secret War Between the FBI and CIA Has Endangered National Security**—and it's more than likely you'll be hooked on reading about the secret and paranoid world of intelligence, where amorality is often the coin of the realm.

As can be seen in British spy thrillers from the 1960s to the present, novelists in this genre have to come to terms with the great betrayals of the period: British intelligence agents who turned out to be Soviet spies. Andrew Boyle's **The Climate of Treason: Five Who Spied for Russia** and **The Fourth Man: The Definitive Account of Kim Philby, Guy Burgess, and Donald Maclean and Who Recruited Them to Spy for Russia** both reflect the dismay, anger, and overpowering sense of betrayal that followed the unmasking of four

Soviet agents high up in British intelligence. Peter Wright's **Spycatcher: The Candid Autobiography of a Senior Intelligence Officer** offers his version of tracking down Russian spies in MI5; and then there's Stephen Dorril's **MI6: Inside the Covert World of Her Majesty's Secret Intelligence Service.**

Nigel West has made a career of writing about British intelligence. Among his best books are **A Matter of Trust: MI5 1945–72** and **Molehunt: The Hunt for the Soviet Spy Inside MI5,** and his collaboration with Oleg Tsarev, a former Russian agent, in **The Crown Jewels: The British Secrets at the Heart of the KGB Archives.**

For two general historical treatments of the secret world of espionage, try Christopher Andrew's **For the President's Eyes Only: Secret Intelligence and the American Presidency from Washington to Bush** and **Her Majesty's Secret Service: The Making of the British Intelligence Community.**

The history of American intelligence is also the subject of G. J. A. O'Toole's **Honorable Treachery: A History of U.S. Intelligence, Espionage, and Covert Action from the American Revolution to the CIA.**

James Bamford has written two extensively researched books about U.S. government agencies that are involved in spying, **The Puzzle Palace** and **Body of Secrets: Anatomy of the Ultra-Secret National Security Agency from the Cold War Through the Dawn of a New Century.**

Allen Weinstein and Alexander Vassiliev offer up history that they feel should not be forgotten, in **The Haunted Wood: Soviet Espionage in America—The Stalin Era.**

Peter Grose writes about the director of the CIA in the opening years of the Cold War, in **Gentleman Spy: The Life of Allen Dulles.**

SPORTS AND GAMES

To me, the best nonfiction sports-writing comes in books that take a wider view of their subject than simply the game itself, so you don't have to be a sports fan, or have much knowledge at all about a particular sport, to enjoy them. The authors of these books use sports as a way to write social history, illuminating the American character or a particular time period or way of life.

In John Feinstein's books like **The Punch: One Night, Two Lives, and the Fight That Changed Basketball Forever** (the Rudy Tomjanovich/Kermit Washington altercation); **The Last Amateurs: Playing for Glory and Honor in Division I College Basketball;** and **A Season on the Brink: A Year with Bob Knight and the Indiana Hoosiers,** it's clear that he's not writing solely about a game (in this case, basketball), but also about the role of sports in American society.

Seabiscuit by Laura Hillenbrand is the thrilling story of one of the greatest race horses of all time, and the men and women who owned, trained, and rode him.

Friday Night Lights: A Town, a Team, a Dream by H. G. Bissinger is the eye-opening story of a high school football team, the Permian Panthers, in the segregated oil-boomtown of Odessa, Texas, in the late 1980s.

Long before he was a senator and a presidential candidate, Bill Bradley was a basketball player, and no book demonstrates better the sort of man that he is than John McPhee's **A Sense of Where You Are: A Profile of William Warren Bradley.**

The Breaks of the Game by David Halberstam follows the 1979–80 Portland Trail Blazers as they play throughout a disappointing season that follows on the heels of their National Basketball Association championship just three years before. (There's a nice correspondence here with **The Punch,** since Kermit Washington was traded to the Trail Blazers from the Los Angeles Lakers following the Tomjanovich punching.)

One of the most beloved books about baseball and life ever written is Roger Kahn's **The Boys of Summer.** Kahn, who covered the Brooklyn Dodgers in the 1950s for *The New York Herald Tribune,* writes of his love affair with baseball and with the 1955 boys of summer: Jackie Robinson, Duke Snider, Gil Hodges, and Peewee Reese.

REX STOUT'S NERO WOLFE: TOO GOOD TO MISS

When he died in 1975 at the age of seventy-nine, Rex Stout had written forty-six detective novels and short stories featuring Nero Wolfe, the rotund (286 pounds, pretty much all of it blubber, since his main exercise is tending his remarkable orchid collection), eccentric stay-at-home genius, and his trusty sidekick, Archie Goodwin. When Stout is on top of his game, which is most of the time, his diabolically clever plotting and his storytelling ability exceed that of any other mystery writer you can name, including Agatha Christie, who invented her own eccentric genius detective, Hercule Poirot.

Although in the years since Stout's death I find myself going back and rereading his entire oeuvre every year or two, I return with particular pleasure to these five novels: **The Doorbell Rang; Plot It Yourself; Murder by the Book; Champagne for One;** and **Gambit.**

If the Nero Wolfe bug bites you, as it did me, you'll also want to read **The Nero Wolfe Cookbook,** by Rex Stout and the editors of Viking Press; and

Nero Wolfe of West Thirty-Fifth Street: The Life and Times of America's Largest Private Detective, by William S. Baring-Gould.

In chronological order, then, here are all the Nero Wolfe books, with the particularly good ones marked by an asterisk:

*Fer-de-Lance, *1934*

The League of Frightened Men, *1935*

The Rubber Band, *1936*

The Red Box, *1937*

Too Many Cooks, *1938*

Some Buried Caesar, *1939*

Over My Dead Body, *1940*

Where There's a Will, *1940*

Black Orchids, *1944*

Not Quite Dead Enough, *1944*

The Silent Speaker, *1946*

Too Many Women, *1947*

And Be a Villain, *1948*

Trouble in Triplicate, *1949*

*The Second Confession, *1949*

Three Doors to Death, *1950*

*In the Best Families, *1950*

*Murder By the Book, *1951*

Curtains for Three, *1951*

Prisoner's Base, *1952*

Triple Jeopardy, *1952*

The Golden Spiders, *1953*

The Black Mountain, *1954*

Three Men Out, *1954*

Before Midnight, *1955*

Might as Well Be Dead, *1956*

Three Witnesses, *1956*

Three for the Chair, *1957*

If Death Ever Slept, *1957*

And Four to Go, *1958*

*Champagne for One, *1959*

Plot It Yourself, *1959*

Three at Wolfe's Door, *1960*

Too Many Clients, *1960*

The Final Deduction, *1961*

Homicide Trinity, *1962*

*Gambit, *1962*

*The Mother Hunt, *1963*

*The Doorbell Rang, *1963*

*A Right to Die, *1964*

Trio for Blunt Instruments, *1964*

*Death of a Doxy, *1966*

*The Father Hunt, *1968*

Death of a Dude, *1969*

Please Pass the Guilt, *1973*

A Family Affair, *1975*

TAKE ME OUT TO THE BALLGAME

For some fans, baseball is not just a metaphor for life, but life itself. And many writers use baseball as a metaphor to explore themes of success, love, and loss.

At the very top of a list of best baseball fiction is **The Natural** by Bernard Malamud. This novel of the rise and fall of Roy Hobbs, who was determined to be the best there ever was, approaches Greek tragedy.

The quartet of novels by Mark Harris featuring pitcher Henry Wiggen includes **The Southpaw;** then **Bang the Drum Slowly; A Ticket for a Seamstitch;** and **It Looked Like for Ever,** which ends on an appropriate elegiac note.

From its evocative title to its perceptive understanding of family relationships, David James Duncan's **The Brothers K** is a winner.

Battle Creek, a first novel by Scott Lasser, is about Gil Davison, the longtime coach of a semiprofessional team, who hopes that the arrival of a hotshot player will give the team what they need to win the national championship.

Nancy Willard's magical-realist **Things Invisible to See,** which takes place in Ann Arbor, Michigan, around World War II, combines the stories of amateur baseball, a good twin and a bad one, and a crippled young woman into a memorable novel.

Robert Coover's **The Universal Baseball Association, Inc., J. Henry Waugh, Prop.** is the story of a man who uses a fantasy baseball league to escape from ordinary life.

The Dreyfus Affair: A Love Story by Peter Lefcourt is the slightly over-the-top story of a professional baseball player, shortstop Randy Dreyfus, who discovers that he is in love with D. J. Pickett, the second baseman on the team.

All the way through **The Last Days of Summer** by Steve Kluger you'll be laughing out loud, but at the end of the book (which is set in Brooklyn just before and during World War II), I'd be surprised if you weren't in tears .Kluger explores the relationship between Joey, a young boy looking for a hero, and Charlie Banks, the phenomenal rookie third baseman for the New York Giants.

If you're still hungry for books about baseball, take a look at **Diamond Classics: Essays on 100 of the Best Baseball Books Ever Published,** by Mike Shannon. It's great.

TEACHERS AND TEACHING TALES

Novels and nonfiction about teachers and their experiences both in and out of the classroom abound. Consider James Hilton's classic novel **Goodbye, Mr. Chips,** set in England in the late nineteenth century, which describes a teacher's influence on three generations of students (and incidentally is directly responsible for such films as *Dead Poets Society* and *Mr. Holland's Opus*).

Two of my favorite novels about teachers, their students, and their battles with bureaucracy are **I'm Not Complaining** by Ruth Adam, set in an English elementary school in the 1930s, and **Up the Down Staircase** by Bel Kaufman, which is, in the minds of many teachers, the story of their professional lives, and as such should be required reading for anyone contemplating a career in education.

It's a shame that most people are probably more familiar with the film of

To Sir, with Love (one of Sidney Poitier's great starring roles) than they are with Edward Ricardo Braithwaite's own story of his teaching experiences in the London slums in the 1950s, but readers of Braithwaite's memoir will discover an even richer portrayal of character and events than the movie offered.

Other good nonfiction about teaching includes Herbert Kohl's **36 Children,** in which he describes his experiences teaching black sixth-graders at an East Harlem elementary school in the 1960s, and Jonathan Kozol's **Death at an Early Age** (a disturbing account of teaching fourth-graders in a predominantly black school in Boston, also in the 1960s).

Educating Esmé: Diary of a Teacher's First Year by twenty-four-year-old Esmé Raji Codell is her very personal account of what it's like to be a young, relatively hip, very inexperienced teacher.

TECHNO-THRILLERS

The unexpected popularity of Dava Sobel's **Longitude** convinced publishers that there was a reading public eager for well-written and interesting nonfiction about science and technology. As a result, ever since Sobel's book was published in 1996, it's hard to turn around with bumping into yet another techno-thriller waiting to be discovered. Here are some surefire choices:

The Thread Across the Ocean: The Heroic Story of the Transatlantic Cable by John Steele Gordon details the history, people, and complications involved with the laying of the transatlantic cable in 1866, an event that made many of the major events of the twentieth century possible.

A request by his editors at *The New York Times* to write an essay about "the best tool of the millennium" led Witold Rybczynski to write the entertaining and informative book **One Good Turn: A Natural History of the Screwdriver and the Screw.**

Henry Petroski, a professor of civil engineering and a well-known historian of technology, wrote about another humble tool of technology in **The Pencil: A History of Design and Circumstance.** Other good books by Petroski include **The Book on the Bookshelf; The Evolution of Useful Things;** and **To Engineer Is Human: The Role of Failure in Successful Design.** Petroski is able to convey the romance of engineering, a phrase some people might consider an oxymoron.

Zipper: An Exploration in Novelty by Robert Friedel describes the life of Whitcomb Judson, a lesser-known contemporary of the great inventors Thomas Edison and Alexander Graham Bell, who made one great contribution to contemporary life.

Who would have thought that the science of measurement could be so interesting that not one but two books would be published nearly simultaneously on the subject? It turns out to be a fascinating topic, particularly in the hands of Ken Alder (**The Measure of All Things: The Seven-Year Odyssey and Hidden Error That Transformed the World**) and Andro Linklater (**Measuring America: How an Untamed Wilderness Shaped the United States and Fulfilled the Promise of Democracy**), both of whom combine history, technology, and biography to open up a new way of thinking about the simple inventions and scientific investigations that have changed our lives.

TEXAS: A LONE STAR STATE OF MIND

Texas history is long, complicated, and endlessly interesting, and few write about it more knowledgeably or better than T. R. Fehrenbach in **Lone Star: A History of Texas and the Texans.**

Contemporary Texas is the subject of Larry McMurtry's **In a Narrow Grave: Essays on Texas.** Published in 1968, it considers the changing realities of the state, including the deaths of small towns (a theme that McMurtry also addressed in his novel **The Last Picture Show**), and what it means to be a writer from and of Texas.

There are three interesting histories of the siege of the Alamo. To get the most bang for your buck, read them sequentially. For the story that most corresponds to the legends that American children grow up with (with little acknowledgment that there are two sides to any issue), try Lon Tinkle's **13 Days to Glory: The Siege of the Alamo.** Jeff Long offers a far more balanced view in **Duel of Eagles: The Mexican and U.S. Fight for the Alamo.** William C. Davis explores the lives of three famous men who died at the Alamo whose stories have long been obscured by legend in **Three Roads to the Alamo: The Lives and Fortunes of David Crockett, James Bowie, and William Barret Travis.**

Probably the best novel ever written about the Alamo and the years leading up to the great Mexican-American conflict played out there is the meticulously researched and very moving **The Gates of the Alamo** by Stephen Harrigan.

Other good Texas novels include, of course, all of Larry McMurtry's fiction, but try Edna Ferber's **Giant** for an oldie-but-goodie. Loula Grace Erdman's novels of pioneer life in West Texas in the late nineteenth century are hard to beat for good old-fashioned storytelling. **The Edge of Time** and **The Far Journey** are two of my favorites, along with her novels for young adults, including **The Wind Blows Free** and **The Wide Horizon: A Story of the Texas Panhandle.** Carol Dawson's **Body of Knowledge** is a delightful novel about a Texas-sized woman and her eccentric family's secrets.

ROSS THOMAS: TOO GOOD TO MISS

Ross Thomas (1926–1995) was an absolute master of the fast-paced, multilayered novel of political corruption, con games, and unlikely loyalties. He could always be counted on for intelligent writing, fascinating characters (both the good guys and the bad), and tortuously complicated stories, filled with unexpected and unpredictable (but perfectly logical, given the situation) plot twists and turns. Plot summaries of his books don't do them justice. His novels are incredibly cynical—the product of a man who possessed a bleak view of human nature in general, especially when that human was a politician.

Although each one of Thomas's novels has its rabid fans, these are my two absolute favorites:

Briarpatch, in which Ben Dill (a great character who unfortunately never appeared in another Thomas novel) encounters all manner of liars and cheats in Oklahoma City when he tries to bring a killer to justice, won Thomas his second Edgar award for best mystery (his first was for **The Cold War Swap,** his first novel, written two decades before).

Chinaman's Chance, published in 1988, introduces two of Thomas's most popular characters—Artie Wu and Quincy Durant—con men and white knights in just about equal measure. Here they set up a great scam, involving a fortune left behind in Vietnam when the war ended, a crooked CIA agent, and a missing woman.

In addition, Thomas has authored the following books:

Ah, Treachery!

Twilight at Mac's Place

The Fourth Durango

Out on the Rim

Missionary Stew

The Mordida Man

The Eighth Dwarf

Yellow-Dog Contract

The Money Harvest

If You Can't Be Good

The Porkchoppers

The Backup Men

The Fools in Town Are on Our Side

The Singapore Wink

Cast a Yellow Shadow

The Seersucker Whipsaw

And writing as Oliver Bleeck, Thomas published these novels: No Questions Asked; The Highbinders; The Procane Chronicle; Protocol for a Kidnapping; and The Brass Go-Between.

THREE-HANKY READS

There's something purely cathartic about crying over a book—it feels less self-centered than tearing up for oneself. Whenever I think that I'm too jaded for tears, I pick up one of these novels and sure enough, no matter how many times I've read the book (many, many times, for most of them), and no matter how much I suspect that I'm being seriously manipulated by the author, I never fail to weep. The best of this type of book maintains that delicate line between pathos and bathos.

Ernest Gaines's **A Lesson Before Dying** is one of the most powerful and disturbing novels I've ever read, in part because of the subject matter—a man convicted and sentenced to death for a crime he didn't commit—but also because of its beautiful writing.

Cancer and other illnesses are of course prime candidates for three-hanky novels, and there are a lot of them around. Three of the best in this category escape sentimentality: Larry McMurtry's **Terms of Endearment; Gus in Bronze** by Alexandra Marshall; and **Souls Raised from the Dead** by Doris Betts.

"Heartfelt" and "sentimental" are the two adjectives to apply to Elizabeth Berg's **Talk Before Sleep** and Patricia Gaffney's **The Saving Graces,** both of which deal with women's friendships and breast cancer and are not overly soppy. (Incidentally, Gaffney's novel has one of the most sensitive and honest descriptions of the experience of undergoing chemotherapy that I've read.)

I cried when I read Sue Miller's **The Good Mother** (no death and dying there) and Lynne Sharon Schwartz's **Disturbances in the Field,** in which the main character realizes that, in fact, there is no consolation in philosophy. The ending of **Tryst,** by Elswyth Thane, continues to bring on the weepies in readers new and old, more than sixty years after it was first published. And what young girl (or older woman, remembering the scene) can hold back the tears when Ruby Gillis dies of consumption (tuberculosis) in L. M. Montgomery's **Anne of the Island** or when Beth dies in Louisa May Alcott's **Little Women**?

Steve Kluger's **Last Days of Summer**—the story of a friendship between a twelve-year-old boy and a baseball player, set in the 1940s and told entirely in letters, scorecards, newspaper articles, and report cards—is a novel that you actually laugh all the way through until the last page, when, still laughing, you realize that you're also crying.

And for a really good, hearty cry, try these dog books aimed at the children's market: **Good-bye, My Lady,** by James Street, William Armstrong's **Sounder,** and **Beautiful Joe: A Dog's Own Story,** by Marshall Saunders.

GORE VIDAL'S HISTORICAL NOVELS: TOO GOOD TO MISS

The multi-, indeed sometimes outrageously, talented Gore Vidal is at his absolute writerly best in his historical fiction, especially in his American Chronicle series, which includes his critically acclaimed and very popular **Burr** and **Lincoln.** They offer readers intelligent, thought-provoking, fully realized re-creations of the first one hundred and fifty years of the United States and the people and events that have come to define that period. Historical fiction certainly doesn't get any better than this. (Besides these two, my personal favorite novel of Vidal's is **Messiah.**)

In **Burr,** which was published in 1973 at the height of the Watergate scandal, Vidal brings vividly to life another tumultuous time in American history, as an aged Aaron Burr looks back over the Revolutionary War period, the early years of the republic, and his famous duel with Alexander Hamilton—offering devastating assessments of his friends and foes (who were legion).

Although Vidal makes clear in his nonfiction that he is not now, nor has he ever been, a fan of Lincoln's (regarding him as stubborn, tyrannical, and dictatorial), in **Lincoln** he presents us with a man who comes very close to being a character in a Greek tragedy, one whose greatest strength becomes his greatest weakness. We grow to know Lincoln mainly through the eyes of the people around him, including his wife, Mary Todd Lincoln; the ambitious governor of Ohio, Salmon P. Chase, and his wife Kate; William Seward, Lincoln's secretary of state; and John Hay, once the babysitter for the Lincoln family, now Lincoln's personal secretary.

VIETNAM

David Halberstam's two books about the Vietnam War are two of the best I've ever read. The earliest, written about his experiences as a young reporter there in the early 1960s when he won a Pulitzer Prize for journalism, is **The Making of a Quagmire: America and Vietnam During the Kennedy Era,** which was first published in 1965 (so the experiences were quite recent). The hefty, riveting, and definitive **The Best and the Brightest** is a study of how John F. Kennedy's cabinet and advisers engineered a losing and disastrous war. Halberstam's style is never stodgy, and he always makes a complex subject easier to understand without minimizing or oversimplifying its complexities.

1973's Pulitzer Prize–winning **Fire in the Lake: The Vietnamese and Americans in Vietnam** by Frances FitzGerald examines in highly readable prose the reasons why it was impossible for the United States to win the war in Vietnam. In studying the series of mistakes made by successive U.S. governments, Fitzgerald also comments indirectly on America's (still strongly held) inclination to see the rest of the world in black-and-white.

Neil Sheehan's brilliant 1989 National Book Award– and Pulitzer Prize–winning **A Bright Shining Lie: John Paul Vann and America in Vietnam** looks at the Vietnam War through the experiences of one of the American combatants, an officer whose ongoing criticism of the military and complaints of political mismanagement of the war made him distinctly unpopular with his superiors.

Tim O'Brien seems fated to have the Vietnam War, in one aspect or another, as the primary subject matter of his books, whether they are fiction (**The Things They Carried, Going After Cacciato,** and **In the Lake of the Woods**) or nonfiction, as in **If I Die in a Combat Zone, Box Me Up and Ship Me Home,** which he wrote shortly after returning home from combat in Vietnam in 1969. Raw and intense, this young man's feelings of outrage and pain would become slightly modulated in his later books.

For vivid and heartbreaking pictures of war, including the combatants on both sides of the battle, devastated villages, and maimed and dying civilians of all ages, take a look at Larry Burrows's **Vietnam,** a collection of photographs by the *Life* magazine photographer, taken from 1962 until 1971, when he died in a helicopter that was shot down on the Vietnam-Laos border.

WESTERN FICTION

G iven the magnificence of the landscape, the vast distances, and the wide scope of the historical events that occurred there, it is not surprising that setting plays an important role in novels about the American West. Each of these books succeeds brilliantly in evoking a particular place and time:

A. B. Guthrie's 1947 novel **The Big Sky** (even better than its sequel, **The Way West,** which won the Pulitzer Prize), **The Ox-Bow Incident** by Walter Van Tilburg Clark (1940), and Jack Schaefer's **Shane** (1949) were all made into well-regarded movies, but these three classics of Western fiction continue to make for wonderful reading.

Larry McMurtry's trio of novels about Duane Moore and Thalia, Texas, in the last half of the twentieth century—**The Last Picture Show; Texasville; and Duane's Depressed**—are bittersweet, frequently funny novels about growing up and growing older in a dusty West Texas town, but it's his historical novels that have really made his reputation. The series that began with **Lonesome Dove,** which won the Pulitzer Prize in 1985 and continued with several sequels and prequels (including **Streets of Laredo; Comanche Moon;** and **Dead Man's Walk**), is considered by many to be the Great American Western Saga.

One of the major pleasures of reading both of James Galvin's novels, **The Meadow** and **Fencing the Sky** (the setting is Colorado in the former and the Wyoming-Colorado border in the latter), is seeing how he writes with care, affection, and poetic detail about place and time. In the one hundred vignettes that comprise **The Meadow,** Galvin mixes fact and fiction while relating the story of the men and women who lived and worked over a hundred-year period on a mountain. **Fencing the Sky** explores issues of greed and idealism, friendship and forgiveness. Take a look also at Galvin's work as a poet, in **Resurrection Update: Collected Poems 1975–1997.**

Pueblo, Colorado, a corrupt and decaying mining town high in the Rockies, is the setting for Heidi Julavits's **The Mineral Palace,** a story of motherhood, a troubled marriage, and the unveiling of long-held secrets.

A failing sheep ranch on the windswept Great Plains seems an odd setting for a tragedy of Greek proportions, but J. Robert Lennon in **On the Night Plain** pulls it off successfully. This novel is the story of Grant Person, who returns home to the Great Plains after World War II and witnesses the wreckage of his once-thriving family.

And no list of Western fiction would be complete without a doff of the hat to Wallace Stegner, and in particular his magnificent novel **Angle of Repose.**

WESTERN MEMOIRS

Wide-open spaces, the last frontier, nature up-close and personal—whatever the draw is, the West has inspired hundreds of memoirs about growing up there.

Here are some of the best:

It's perhaps a reach to include Mark Twain's **Roughing It** in this list of memoirs, since it's a mixture of fact and fiction, but I couldn't resist. This is a truly wonderful American classic about traveling through the American West in the second half of the nineteenth century.

Ivan Doig proves himself to be a great chronicler of the American West in **This House of Sky: Landscapes of a Western Mind** and **Heart Earth: A Memoir,** both of which are set in small towns in Montana.

Mark Spragg grew up on a dude ranch in Utah, and in **Where the Rivers**

Change Direction he ruminates on how that landscape helped shape who he has become.

Hole in the Sky: A Memoir is William Kittredge's sometimes exalted, sometimes heartbreaking search for self-understanding, as he comes of age on a huge ranch in Warner Valley, Oregon.

In Breaking Clean, Judy Blunt looks back on her childhood and early married life in the 1950s and '60s on cattle ranches in northeastern Montana, and explores what it meant to be female in that place and time.

WHAT A (NATURAL) DISASTER

Many of the books listed below describe the terrible devastation caused by natural disasters (flood, earthquake, hurricane) and exacerbated by human failure: bad engineering, greed, or hubris.

Before David McCullough went on to fame, fortune, and literary awards with books like John Adams and Mornings on Horseback, he wrote a tragic and riveting account of the great 1889 flood in Pennsylvania, The Johnstown Flood. Kathleen Cambor describes the same disaster in a novel, In Sunlight, in a Beautiful Garden.

John Edward Weems's A Weekend in September vividly describes the 1900 hurricane that hit Galveston, Texas, an event that's also the subject of Isaac's Storm: A Man, a Time, and the Deadliest Hurricane in History by Erik Larson.

Norman Maclean writes about the deadly 1949 Mann Gulch fire in Montana in Young Men and Fire. His son, John N. Maclean, is also fascinated by fire, as seen in his Fire on the Mountain: The True Story of the South Canyon Fire, the story of the 1994 Colorado conflagration.

Stephen J. Pyne draws on his own many years of experience fighting fires in **Fire on the Rim: A Firefighter's Season at the Grand Canyon.**

Sebastian Junger's **The Perfect Storm: A True Story of Men Against the Sea** is the heart-stopping story of men fighting against the elements for their lives during a huge storm that hit the East Coast of the United States in 1991.

WHAT A TRIAL THAT WAS!

We expect trial scenes—probing cross-examinations, surprises during the summation, an unexpected but telling witness—in mysteries as well as in that category of fiction known as legal thrillers; indeed, we read legal thrillers for that very reason. One of the very earliest in this category, published more than fifty years ago but is still riveting reading today, is Robert Traver's **Anatomy of a Murder,** a detailed account of a trial in Michigan's Upper Peninsula. This book set a high bar for writers like John Grisham and Steve Martini. I'm not convinced that anyone has succeeded in besting it.

One of the greatest trial scenes in literature is actually nonfiction, occurring in Plato's dialogue **The Apology,** in which the author describes the trial of Socrates, who was accused and found guilty of corrupting the youth of Athens.

Another brilliant trial scene (pretty much the whole second half of the play) is found in *Inherit the Wind,* a play by Jerome Lawrence and Robert E. Lee (not the Confederate general) about the 1925 Scopes "monkey" trial, in which two great minds—Clarence Darrow and William Jennings Bryan—fought over the idea of evolution.

Other good trials can be found in George Eliot's **Adam Bede,** John Galsworthy's many chapters about the Forsyte family's legal travails in **The**

Forsyte Saga, Susan Glaspell's **A Jury of Her Peers** (based on a real murder trial that the author covered as a court reporter in Iowa), David Guterson's **Snow Falling on Cedars** (which deals with racism, World War II, and the internment of Japanese Americans), Chris Bohjalian's **Midwives** (a remarkable mother-daughter novel, too), **The Reader** by Bernhard Schlink, Herman Wouk's **The Caine Mutiny**, Ivan Klíma's **Judge on Trial** (a chilling portrait of Cold War internal politics in Prague), Ernest Gaines's **A Lesson Before Dying**, Agatha Christie's brilliant story **The Witness for the Prosecution**, and of course Harper Lee's **To Kill a Mockingbird**.

WILD LIFE

One of the best books about wildlife, humans, and nature is Henry Beston's account of a year he spent living on Eastham Beach, on Cape Cod, **The Outermost House: A Year of Life on the Great Beach of Cape Cod,** a timeless treasure and a classic in the literature of natural history, originally published in 1928. In that book he says: "We need another and a wiser and perhaps a more mystical concept of animals. They are not underlings, they are other nations, caught with ourselves in the net of life and time, fellow prisoners of the splendor and travail of the earth." These nature writers would subscribe wholly to Beston's view of the relationship between man, nature, and animals:

Craig Childs is a naturalist and a wilderness guide. His book **Crossing Paths: Uncommon Encounters with Animals in the Wild** details his meetings with a variety of animals, both large and small, from grizzly bears to mountain lions, from mosquitos (a great chapter) to mice. Childs is funny, informative, and in love with whatever is wild in nature.

In **A Most Dangerous Journey: The Life of an African Elephant,** Roger A. Caras makes a moving case for ending the killing of African elephants and a plea that humankind get its act together to conserve the wilderness and the animals therein. (For a fictional view of elephants—indeed, a surprisingly successful novel told from the point of view of an elephant—try Barbara Gowdy's **The White Bone**).

Hope Ryden documents the lives of a pair of beavers and their offspring in the delightfully informative **Lily Pond: Four Years with a Family of Beavers.**

Any list of great writings about animals and nature would be incomplete without something by Peter Matthiessen, particularly **The Snow Leopard.** His **Tigers in the Snow,** the story of the Siberian Tiger Project, set up to study and protect the rapidly dwindling population of these animals in the Far East of Russia, is also great reading.

Lynn Sherr is tall and blonde and in love with giraffes, also tall and (somewhat) blonde. In **Tall Blondes,** she captures all sorts of facts and fancies about the species, which she presents in a breezy but knowledgeable manner. Another hidden gem of a book about giraffes is Michael Allin's **Zarafa: A Giraffe's True Story, from Deep in Africa to the Heart of Paris.**

Robert Sapolsky's **A Primate's Memoir: A Neuroscientist's Unconventional Life Among the Baboons** introduces readers to an incredibly humane scientist.

CONNIE WILLIS: TOO GOOD TO MISS

Although her books usually get shelved in the science fiction/fantasy section of bookstores and libraries, nonfans of science fiction shouldn't be put off by the label; Connie Willis writes speculative fiction with heart.

Her novels are anything but repetitive, so each time you pick up a new Willis novel you can't be sure if it'll be serious, on the order of **Lincoln's Dreams** and **Passage,** or more lighthearted, in the style of **To Say Nothing of the Dog** and **Bellwether.** (And even her most amusing novels offer some captivating ideas to mull over.)

The title of the indescribable but very funny **To Say Nothing of the Dog** comes from a classic humorous novel, Jerome K. Jerome's **Three Men in a Boat (To Say Nothing of the Dog),** but Willis's madcap plot is entirely her own—a group of people from the future have to go back into the past to locate a missing relic, and come up against the inconsistencies inherent in time travel.

About halfway through **Passage,** which tells the story of a young female scientist researching life after death, you'll encounter a stunning and unexpected plot twist. (It actually took me a day or two to get over it and get back to finishing the novel.) **Doomsday Book,** which many people believe is Willis's most accomplished novel, takes place sometime in our future, when the main character travels back to the late Middle Ages and finds herself marooned in England during the height of the Black Plague.

But my favorite Willis novel is **Bellwether,** which improbably blends chaos theory, sheep, and fads (the hula hoop and bobbed hair, among others) into what can only be described as a very sweet intelligent love story.

Willis also writes wonderful short stories; the two especially not to miss are "At the Rialto" and "Ado," a sly appraisal of where political correctness is taking us.

In addition to these books, Willis is the author of **Fire Watch; Impossible Things; Uncharted Territory; Remake;** and **Miracle and Other Christmas Stories.** In collaboration with Cynthia Felice, Willis wrote **Light Raid; Promised Land;** and **Water Witch,** which are purely science fiction.

WOMEN'S FRIENDSHIPS

The close relationship between women is a tried-and-true plot in domestic fiction, but in talented hands can still feel fresh and original, as these novels demonstrate:

Christina Schwarz's **All Is Vanity** is a delightful novel about what happens when Margaret decides to give up her high-school teaching job to take a crack at writing a novel, and begins by appropriating her best friend Letty's life as the subject—with hilarious but sometimes uncomfortable results.

In Alice Mattison's **The Book Borrower,** Toby and Deborah meet as young mothers, and over the next twenty years they discuss their children, marriages, God, death, and the whereabouts of a book Deborah lent to Toby when their friendship began.

Three women on the verge of turning thirty who have been friends since fifth grade face choices that put their relationship at risk in **Friends for Life** by Meg Wolitzer.

Maria Thomas's **Antonia Saw the Oryx First** is the story of the unlikely friendship between a white African, Harvard-trained physician and her African patient, Esther, a prostitute and traditional healer, set against the background of a newly independent Tanzania.

A trio of high school friends, whose lives have gone in radically different directions, find that a trip to London offers each of them unexpected opportunities, as related in **London Holiday** by Richard Peck.

Augusta Trobaugh, in **Resting in the Bosom of the Lamb,** tells the story of four elderly women who spend all their time together, with only Pet, an African American who has worked for the families of the other three all her life, knowing the secret that unites their lives with hers.

Margaret Atwood reveals the ambiguous nature of women's friendships in two novels: **Cat's Eye,** in which Elaine Risley, a Canadian artist, returns home to Toronto and finds that she cannot forget (or forgive) her childhood friend, Cordelia; and **The Robber Bride,** the story of three friends, now in their fifties, who have all had to cope with the various nasty behaviors of their so-called friend, Zenia.

Fay Weldon sets up an intriguing situation in **Life Force:** four ex-lovers of Leslie Beck's reconnect after the death of Leslie's second wife, inspiring one of the four to record the history of their entanglements.

In Lane Von Herzen's delicious **The Unfastened Heart,** a group of well-meaning lovelorn women concoct a scheme to make their beloved friend Anna fall in love with the widower who lives next door to her.

Other novels exploring women's friendships include Alice Adams's **Superior Women;** Terry McMillan's **Waiting to Exhale;** Rebecca Wells's **Divine Secrets of the Ya-Ya Sisterhood;** Louis Auchincloss's **The Book Class;** Whitney Otto's **How to Make an American Quilt;** Talk Before Sleep by Elizabeth Berg; and Fannie Flagg's **Fried Green Tomatoes at the Whistle Stop Cafe.**

WORDS TO THE WISE

The best writers love words. They appreciate the myriad ways in which words can fit together, the ways their meanings can stretch and narrow, words' power to evoke emotions, pictures, and ideas. Where would writers (and readers) be without words? There are some wonderful books about words and language, ranging from books about grammar and punctuation, to histories of dictionaries, to deciphering and decoding texts.

Karen Elizabeth Gordon's **The New Well-Tempered Sentence: A Punctuation Handbook for the Innocent, the Eager, and the Doomed** and **The Deluxe Transitive Vampire: The Ultimate Handbook of Grammar for the Innocent, the Eager, and the Doomed** are not only among the most entertaining books you'll read, they're also incredibly useful in dealing with those pesky details of comma usage, "which" vs. "that," and other conundrums of language.

In **Caught in the Web of Words: James Murray and the Oxford English Dictionary**, Elisabeth Murray offers an unassuming biography of her grandfather, the first editor of the dictionary—a labor of love on which he worked for over thirty years—who died before it was completed.

The Professor and the Madman: A Tale of Murder, Insanity, and the Making of the Oxford English Dictionary by Simon Winchester looks at the relationship between Professor James Murray (see above) and Dr. W. C. Minor, whose learned and extensive contributions to the Oxford English Dictionary gave no hint of his deranged mental state.

Barbara Wallraff, who writes the Word Court column for *The Atlantic Monthly*, offers up *con brio* a career's worth of information about language and advice for writers in **Word Court: Wherein Verbal Virtue Is Rewarded, Crimes Against Language Are Punished, and Poetic Justice Is Done.**

The Word Museum: The Most Remarkable English Words Ever Forgotten by Jeffrey Kacirk is an alphabetical listing of words no longer in common currency. And what a shame; the English language is much weaker for having left behind words like *prunk* (proud, vain, saucy), *laced-mutton* (a prostitute; a bad woman with a bright showy dress), *jemmie duffs* (weepers, who followed funerals around), and *dwang* (to oppress with too much work) in common currency. Whatever happened to *thenadays* (we still have nowadays), *stelliscript* (that which is written in the stars), and *haimsucken* (the crime of beating or assaulting a person in his own house)?

WORLD WAR I FICTION

Probably the best-known and, for many readers, simply the best novel about World War I is Erich Maria Remarque's **All Quiet on the Western Front,** an unsentimental yet moving account of a German soldier's experiences, from enlistment through combat and beyond.

Both **Birdsong** by Sebastian Faulks and Robert Goddard's **In Pale Battalions** are great for fans of historical fiction who also love thick English novels, *Masterpiece Theatre,* and Merchant-Ivory films.

Although Patricia Anthony is best known as a science fiction writer, **Flanders** is a powerful and haunting novel of a young American's experiences as a sharpshooter in the British army during the Great War, as seen through his letters home.

Pat Barker's outstanding Great War trilogy, composed of **Regeneration; The Eye in the Door;** and **The Ghost Road,** explores how the lives of her characters (including the poet Siegfried Sassoon) were affected by their experiences during the war.

The loss of innocence is the subject of Paul West's beautifully written **Love's Mansion,** in which the novelist-narrator considers his parents' marriage in the years following World War I.

And mystery lovers won't want to miss the series by Charles Todd, beginning with **A Test of Wills** and **Wings of Fire,** in which the detective, a shell-shocked veteran of World War I, struggles to do his job and at the same time deal with the mental and emotional scars left by his combat experience.

WORLD WAR I NONFICTION

I've always felt that World War I (also known as "The Great War") has its own special sadness. Trench warfare, with young men fighting in muck and mud over inches of land, conjures up an almost unbearable picture of suffering and death. And, of course, some of the best war poetry ever written was composed by English soldiers during the war, several of whom—including Rupert Brooke and Wilfred Owen—died in the fighting, Owen just a week before the Armistice.

There are many good general military histories of World War I, including John Keegan's **The First World War** and **The Pity of War** by Niall Ferguson, but two of the best books about the war are not strictly histories of the conflict but about the lives of combatants and their families and friends.

The first is Paul Fussell's **The Great War and Modern Memory,** which was awarded the 1976 National Book Critics Circle Award and the National Book Award. It examines the literature of World War I in a style that is scholarly yet totally accessible.

The second is a lesser-known book called **Children of the Souls** by Jeanne McKenzie, which looks at the effects of World War I on a group of upper-class intellectuals, the best and the brightest of Britain's young men, all of whom were in school at Cambridge when war broke out—a group that included Raymond Asquith, Julian and Billy Grenfell, and the Charteris brothers.

Another outstanding account of the Great War is from novelist Winston Groom (**Forrest Gump**), a Vietnam veteran who has also written top-notch military histories, including **A Storm in Flanders: The Ypres Salient, 1914–1918.** Here he shows his deep compassion for the ordinary soldiers who fought at the whims of generals and commanders who were themselves far from the front lines of death.

Vera Brittain's **Testament of Youth: An Autobiographical Study of the Years 1900–1925** offers a moving account of how the war affected soldiers and civilians alike.

WORLD WAR II FICTION

E very list of great World War II fiction should begin with—in alphabetical order—two classic novels of men at war: James Jones's **From Here to Eternity** and Norman Mailer's first novel, **The Naked and the Dead,** written when he was only twenty-five.

Other good fiction about the Second World War includes Herman Wouk's **The Winds of War** and **War and Remembrance;** W. E. B. Griffin's series about the Marines, *The Corps,* which includes **Under Fire; In Danger's Path; Behind the Lines; Close Combat; Line of Fire; Battleground; Counterattack; Call to Arms;** and **Semper Fi;** Thomas Fleming's **Time and Tide;** Marge Piercy's **Gone to Soldiers;** Walter J. Boyne's novels, including **Trophy for Eagles** and **Eagles at War;** John R. McCormick's **The Right Kind of War;** Edward L. Beach's classic novel of submarine warfare, **Run Silent, Run Deep;** Martin

Booth's **Hiroshima Joe**; and two Pulitzer Prize–winning novels, **The Caine Mutiny** by Herman Wouk, and **Guard of Honor** by James Gould Cozzens.

Some of the best World War II thrillers are Jack Higgins's **The Eagle Has Landed** and **The Eagle Has Flown**. Alan Furst has also made a career of writing atmospheric novels set in Europe in the late 1930s and '40s, including **Night Soldiers** and **The Polish Officer**.

There are also some moving sections about World War II in Anthony Burgess's **Any Old Iron**, Nora Okja Keller's **Comfort Woman**, Kit Reed's **At War As Children**, Chang-rae Lee's **A Gesture Life**, **Empire of the Sun** by J. G. Ballard, and Nancy Willard's **Things Invisible to See**.

WORLD WAR II NONFICTION

The fiftieth anniversary years of World War II propelled publishing companies to release a huge number of books on the subject. It would take another fifty years to read them all, so you might want to limit yourself to these outstanding works:

The best place to begin is with almost any book by either of two prolific British historians: John Keegan, a professor at Sandhurst, the British equivalent of West Point, or Martin Gilbert, the official biographer of Winston Churchill. For an overview of the war, try Keegan's **The Second World War** or Gilbert's **The Second World War: A Complete History**. A noted American historian is Stephen Ambrose, whose books range from accounts of specific battles, such as **D-Day June 6, 1944: The Climactic Battle of World War II**, or accounts of individual combatants, as in **Citizen Soldiers: The U.S. Army from the Normandy Beaches to the Bulge to the Surrender of Germany, June 7, 1944 to May 7, 1945; Band of Brothers: E Company, 506th Regiment, 101st**

Airborne from Normandy to Hitler's Eagle's Nest; or **The Wild Blue: The Men and Boys Who Flew the B-24s over Germany.**

If you're looking for something beyond a chronology, however expanded by narrative, of the war, try these winning titles:

Hampton Sides tells the dramatic story of the rescue from a Philippine prison camp of Bataan death-march survivors, in **Ghost Soldiers: The Forgotten Epic Story of World War II's Most Dramatic Mission.**

Flags of Our Fathers by James Bradley tells the story of the six men—one of whom is the author's father—who were immortalized by the famous World War II photograph of the Marines raising the American flag on Iwo Jima.

Cornelius Ryan's **The Longest Day: June 6, 1944** deserves its reputation as one of the classic accounts of World War II battles. Follow up with his **A Bridge Too Far** and **The Last Battle.**

The Last 100 Days by John Toland is the dramatic story of the last days of Nazi Germany.

And for an oral history, you can never do better than Studs Terkel's **"The Good War": An Oral History of World War II.**

ZEN BUDDHISM AND MEDITATION

Probably the best book written about meditating—appropriate both for the beginner and for someone who's already done some reading on the subject—is Patricia Carrington's **Freedom in Meditation.** Her book is an impressive blend of scientific objectivity and personal enthusiasm (she is a longtime meditator).

A highly respected Sri Lankan Buddhist monk and meditation teacher, Henepola Gunaratana, offers some useful information in **Mindfulness in Plain English,** intended as a beginner's manual for the learning of Vipassana (mindfulness) meditation, especially for those without access to a teacher. Gunaratana's book is much less theoretical, vis-à-vis Buddhist philosophy and psychology, than is Joseph Goldstein et al.'s **Seeking the Heart of Wisdom: The Path of Insight Meditation,** but more practical and systematic in its presentation of technique.

Charlotte Joko Beck didn't begin the practice of Zen until she was well into her forties. Probably because she's an American and lived a "conventional" life—marriage, divorce, children, career—**Everyday Zen: Love and Work** is especially accessible and meaningful to readers who are somewhat put off by reading the great Asian masters. This is a good first book to read on Zen and Buddhist meditation generally since it consists of talks given to American Zen students. It would be a good accompaniment to a reading of Shunryu Suzuki's **Zen Mind, Beginner's Mind.**

For an excellent general introduction to Buddhism, read Walpola Rahula's **What the Buddha Taught,** an easily understood yet authoritative introduction to the teachings of the Buddha.

And no list of books on Buddhism, however short, would be complete without recommending Hermann Hesse's deceptively simple novel **Siddhartha,** "the story of a soul's long quest in search of the ultimate answer to the enigma of man's role on this earth."

ZERO: THIS WILL MEAN NOTHING TO YOU

There are some books that are simply about nothing. At all. Zero. Zip. Nada. Zilch. But wait, you ask, how can a book be about nothing? Easy—if it's one of a group of nonfiction books about the concept of zero. These are among the best sort of popular science books: totally accessible, eminently readable, and filled with interesting facts, theories, and ideas. Each covers the history of zero from its not-so-humble beginnings in Babylonia to its central place in the world of astrophysics and mathematics, and how its use and discovery changed the way we look at and deal with the world around us. Although there is, perforce, some duplication of the history and topics from book to book, each offers the interested reader enough new information (or different interpretations) to make reading them all a valuable (albeit time-consuming) experience.

For plenty of nothing, try these:

K. C. Cole's **The Hole in the Universe: How Scientists Peered over the Edge of Emptiness and Found Everything;** John D. Barrow's **The Book of Nothing: Vacuums, Voids, and the Latest Ideas About the Origins of the Universe;** Charles Seife's **Zero: The Biography of a Dangerous Idea** (in which he offers a mathematical proof that Winston Churchill is equal to a carrot); and Robert Kaplan's **The Nothing That Is: A Natural History of Zero.**

INDEX

ABOUT THE AUTHOR

Nancy Pearl has worked as a librarian in Detroit, Tulsa, and Seattle. She is currently the Director of Library Programming and the Washington Center for the Book at the Seattle Public Library, where she initiated the program "If All of [you name the city] Read the Same Book." Pearl reviews books weekly on Seattle's NPR affiliate, KUOW. She is the author of two books for librarians, *Now Read This: A Guide to Mainstream Fiction, 1978–1998*, and *Now Read This II: A Guide to Mainstream Fiction, 1998–2001*. She also reviews books for both local and national publications. She lives with her husband, Joe Pearl, in Seattle.